When Work
Is Not Enough

When Work
Is Not Enough

*State and Federal Policies
to Support Needy Workers*

Robert P. Stoker
Laura A. Wilson

BROOKINGS INSTITUTION PRESS
Washington, D.C.

Copyright © 2006
THE BROOKINGS INSTITUTION
1775 Massachusetts Avenue, N.W., Washington, D.C. 20036
www.brookings.edu

Library of Congress Cataloging-in-Publication data
Stoker, Robert Phillip, 1954–
  When work is not enough : state and federal policies to support needy workers / Robert P. Stoker, Laura A. Wilson.
     p.   cm.
  Summary: "Examines a broad range of state and federal programs providing cash or in-kind benefits to low-wage workers, low-income families, and families making the transition from welfare to work to assess the ability of the work support system to lead to self-sufficiency"—Provided by publisher.
  Includes bibliographical references and index.
  ISBN-13: 978-0-8157-8191-2 (pbk. : alk. paper)
  ISBN-10: 0-8157-8191-1 (pbk. : alk. paper)
  1. Working poor—Government policy—United States. 2. Working poor—Services for—United States. 3. Public welfare—United States. I. Wilson, Laura Ann. II. Title.
  HD8072.5.S76 2006
  362.85'5610973—dc22   2005027257

9 8 7 6 5 4 3 2 1

The paper used in this publication meets minimum requirements of the American National Standard for Information Sciences—Permanence of Paper for Printed Library Materials: ANSI Z39.48-1992.

Typeset in Minion

Composition by OSP, Inc.
Arlington, Virginia

Printed by R. R. Donnelley
Harrisonburg, Virginia

Contents

Appendixes

Preface

This book examines whether the work support system is an effective means of helping needy workers (including former welfare recipients) escape poverty and privation. We initiated the project in the late 1990s, following the implementation of federal welfare reform. Cash assistance welfare rolls had declined markedly, as former welfare recipients left for work or quietly went away. A bipartisan celebration broke out in Washington. Yet there was evidence suggesting that many former welfare recipients were struggling to make ends meet—they had left the welfare system to join the ranks of the working poor.

Policymakers did not ignore the working poor. During the 1990s a series of policy reforms were enacted (at both the state and federal levels) to enhance various forms of government assistance for needy workers or their dependents. These "work supports" offered needy workers the opportunity to receive means-tested benefits while working. As welfare reform pushed people into the labor market, work supports pulled them in. However, little was known about the "system" of work supports. While there was evidence that needy workers could experience significant income gains if they received work supports, research also suggested that few needy workers did in fact receive work supports.

When we initiated this project the federal government was flush with resources. In the late 1990s, the Congressional Budget Office was predicting a flood of black ink far into the future. For a brief period, people around Washington wondered how to best make use of the federal surplus. We saw the surplus as an opportunity to enhance the assistance provided to needy workers in order to complement and complete welfare reform. Times have changed. Slower economic growth, tax cuts, and an explosion of federal spending have created record federal budget deficits. We have responded by proposing reforms that reflect the current fiscal environment. Despite these limitations, we believe that the work support system has tremendous potential to assist needy workers and that opportunities exist to enhance the system's effectiveness. We hope this project will contribute to that endeavor.

Many people at the Brookings Institution Press made valuable contributions to this project. We would both like to thank Christopher Kelaher, Mary Kwak, and Tanjam Jacobson for their editorial assistance, and Susan Woollen for the cover design. We also thank the anonymous reviewers for their helpful comments and suggestions.

Robert Stoker appreciates the support he received for this project as a policy research scholar at the George Washington Institute for Public Policy. Many of the faculty associated with the institute, including Joseph Cordes, Marcus Raskin, Clarence Stone, Michael Wiseman, and Harold Wolman, were encouraging and helpful. Cordes deserves special thanks for his patient tutorials on economics. Stoker also is grateful to George Washington University for the Dilthey Award, which provided summer support for this project.

Laura Wilson would like to acknowledge the support she received from Norman Zucker of the University of Rhode Island and Robert Durant of American University. In addition, she would like to thank Larry Thomas and staff at the Schaefer Center for Public Policy at the University of Baltimore for their assistance.

It is not possible to complete a project like this without the cooperation and support of loved ones. Our greatest debt is to our families: Pat, David, Greg, and Kate Stoker and Dean, Steven, and Justin Gentry.

1

Redistribution through Work

Millions of American workers live between dependency and self-sufficiency. Despite significant effort, they cannot earn enough to support themselves and their families. Policymakers have not ignored the plight of those workers who must struggle to make ends meet. A number of recent federal policy changes have multiplied and enhanced the opportunities for needy workers to combine earned income with means-tested tax and transfer benefits. State-level policy choices vary, but many state governments have also created or expanded programs to assist needy workers. These programs are referred to collectively as the work support system.[1]

The work support system serves three overlapping target groups: low-wage workers, low-income workers, and people making the transition from welfare to work. It has two related objectives: to discourage welfare dependency and to help needy workers escape poverty and achieve self-sufficiency. With those purposes in mind, we define the work support system as follows: a collection of policies and programs that redistribute income by providing material assistance (in the form of cash or in-kind benefits) to low-wage workers, low-income working families, and families making the transition from welfare to work. On the basis of this definition, we analyze the following work support policies and programs (we explain program selection in detail in chapter 2): state and federal minimum wage rates; state and federal earned income tax credit (EITC) programs and the child tax credit; medical assistance programs, including transitional medical assistance (TMA), Medicaid, and state Children's Health Insurance Programs (CHIP); food programs, including food stamps and free or reduced-price school meals; Temporary Assistance for Needy Families (TANF) earned income disregards; child care grants; and rental assistance.

This book describes and evaluates the work support system in theory and in practice. Although the system is quite significant in terms of theory because it challenges and reforms many of the ideas that have influenced U.S. social policy, in practice the system is performing far below its potential. We describe work support programs and estimate the benefits that selected programs provide in the fifty states and the District of Columbia. We evaluate the system's performance at the national and state levels and discuss its potential and limitations as a means to alleviate poverty and realize self-sufficiency among needy working families. (We typically use the terms "needy workers" or "needy working families" to refer to the combination of the work support system's three target groups.)

Our research addresses the following questions:

—What is the work support system and how has it changed over time?

—Who is eligible, under what circumstances, to receive work support benefits?

—How do benefits vary from state to state? How do benefits vary with work effort, family composition, and contact with the welfare system?

—Do work support benefits, in conjunction with earned income, provide an adequate living for needy workers and their families?

—Is the work support system a complementary set of policies and programs that meets the needs of struggling workers? Or is it merely a disjointed collection of programs that fails to provide adequate income support for many needy workers and their families?

Redistribution through Work

The work support system was shaped by the influential social policy trends of the 1990s. The "devolution revolution" empowered states to make significant policy choices, especially in the areas of cash welfare payments, child care grants, and medical assistance programs.[2] As a result, significant variation exists in the nature and generosity of work support programs from one state to another. The development of the work support system also reflects the "personal responsibility" movement.[3] Policymakers used program benefits as

2. Winston (2002); Meyers, Gornick, and Peck (2001).
3. Mead (1986, 1997); Handler (1995); Melnick (1994).

leverage to encourage people to behave responsibly. Although personal responsibility was demanded in many areas, such as education, child support, and teenage pregnancy, the notion was expressed most often as an expectation that able-bodied people must work. By linking the receipt of means-tested benefits to earned income, policymakers intended to encourage and reward work. However, they also (perhaps unintentionally) linked the well-being of needy workers to the performance of the economy, especially to the employment prospects of workers at the bottom of the labor market. If employment contracts in an economic downturn, needy workers may find their job loss compounded by the loss of work support benefits.

Despite the influence that devolution and personal responsibility have had on the structure and development of the work support system, in many ways the system's recent history contrasts with the welfare policy trends that dominated the 1990s. First, while the welfare system was reshaped by the devolution of policymaking authority to the states, the work support system was influenced by devolution, the expansion of national programs, and the creation of federal mandates to the states.

Second, whereas welfare benefits were reduced at the state and federal levels, many work support benefits grew more generous. These gains were evident both in terms of eligibility to receive benefits and the value of benefits provided. Decisions to enhance benefit generosity were made by both the federal and the state governments. In addition, whereas cash assistance welfare payments were reduced and time limited, some of the cash assistance benefits from the work support system, benefits that can be enjoyed indefinitely, were made more generous. Finally, the widespread fear that devolution of welfare policy would initiate a destructive "race to the bottom" was not borne out for work supports. Many states used their discretion to enhance the value of the means-tested benefits they provided to needy workers.

Third, although welfare recipients were disciplined by reforms that created work requirements and time-limited benefits, they were also granted privileged status as work support beneficiaries. People who make the transition from welfare to work enjoy exclusive eligibility for some work support benefits and priority eligibility for others.

Finally, as welfare recipients were told to leave the welfare system and enter the labor market to earn their own keep, the opportunities to combine means-tested benefits with earned income were expanded and enhanced. The ability to receive means-tested benefits while working, or to continue to receive means-tested benefits after making the transition from welfare to work, calls into question the association between the receipt of means-tested benefits and dependency that motivated critics of the welfare system and animated its reform.

Rethinking Dependency and Self-Sufficiency

Many American workers live between dependency and self-sufficiency because the income and benefits they receive from the labor market are insufficient to support their families. These workers are beyond dependency because they work, but they do not earn enough to be self-supporting. They require material assistance to make ends meet, and the work support system provides that assistance in a variety of different ways. However, the programs that compose the system are not welfare traps; work supports combat poverty and promote self-sufficiency simultaneously by redistributing income through work.

Redistribution through work may be a provocative idea to some readers, because it challenges influential views of dependency and self-sufficiency. Some social policy analysts have identified receipt of means-tested benefits with dependency: you are dependent if you receive means-tested benefits, you are self-sufficient if you do not. Charles Murray has associated participation in means-tested programs with the irresponsible, antisocial behaviors (particularly, failure to work) that result in dependency and perpetuate the cycle of poverty.[4] Work, on the other hand, is associated with self-sufficiency. Lawrence Mead has claimed: "If low-income men and welfare mothers worked regularly, the underclass would be well on its way to dissolution."[5] While it is doubtlessly true that some welfare clients use means-tested benefits as a way to evade work responsibilities, it is also true that millions of needy working families combine means-tested benefits with earned income to mitigate the limitations of their earning power.

The distinctive nature of redistribution through work is reflected in the welfare dependency literature. The Department of Health and Human Services, in response to the Welfare Indicators Act of 1994, convened a bipartisan advisory board to define welfare dependency in relation to cash assistance—Aid to Families with Dependent Children (AFDC) and TANF—food stamps, and Supplemental Security Income (SSI). Three criteria for determining welfare dependency were proposed:

1. The extent to which means-tested benefits contribute to family income: families are more dependent if they receive a larger share of their total income from means-tested government benefits.

4. Murray (1984).
5. Mead (1986, p. 70).

2. The length of time benefits are received: families are more dependent if they receive means-tested benefits for a long period of time.

3. The exclusion of work-related benefits: work supports received by the family are not counted as contributions to welfare dependency.

According to the Department of Health and Human Services' report to Congress: "A family is dependent on welfare if more than 50 percent of its total income in a one-year period comes from AFDC/TANF, Food Stamps and/or SSI, and this welfare income *is not associated with work activities.*"[6]

The definition implies that means-tested programs contribute to dependency when receiving benefits is an alternative to work. However, when means-tested benefits complement and support work, the link between participation in means-tested programs and dysfunctional, antisocial behavior—the link that defined the underclass and the welfare dependency problem —is broken.[7]

It is difficult to defend the proposition that means-tested benefits are an alternative to work in the wake of welfare reform and the expansion of the work support system. As eligibility for means-tested benefits is linked to work requirements and as means-tested benefits become available to needy working families, it is no longer plausible to consider means-tested programs and work as alternatives. Recent policy changes have subjected welfare programs, such as cash assistance and food stamps, to ever more demanding work requirements. At the same time, programs that provide child care and medical assistance support people who are moving from welfare to work. In addition, millions of needy workers receive means-tested cash benefits through the earned income tax credit; millions of children from low- and moderate-income families receive medical assistance benefits through state Children's Health Insurance Programs. Beyond this, many middle-class and upper-middle-class families receive the child tax credit, a conditionally refundable means-tested tax benefit—no one would call these families "dependent"; the adults are working, paying taxes, and struggling to support their families.[8]

Although workers strive to be self-sufficient, the income and benefits they command in the labor market may not allow them to be fully self-supporting. When work is not enough, work support programs can help needy working

6. Department of Health and Human Services (1997, p. I-3), emphasis added.

7. On the underclass, see Wilson (1987); on welfare dependency, see Murray (1984), Mead (1986).

8. According to Internal Revenue Service publication 972 ("Child Tax Credit"), in 2004 married couples filing jointly could receive the credit if their modified adjusted gross income is less than $110,000.

families to make ends meet. In that sense, work supports contribute to self-sufficiency: a family is minimally self-sufficient when the combined income and benefits it receives from work and work support programs meet its needs.[9] As work support programs become more generous, opportunities for needy working families to escape poverty and privation are created. By combining means-tested benefits with work, the work support system can alter the established relationships among work, welfare, and poverty and create new possibilities for redistribution in the United States.

Work, Welfare, and Poverty

In one sense, the relationship between work and poverty in the United States is clear—workers are much less likely to be poor than nonworkers. The Census Bureau reports that in 2001 only 5.6 percent of American workers were poor, but 20.6 percent of nonworkers were poor.[10] Families with at least one worker had a poverty rate of 7.6 percent as compared to a poverty rate of 30.5 percent for families in which no one worked. This relationship is consistent, regardless of family type, implying that work is a powerful means of avoiding or escaping poverty. However, two important facts are obscured by this clear relationship: many poor people work and many workers are poor.

The Department of Labor (DOL) estimates the number of "working poor" on the basis of income and workforce participation. The working poor are "individuals who spent at least 27 weeks in the labor force (working or looking for work), but whose incomes fell below the official poverty level."[11] Although the number of working poor declined in the late 1990s as conditions in the labor market improved, 6.4 million people still fit this definition in 2000.[12] Women, young people, and members of minority groups were more likely to be among the working poor. Those with low educational achievement, those who worked in the service sector, and those with children were also more likely to be among the working poor. Although full-time workers were less likely to be poor, full-time work was not always a ticket out of poverty; three-fifths of the working poor were full-time workers.

---

9. We consider two different need standards to assess self-sufficiency: the federal poverty standard and basic family budgets. See Bernstein, Brocht, and Spade-Aguilar (2000); Boushey and others (2001).

10. Census Bureau (2002b).

11. Bureau of Labor Statistics (2002).

12. The definition of income used by the Department of Labor in this estimate does not include taxes or transfer programs that may benefit the working poor and increase family income.

Gregory Acs, Katherin Ross Phillips, and Daniel McKenzie have identified and described low-income working families using data from the 1997 Survey of America's Families.[13] Although they considered several possibilities, the definition they prefer includes people in families with incomes below 200 percent of the federal poverty standard, with the adults working an average of at least 1,000 hours per year. Acs, Phillips, and McKenzie doubled the poverty standard because many families above the poverty level are eligible for a variety of means-tested government benefits and still struggle to make ends meet. Moreover, they argue that the federal poverty standard is too low to identify all of the working poor, because it does not account for the additional expenses incurred when working, such as for child care and transportation.[14] Their standard for work also excludes people who are merely "looking for work."

Using these criteria, Acs, Phillips, and McKenzie estimate that 16.7 percent of all nonelderly persons in the United States live in low-income working families. Low-income working families are likely to contain young children; 82.1 percent of people in low-income working families live in families with children. Low-income working families are likely to be headed by a person with low educational attainment; 68.1 percent of people in such families live in a family headed by a person with a high school education or less. Although work effort among the primary earners in low-income working families is significant, such families are less likely to have secondary workers; most of the primary earners in low-income working families work full time (an average of 2,080 hours per year).

Using data from the Panel Study on Income Dynamics, Anthony Carnevale and Stephen Rose found that 32 percent of all workers were "low earners"; that is, they made less than $15,000 in 1998.[15] A majority of low earners had limited education, having attained a high school diploma or less. Women and members of minority groups were more likely to be low earners. Most low earners suffered from both low wages and limited work opportunities (less than full-time, year-round employment). Although many low earners were secondary income sources in more affluent families, the authors estimated that 15.6 million low earners were responsible for providing a significant contribution to total family income in low-income families; more than one-third of such families had children to support.

13. Acs, Phillips, and McKenzie (2001).
14. Research on basic family budgets estimating the income required for a decent, minimal standard of living in various localities around the United States suggests that even incomes of twice the poverty standard are insufficient. See Boushey and others (2001).
15. Carnevale and Rose (2001).

Using different standards and data sources, these studies reach a common conclusion: for millions of working Americans, work income is not enough to make ends meet. Despite significant effort, many workers cannot escape poverty or achieve self-sufficiency. The studies also agree on many of the common characteristics of needy workers: they are more likely to be women and minorities; most have limited educational attainment, which limits their ability to find gainful employment and to advance through the ranks when they are working; and many are struggling to support families with children.

Although there is widespread consensus that millions of working Americans cannot make ends meet, the studies also suggest that the choice of standard used to identify needy workers is an important consideration. One of the most commonly used is the federal poverty standard. However, by using the federal poverty standard one may understate the number of low-income people and families, because it does not really reflect the income required to live a decent life, and it fails to take into account the additional expenses that work requires.[16] On the other hand, by using the federal poverty standard one may overstate the number of low-income people and families, because it does not take into account the income support provided by government transfer programs.[17]

The Census Bureau has developed a number of alternate measures of poverty that account for differences in the measured cost of living and in the composition of income. Originally, the poverty standard was based upon the Department of Agriculture's Thrifty Food Plan. A poverty-level income was defined as the cost of the Thrifty Food Plan multiplied by three, because middle-class families in the early 1960s paid about one-third of their income for food. As the cost of purchasing this food plan changed over time, the poverty level changed. Since 1969 the poverty threshold has been adjusted for changing living costs on the basis of the Consumer Price Index. The CPI measures living costs over time by tracking the retail costs of various products (such as housing, food, transportation, and electricity). However, the CPI has been criticized for overstating changes in living costs, in particular, housing costs. In 1983 the Bureau of Labor Statistics developed an alternative cost-of-living index that was based upon estimated differences in the cost of rental housing. When this measure was projected backward to create a consistent cost-of-living adjustment factor (the CPI-U-XI), the estimated increases in the

---

16. On income level, see Bernstein, Brocht, and Spade-Aguilar (2000), Handler (1995); on additional expenses, see Acs, Phillips, and McKenzie (2001).

17. U.S. House of Representatives, Committee on Ways and Means (2000) (hereafter, *Green Book*); Handler (1995).

cost of living were reduced, lowering the poverty threshold. This, in turn, reduced the estimated number of individuals and families living in poverty.[18]

The Census Bureau also has introduced alternative measures of income that do account for tax and transfer programs (including noncash income) and the effects of such benefits on estimates of poverty. When taxes, transfers, and in-kind benefits such as food, medical assistance, housing assistance are included, the incomes of beneficiary populations increase and estimates of the population in poverty decline.[19] Estimates presented in the House Committee on Ways and Means' *Green Book* (which details a variety of means-tested government programs) suggest that adjusting the cost of living by using the CPI-U-XI index and accounting for noncash benefits reduces official poverty estimates by approximately one-third.[20] Most of this reduction comes from tax and transfer payments (including noncash income), suggesting that government programs are important antipoverty tools. These revised poverty estimates confirm that an accurate understanding of the relationship between work and poverty depends upon accounting for the government benefits that workers receive to supplement earned income.

Labor Market Rewards

The relationship between work and poverty reflects the income and benefits provided to workers at the bottom of the labor market, and since the mid-1970s these have been declining. Although real gross domestic product per capita grew 68 percent and real disposable personal income increased 59 percent between 1975 and 1998, prosperity was a blessing bestowed unevenly. During that same period, income and wage inequality increased because of declines in the rewards for low-wage and low-skill work.[21] This inequality was mitigated somewhat in the late 1990s, when unemployment rates fell below what some perceived as their "natural" limit and gains in wage and income equality were realized; but for many workers these gains were insufficient to overcome decades of decline in real wages and incomes.[22]

18. *Green Book* (2000).

19. Haskins (2001); Handler (1995).

20. *Green Book* (2000, p. 1291).

21. Blank (1997); Haveman (1997); Handler (1995); Solow (1994); Burtless (1994); Baily, Burtless, and Litan (1993).

22. Among economists it was widely believed that the economy will stabilize at an unemployment rate of approximately 5 percent. The performance of the labor market in the late 1990s suggested otherwise.

The struggles of needy workers in the face of aggregate prosperity are curious, because economic expansion is supposed to benefit poor and near-poor workers. Growth promotes employment opportunities. The poor and near-poor are more likely than others to be unemployed or underemployed; economic growth expands their opportunities and assists them by providing regular work, the opportunity to earn income. Because work is the primary income source in the United States, economic growth is expected to benefit low-income people who are willing to work. However, in the 1980s and 1990s, the link between economic growth and the material well-being of low-income workers was broken, undermining the idea that the struggles needy workers experience can be addressed exclusively by encouraging the economy to grow and encouraging people to work.[23]

Rebecca Blank has examined the relationship between economic growth and poverty and concludes that recent economic history contradicts "trickle down" theory, the view that economic growth helps everyone, including the poor.[24] During the 1980s poverty declined only slightly while the economy grew and poverty remained higher than it had been during the 1970s. During the early 1990s, poverty actually increased during a period of economic expansion. Blank notes that this is unprecedented in modern U.S. economic history and asks, "What happened over these years that caused economic growth to decline as an effective antipoverty tool?" Blank examined the components of earned income: work effort and wages. She contends that work effort was not the problem: "Adults in low-income households took advantage of growing employment opportunities in the 1980s even more than they did in earlier decades. Work effort was *more* responsive to changes in the economy in the 1980s than in the 1960s." That leaves wages. During the expansion of the 1960s, real wages increased throughout the entire income distribution. However, during the 1980s, among the poorest members of the population "real wages actually *fell* with economic growth." In the 1980s the poor worked more but earned less. Blank concludes that "the difference between the responsiveness of poverty and of the income distribution to economic growth between the 1960s and the more recent decade is entirely due to these wage changes."[25]

Robert Haveman has documented inequality among working-age males (18 to 64 years old) and contends that growing inequality is due in part to wage declines and in part to reductions in work effort.[26] He reports that between 1973 and 1988, wages among male workers stagnated or declined,

23. Blank (1997); Haveman (1997); Burtless (1994).
24. Blank (1997). See also Haveman (1997).
25. Quotes are from Blank (1997, pp. 27, 31, 32).
26. Haveman (1997).

and both for all working-age males and for all male workers, income distributions in 1988 were less equal than those for 1973. However, his data also show two significant changes in the patterns of male employment between 1973 and 1991. First, there was a decline in full-time, year-round employment; the proportion of working-age males with this work pattern declined from 66.8 to 60.5 percent. Among working males, full-time, year-round employment declined from 72.3 percent in 1973 to 69.3 percent in 1991. During this same period, among all working-age males and male workers, part-time, year-round and part-time, part-year work patterns became increasingly common. Second, there was significant growth in the proportion of working-age males who reported no earned income. The proportion of males who did not work at all increased from 7.4 percent in 1973 to 12.7 percent in 1991. Haveman concludes that changing work patterns are contributing to the growth of wage and income inequality among males.

Gary Burtless has examined the interaction between low-wage work and the opportunity to earn income and argues that changing work patterns are correlated with participation in low-wage work.[27] "Contributing to the growth in annual earnings inequality has been a rise in the correlation between low weekly hours and low annual weeks at work, on one hand, and low hourly wage rates, on the other." People who work irregularly (a few hours per week or a few weeks per year) are also likely to earn low wages. He concludes: "Men paid low hourly wages have not only suffered an absolute decline in their real wages, if they work, they have suffered declines in their ability to find work."[28]

Jared Bernstein and Heidi Hartmann argue that the U.S. labor market is becoming segmented.[29] The primary labor market offers decent wages; benefits linked to employment, such as health insurance and paid vacations; and possibilities for advancement. However, there is also a secondary labor market, characterized by low wages, few benefits linked to employment, irregular employment opportunities, and limited upward mobility. Whether work is the road up and out of poverty depends upon whether you are employed in the primary labor market. Bernstein and Hartmann describe participants in the secondary job market in this way: "Compared to the overall workforce, low-wage workers are more likely to be women, minority, non-college-educated, nonunion, in the retail trade industry, and in low-end sales and service occupations."[30] Participants in the secondary labor market have a difficult time earning enough to lift themselves out of poverty even when aggregate wages

27. Burtless (1994).
28. Quotes are from Burtless (1994, pp. 19, 20).
29. Bernstein and Hartmann (2000).
30. Bernstein and Hartmann (2000, p. 23).

are rising, because they are more likely to suffer unemployment, limiting their work hours. Bernstein and Hartmann report that job "churning" is common in the secondary labor market. However, in contrast to the primary labor market, this tendency of workers to move from one job to another does little to contribute to upward mobility unless they are able to make the transition from the secondary to the primary labor market. Unfortunately, the secondary labor market has been growing. Bernstein and Hartmann find that the proportion of workers earning wages at or below the poverty level increased from 23.7 percent in 1973 to 28.6 percent in 1997. They attribute growth in this segment of the labor market to two factors: declines in the demand for low-wage workers and declines in the institutions that support their economic well-being, such as minimum wage laws, trade unions, monetary policy, and trade regimes.

Is being a low-income worker a stage through which people pass on their way to prosperity, or are some workers likely to be low earners for extended periods of time? Carnevale and Rose have analyzed the prospects of low earners (people earning less than $15,000 annually) and observe that although some are young people who are seeking their niche in the labor market, "many low-earners never break out of low-paying jobs."[31] They examine the income dynamics among low earners for five- and ten-year periods and conclude that many low earners "have only isolated bad years" and are able to earn larger incomes over time.[32] About half of male low earners had improved their earnings within five years, but about one-third continued to earn less than $15,000 annually; after ten years, about one-fourth remained low earners. More than half of low-earning women were still low earners five years later; however, after ten years only about one-fifth of female low-earners were still low earners. The authors estimate that 5 percent of all workers who are responsible for a significant share of family income are permanently mired in low-earning jobs.

Lower lifetime earnings are particularly likely for poorly educated young males. Daniel McMurrer and Isabel Sawhill report that young men have experienced "a precipitous drop" in average earnings.[33] "Men born between 1940 and 1949, who were ages 25 to 34 in 1974, had average incomes of almost $30,000 that year (in 1994 dollars). Men born between 1960 and 1969, by contrast, who were 25 to 34 in 1994, averaged less than $23,000." The authors attribute this change to slower economic growth (in particular, slower pro-

31. Carnevale and Rose (2001, p. 46).
32. Carnevale and Rose (2001, p. 58).
33. McMurrer and Sawhill (1998, p. 39).

ductivity growth) since 1973 and to growing inequality. They conclude that the rate of economic growth and rising earnings inequality since the 1970s have diminished social mobility and lifetime earnings for all males and particularly for younger, less-educated males.

Although they examine different market segments at different points in time, these analysts agree that there are serious problems at the bottom end of the labor market. Despite aggregate prosperity, there was a decline in the rewards the labor market provided to many workers—wage and income inequality grew as real wages, benefits, and work opportunities for low-wage workers declined. Consequently, for a large number of Americans, work is not enough to avoid or escape from poverty.

From Welfare to Work

Ignoring the apparent problems at the bottom of the labor market, the Personal Responsibility and Work Opportunity Reconciliation Act of 1996 (PRWORA) put in place a national policy to end welfare dependency and make welfare recipients self-sufficient by encouraging them to work. The clear message was, "Get a job, any job." Instead of acknowledging the plight of low-income workers, the PRWORA promoted work as a solution to the problem of welfare dependency.[34] By some measures the PRWORA was a roaring success; welfare caseloads declined so much that political leaders now compete to claim credit for this accomplishment. But this policy placed faith in the labor market as a means to achieve self-sufficiency even as the plight of low-income workers grew.[35]

Ironically, many provisions of the 1996 "welfare reform" reflect the established historic relationships among work, welfare, and poverty. Joel Handler observes that the core of the U.S. social contract is that people will work to support themselves and their family.[36] Consequently, the U.S. welfare system is and always has been premised on the idea that poor women, even poor women with young children, should work. Not working is viewed as deviant behavior that is related to other forms of deviancy, such as crime and vice; not working is a threat to the social and economic order; not working is a personal moral failure; not working makes the able-bodied poor unworthy of assistance. These core beliefs imply that means-tested programs must discipline

34. Joel Handler (1995) reports that the original meaning of self-sufficiency in the Work Responsibility Act of 1994 (President Clinton's welfare reform proposal) was the absence of cash assistance welfare participation.
35. Solow (1998); Haveman (1997).
36. Handler (1995).

and direct adults (no matter what the consequences for their children), and that the welfare system must be so miserly and demeaning that people will prefer to work rather than receive government assistance.

Those people who make the transition from welfare to work typically join the ranks of low-income workers, and consequently many former welfare recipients cannot earn enough to escape poverty despite their work effort.[37] In their study of the consequences of welfare reform, McMurrer and Sawhill found that although most former welfare clients who found jobs in the late 1990s earned between $7 and $8 per hour, few gained full-time, year-round employment. As a result, annual earnings for former welfare clients were typically between 70 and 95 percent of the federal poverty standard. Although some former welfare clients managed to move up and earn their way out of poverty, others were slow to climb the economic ladder. Many former welfare recipients, particularly minority females with little education, were likely to work low-wage jobs "for extended periods with little or no increase in pay."[38]

Pamela Loprest has examined the economic prospects of people making the transition from welfare to work and concludes that despite significant work effort, many former welfare recipients have difficulty making ends meet.[39] Using data from the National Survey of American Families, she reports that about 50 percent of those who had left welfare since 1997 were still working when they were interviewed for the survey in 1999. Because many former welfare clients had little education and experience, they were often employed "in low-wage jobs with few benefits." More than two-thirds of these former welfare recipients were employed for thirty-five hours per week or more; they earned a median hourly wage of $7.15. She notes that this wage, in conjunction with the EITC, provides an annual income of nearly $17,000, more than the federal poverty standard for a family of three. Other programs, such as food stamps and Medicaid, can also help. However, she also reports that only a fraction of those making the transition from welfare to work receive such benefits: 23 percent receive food stamps, while 34 percent of former recipients and 53 percent of their children receive Medicaid. Loprest concludes that "a substantial number of former recipients and their families remain in poverty after going off welfare."[40]

Vicki Lens summarized the literature on the success of TANF in this way: "Virtually every study conducted by individual states tracking former recipients has found that these recipients remain mired in low-paying employment

37. Lens (2002); Loprest (2002); Brauner and Loprest (1999).
38. McMurrer and Sawhill (1998, p. 57).
39. Loprest (2002).
40. Loprest (2002, p. 20).

that does not provide enough to live on." Lens attributes this failure to achieve self-sufficiency to the structure of TANF itself and argues that the "insistence that work, not training and education, is the route to self-sufficiency" is the root of the problem.[41]

The work support system is the programmatic link between welfare and work. In their survey of programs in twelve states, Acs and his coauthors report that a half-time, minimum-wage worker who combines her earnings with cash welfare, the EITC, and food stamps can increase her income by more than 50 percent when making the transition from welfare to work.[42] Sheila Zedlewski has examined the effects of several work support programs on low-income families and observes that the "patchwork of income support policies can have a major effect on family income," but the "picture is less rosy for families that do not receive these supports."[43] However, Zedlewski reports that although the EITC was widely used, participation in other programs, such as TANF, food stamps, and Medicaid, decreased between 1996 and 1998. For the lowest-income families, two changes were evident during this period: (1) low-income families received fewer government benefits, and so gained a larger share of their total income from private sources; and (2) income gains from the combination of earned income and government benefits were about 7 percent, significantly less than the possibilities estimated by Acs and coauthors. Clearly, the extent to which the work support system is realizing its potential to assist needy workers, including those making the transition from welfare to work, is an important question.

Although welfare caseloads have been reduced, the continuing struggles of former welfare clients to escape poverty and achieve self-sufficiency have caused some to rethink the wisdom of policies that emphasize quick job search and placement.[44] Self-sufficiency may be better achieved by strategies that consider retention and advancement during the initial job placement.[45] Training and work support services also can help to keep former welfare clients on the job.[46] Earnings supplements are another important part of the picture; such supplements as the EITC and child care grants encourage work and defray some of the costs of working.[47] Programs that reward low-income

41. Lens (2002, pp. 281, 283).
42. Acs and others (1998).
43. Zedlewski (2002, p. 60).
44. Lens (2002).
45. Rangarajan (2001).
46. Lens (2002); Strawn and Martinson (2001).
47. Lens (2002); Strawn and Martinson (2001); Michalopoulos (2001)

workers and their dependents and encourage work can be an important part of efforts to combat welfare dependency and recidivism.[48]

The Work Support System

The work support system aims to "make work pay" by providing cash and in-kind benefits to needy workers. Although most work support programs have been in place for a long time, the scope and generosity of the system were expanded significantly during the 1990s. During the Reagan presidency in the 1980s, by contrast, there was little change. Targeting needy workers for means-tested government benefits was inconsistent with Reagan's social policy agenda; benefits to the working poor were reduced in order to concentrate assistance on the "truly needy." Although the 1986 Tax Reform Act did enhance the generosity of the EITC and indexed benefits and eligibility standards to inflation, other tax policy changes, in particular the expansion of payroll taxes as part of the plan to restore fiscal solvency to the Social Security system, diminished the gains enjoyed by needy workers and their families.

Expansion of work support system generosity was initiated in earnest during the presidency of George H. W. Bush through several key policy changes. First, EITC generosity was enhanced. Second, the minimum wage was increased. And third, the federal government mandated changes in Medicaid eligibility that allowed more low-income children to enjoy access to medical assistance (though this change was phased in gradually over several years).

The pace of work support system development increased later in the 1990s. President Clinton's social policy agenda tried to link expansion of the EITC, access to health care, public employment, and child care subsidies to welfare reform.[49] Although Clinton's health care reform foundered in Congress and the public employment provisions he favored were not included in the PRWORA, several national policy changes during his presidency did enhance the generosity of the work support system. The federal minimum wage was increased. The EITC was made more generous, especially for low-income workers with children.[50] As part of the 1993 budget agreement, provisions requiring that 50 percent of income be "earned" were dropped, making more recipients of means-tested benefits eligible for the EITC; benefit generosity was increased; and EITC benefits were excluded from income in the determination of eligibility for most means-tested transfer benefits.[51] Moreover,

48. Haskins (2001); Greenstein and Guyer (2001).
49. Handler (1995).
50. Zedlewski (2002); Greenstein and Guyer (2001).
51. Handler (1995).

several important policy developments influenced access to medical assistance for needy workers. The PRWORA extended medical assistance to low-income working families moving from welfare to work.[52] Access to health care for low-income children was enhanced further in 1997 by the creation of the Children's Health Insurance Program.[53] Beyond this, the PRWORA also enhanced needy working families' access to child care by consolidating programs and increasing federal financial support. At the same time however, the PRWORA repealed the entitlement to child care assistance of people making the transition from welfare to work.

Although the pace of development has slowed since the 1990s, recent federal policy changes continue to expand work support system generosity. President George W. Bush's tax reductions included a more generous child tax credit that is conditionally refundable and reduced marginal tax rates for low-income workers. In addition, the Farm Security and Rural Investment Act of 2002 took several significant steps to reform the Food Stamp Program to encourage participation among low-income workers.

There is substantial evidence that during the 1990s the states also embraced the mission of supporting low-income workers. Marcia Meyers, Janet Gornick, and Laura Peck have examined interstate variation in "the subset of policies that influences the economic resources and poverty risks of families with children" between 1994 and 1998.[54] Through analysis of eleven different programs that feature substantial state-level discretion over program finance, eligibility, benefit generosity, and administration, they identify several state policy regimes. Although they document variation in state social policies, Meyers, Gornick, and Peck see a pattern in recent state policy changes: "States appear . . . to be moving in directions that contract traditional, welfare-based assistance, and expand support for the working poor."[55]

We agree with their conclusion; state discretionary policy decisions are an important influence on work support system generosity. However, the program set that we examine in this research differs from that examined by Meyers, Gornick, and Peck in two important ways: we focus on means-tested programs that are connected to work and we include programs that are governed by national eligibility and benefit standards. The work support system combines state discretionary and national programs. It is important to understand the mix of national and state discretionary programs that composes the

52. Zedlewski (2002); Greenstein and Guyer (2001).
53. Gruber (2003).
54. Meyers, Gornick, and Peck (2001, p. 457).
55. Meyers, Gornick, and Peck (2001, p. 477).

work support system when considering how the system performs at the state level.

Many state governments have used their discretion to increase the generosity of the work support system. Several states have established minimum wage rates higher than the federal requirement. Several states have created and funded EITC programs to provide refundable tax credits to low-income workers or otherwise reduced the tax liabilities of low-income workers. Welfare reform also created opportunities for recipients in a number of states to make the transition from welfare to work with medical assistance and TANF earned income disregards. Beyond this, many states have used the flexibility provided by welfare reform to establish diversion grants to help low-income workers stay in the labor market or to expand child care funding.[56] Finally, many states have helped low-income workers by expanding eligibility for medical assistance beyond federal requirements.[57]

More of the Same?

Readers who are familiar with U.S. social policy may suspect that the work support system is little more than a new label for "workfare" programs that promote or require work among the able-bodied poor. Although work requirements for welfare recipients are not new, creating or expanding opportunities to link means-tested benefits to work for people inside and outside the welfare system does put a new twist on an enduring policy debate about the relationships among work, welfare, and poverty.[58] To what extent are people responsible for working and earning their keep in the marketplace? In what circumstances should government intervene to protect people from privation? Do means-tested programs undermine the incentives for people to work and care for themselves and their families? Do means-tested programs create a haven that insulates participants from the labor market? Do means-tested programs create a trap that contributes to poverty among participants? If means-tested benefits complement rather than compete with the rewards that the labor market provides, new and unexpected answers to these questions are possible.

56. Adams and Rohacek (2002); Zedlewski (2002); General Accounting Office (2002b). According to the Urban Institute's Assessing New Federalism project, by July 2000 twenty-six states and the District of Columbia had established formal diversion programs that allowed a family to receive a lump sum payment in lieu of TANF benefits; eligibility requirements and benefits vary from place to place.

57. Broaddus and others (2002).

58. On work requirements, see Wilensky (2002); Handler (1995).

In particular, three influential ideas must be reexamined in light of the new possibilities created by the work support system: the "less eligibility" principle, the doctrine of laissez-faire, and the distinction between the deserving and the undeserving poor. The less eligibility principle holds that the material condition of welfare clients must be worse than that of the lowest worker.[59] A miserly, demeaning welfare system disciplines and motivates the poor to work by preventing them from living better on welfare than they could live as workers. Welfare recipients are redeemed by work; through work, they can escape welfare dependency and join the social and economic mainstream. Handler's observation that the lives of many welfare recipients are inconsistent with this belief—many welfare recipients do work and yet cycle in and out of the welfare system as their job prospects rise and fall; and because labor market prospects of welfare recipients are so limited, their work efforts are unlikely to allow them to escape poverty or end welfare dependency—has not diminished the influence of the less eligibility principle. As he notes, it shaped the debates concerning welfare reform during the 1990s.[60]

Laissez-faire doctrine views the market and the government as alternative means of distributing income and material rewards and divides the world into two distinct groups: "amply productive workers," capable of supporting themselves; and "wholly unproductive" people, who require charity or public assistance to survive.[61] The doctrine implies that the rewards of work come exclusively from the market (the income and benefits provided by employers), and government intervention must be constrained and carefully targeted so that people who can work will work. The extension of means-tested benefits to people who are able to work undermines work incentives, creates a dependent population, and perpetuates the cycle of poverty: The more generous the benefits, the greater the problem.[62] However, Edmund Phelps identifies a third category of people that is overlooked by the dichotomy that undergirds laissez-faire doctrine: "workers whose employment and wage prospects are too poor to support a lifestyle remotely approaching that of the middle class."[63] Although they are willing and able to work, the opportunities these workers are offered in the labor market do not provide enough to support their families.

59. Handler (1995); King (1995); Piven and Cloward (1993).
60. Handler (1995).
61. Phelps (1997); Tullock (1997); Okun (1975). The categorization is from Phelps (1997, p. 17).
62. Murray (1984).
63. Phelps (1997, p. 17).

Laissez-faire doctrine and the less eligibility principle converge in their presentation of work and means-tested programs as alternative, mutually exclusive sources of income, so that one can be used only at the expense of the other. The work support system denies this dichotomy by providing redistributive benefits that complement rather than compete with income earned through labor market participation. This creates two important new possibilities for redistribution. First, the poor can be motivated to work by the generosity of the work support system, instead of by the harshness of the welfare system. Unlike welfare benefits, generous work support programs are in harmony with the less eligibility principle; redistributive generosity in support of work is not constrained because an effective work support system alters and improves the lowest conditions in the labor market. Second, the less eligibility principle and laissez-faire doctrine imply that the generosity of the welfare system can and must be evaluated relative to the rewards of work. By complementing the rewards that marginal workers receive from the labor market, a generous work support system opens the possibility of increased welfare generosity for those who do not work. As the rewards of work are enhanced, the rewards of welfare participation decline in comparison. A generous and effective work support system makes it unnecessary to reduce the generosity of the welfare system in order to maintain work incentives.

U.S. politicians benefit from bashing the welfare system because welfare recipients are isolated in programs that can be identified as serving the undeserving poor.[64] Popular opinion in the United States is thought to be hostile to redistribution because programs to assist the poor are thought to conflict with core American values, such as individualism and self-reliance. Ladd and Bowman report that both in 1985 and again in 1996 a majority disagreed when the National Opinion Research Center asked if "reducing the differences in income between people with high incomes and those with low incomes was a government responsibility."[65] There is a well-established norm of distinguishing the deserving and undeserving poor on the basis of work: workers are seen as deserving, whereas the unworking poor are not.[66]

Another reason Americans may disfavor redistribution is because they think only the poor benefit from it. Although redistributive programs transfer income or services from the more affluent to the less affluent, the overall distribution of benefits is less clear-cut. Redistribution that promotes responsible behavior can combat social ills such as idleness, crime, substance abuse,

64. Wilensky (2002); Handler (1995); Jencks (1992).
65. Ladd and Bowman (1998).
66. Wilensky (2002); Handler (1995); Piven and Cloward (1993); Gilens (1999).

and delinquency that affect rich and poor alike.[67] Phelps argues that only the private benefit of employment is reflected in labor market rewards (the income and benefits employers provide), and the private benefit fails to account for the social benefits of employment and the social consequences of unemployment and idleness. This suggests that work is not only a personal, moral responsibility; it is also a public good.[68] Work regulates life and assigns social roles and status within communities and families.[69] Work is a source of personal identity that creates expectations and models lives for children.[70] Work creates and shapes attitudes and interests through social experience and the identification of individuals with larger social institutions. The isolation of those outside the work world contributes to antisocial behavior.[71] In this way, affluent people and poor people alike benefit from redistribution that encourages work.

William Julius Wilson observes that because Americans favor individualistic over structural explanations of poverty, they tend to blame the poor for their circumstances.[72] However, most Americans distinguish "aiding the poor" from expanding "welfare." From 1983 to 1991, National Opinion Research Center surveys found that a majority of respondents felt too little was being spent to help the poor, but only about 20 percent felt too little was being spent on welfare. "Paradoxically, it would seem that helping the poor is good, but helping them through established channels—that is, through welfare—is not."[73] If Wilson is correct, the public's attitude toward aiding the poor reflects, in part, the nature of the programs that government uses to accomplish redistribution. Redistribution through work is likely to be viewed more favorably.

The work support system promotes a new, more positive image of redistribution by providing means-tested benefits to needy workers and people making the transition from welfare to work. This can bring about a fundamental shift in public perceptions of poverty, work, and welfare, replacing the powerful image of the welfare queen with the working mother struggling to support her family and make ends meet.[74] The politics of redistribution can be transformed by connecting means-tested assistance to the American

67. Wilson (1997); Phelps (1997).
68. Phelps (1997).
69. Wilson (1997); Handler (1995); Piven and Cloward (1993); Mead (1986).
70. Handler (1995); Phelps (1994).
71. Wilson (1997); Mead (1986).
72. Wilson (1997).
73. Wilson (1997, p. 162).
74. Winston (2002).

impulse to assist the working poor.[75] However, this transformation is dependent upon the current work support system effectively delivering material assistance to needy workers and their families: whether it can do so is the central question of this book.

Outline of the Book

Our argument is presented in three parts. Part 1 describes the work support system. Chapter 2 elaborates on our definition of the work support system, describes federal and state work support policies and programs, and provides a historical overview of program development with emphasis on recent policy changes that have affected the generosity of the work support system. Chapter 3 examines the basic functions and design of work support programs and explains how the various components of the system strive to balance income supports and social controls.

Part 2 presents estimates of work support program benefits. The benefits provided by work support programs vary from place to place and according to earnings, family structure, family size, and work patterns. Of course, the extent of participation in work support programs is also a crucial factor. We present benefit estimates as nominal values and as values transformed to account for cost-of-living differences at the state and the substate levels. Cost-of-living differences are important because high cost-of-living states tend to use their discretion to provide nominally more generous benefits and low cost-of-living states tend to do the opposite. However, analysis of cost-adjusted benefits suggests that the influence of state-discretionary policies is limited, because the more generous benefits provided by high-cost states are insufficient to compensate needy workers for higher living costs. This implies that federal programs that feature national eligibility and benefit standards influence the generosity of the work support system by raising the bottom rung of the economic ladder regardless of state policy choices.

Chapter 4 presents nominal estimates of the income and benefits that workers can gain from minimum wage work and work support program participation in the fifty states and the District of Columbia. Chapter 5 revises the nominal estimates to more accurately reflect the real value of work support program benefits by adjusting them to reflect cost-of-living differences. Chapter 6 examines the effectiveness of the work support system as a means to encourage welfare recipients to make the transition from welfare to work.

75. Weir (2004).

Part 3 evaluates the performance of the work support system. Chapter 7 evaluates the work support system at the national level, in terms of the assistance it provides to poor and near-poor working families, including families making the transition from welfare to work. Chapter 8 evaluates the performance of the work support system at the state level. We construct a state work support system generosity index and present a regression analysis to explain the variation in generosity. We conclude that residents in states that have done nothing to enhance the generosity of work support benefits are likely to enjoy more generous work support benefits. This counterintuitive result follows from the fact that many of the most important work support programs (such as the EITC, school meals, and food stamps) have national eligibility and benefit standards that provide (with few exceptions) consistent benefits across the nation.[76] States that do nothing to enhance work support benefit generosity also tend to have low living costs. When the estimates of benefit generosity are adjusted to reflect differences in living costs, residents in "do nothing" states receive more generous benefits because the benefits provided by national programs are worth more in low-cost-of-living states and the adjusted national program benefits outweigh the generosity of state-discretionary benefits provided by other states.

We present our conclusions and proposals for reform in chapter 9. Our main conclusion is that the work support system is a work in progress. Despite the fact that the system serves the deserving poor, there is significant overlap between the welfare system and the work support system, and consequently work support programs have not been able to separate themselves from the "welfare mess."[77] Although strides have recently been made to enhance the generosity of the work support system, our evaluation suggests that few needy working families enjoy the full benefits the system has to offer.

---

76. Melnick (1994). These programs are important because they provide generous benefits and enjoy widespread participation in comparison to many other work supports.
77. Wilensky (2002).

Part 1

Describing the Work Support System

2

Work Support Programs

To identify the programs and benefits that compose the work support system is a devilish problem for two reasons: (1) it is difficult to know what programs to exclude, because government has a broad mandate to promote and support employment opportunities; and (2) many of the same programs serve needy workers and nonworking welfare recipients. How can the work support system be distinguished from more general efforts by government to promote and support employment? How can the welfare system and the work support system be distinguished? To overcome these ambiguities, we propose a number of standards that elaborate and clarify the definition of the work support system presented in chapter 1 and explain why programs and program benefits have been classified as either within or outside the work support system for the purposes of this research.

Work support programs and benefits must specifically target needy workers or their dependents, rather than assisting workers in general. We exclude from the work support system the many government programs that provide material assistance to workers or people with a work history but do not specifically target needy workers. Two large-scale social programs that are excluded from the system by this standard are the Old Age, Survivors, and Disability Insurance (OASDI) programs (commonly referred to as "Social Security") and the Unemployment Insurance (UI) program. Although aspects of Social Security are redistributive and many needy workers qualify for OASDI payments—Social Security is an important income source for many needy people (particularly retirees)—OASDI benefits do not specifically target needy workers or their dependents. For the same reason, this standard excludes unemployment compensation.[1] Although UI provides benefits to qualified workers who lose their jobs through no fault of their own and this program does benefit many needy workers, people qualify for UI on the basis of their work and earnings history, the circumstances of their job loss, and their willingness to comply with the program's work requirements; UI does not target needy workers, though it does serve workers in need of temporary income support.

This standard also has implications for which benefits within means-tested programs are considered to be part of the work support system. It establishes two key conditions: work support beneficiaries must be workers or dependents of workers and work support beneficiaries must be needy. Payments under Temporary Assistance for Needy Families (TANF) or food stamp benefits provided to people without earned income are not work supports. However, benefits from these same programs are work supports when they complement earned income. School meal subsidies (for the school lunch or breakfast programs) provided regardless of income are not work support benefits because they are not targeted to needy working families. However, subsidies that pay for free or reduced-price breakfasts and lunches are work supports because these benefits target low-income families.

Work support programs must broadly target needy workers or their dependents, rather than special subcategories of needy workers. Many means-tested government programs are designed to provide benefits to specific categories of needy people, such as veterans, the elderly, disabled people, or people with health concerns.[2] We exclude categorical programs from the work support system because they do not broadly target needy working families. This standard excludes Supplemental Security Income (SSI). Although SSI benefits are means tested and may supplement earned income, the purpose of the SSI program is to ensure that elderly, blind, or disabled people have an adequate minimum income, whether they work or not.[3] The Special Supplemental Nutrition Program for Women, Infants, and Children (WIC) is also excluded by this standard. Although WIC benefits may supplement earned income, the program targets pregnant women and others, including low-income children under age five, who experience specific nutrition risks.[4]

1. It was difficult to decide whether to include unemployment compensation as a work support. Sawhill and Haskins (2002b) are ambiguous about its status. They do not list it among the work support programs they describe, but they do discuss the significance of reforming the unemployment insurance system as a means of assisting those making the transition from welfare to work.

2. Melnick (1994).

3. Daly and Burkhauser (2003).

4. U.S. House of Representatives, Committee on Ways and Means (2000) (hereafter, *Green Book*).

Work support programs may provide benefits to third parties on behalf of needy workers or their dependents. This standard acknowledges the role that third parties often play in the implementation of work support programs. Although work support benefits must be provided on account of particular needy workers or their dependents, a third party may be the direct beneficiary. Medical assistance programs typically make payments to insurance companies, medical practitioners, or health maintenance organizations on behalf of program beneficiaries to provide access to medical treatment. Child care grants are often provided as payments directly to child care providers. Similarly, local housing authorities pay rent subsidies to landlords for the benefit of program participants. However, assistance to third parties that is not provided on account of a particular needy worker or working family is not considered a work support. For example, project-based housing assistance provided to developers in the form of tax credits in order to encourage the creation of affordable housing that may or may not benefit needy workers is excluded from the work support system.

Although work support benefits may vary with income, any nontrivial income must be sufficient to qualify for benefits. Work support programs distribute benefits in relation to income, and within limits may even provide more generous benefits to people who enjoy higher incomes, as does the earned income tax credit (EITC). However, we exclude programs that require a minimum income to qualify for benefits. For example, the federal government provides various forms of mortgage assistance to low-income families who wish to purchase homes (such as mortgage insurance, financial support for secondary mortgage markets, and closing cost assistance). However, to qualify for such assistance, one must have sufficient income to create a reasonable expectation that the loan will be repaid. Thus many needy working families are excluded because they are not affluent enough to fulfill this condition.[5] We exclude as work supports programs that have minimum income standards as a basis for eligibility.

On the basis of our earlier definition and these standards, we propose the following list of work support policies and programs: state and federal minimum wage rates; state and federal EITC programs and the child tax credit; medical assistance programs, including transitional medical assistance (TMA), Medicaid, and the Children's Health Insurance Program (CHIP); food programs, including the Food Stamp Program and free or reduced-price school meals; TANF earned income disregards; child care grants; and tenant-

5. It is also noteworthy that possession of an asset such as a home disqualifies needy workers from participation in many other work support programs.

based rental assistance programs. While we do not claim that this is a comprehensive list of programs that meet our definition and standards, it does include the major sources of material support for needy workers in the United States.

Analysts of social policy have long had concerns about the scope and effectiveness of work support programs. Over the years, they have proposed different lists of programs to define the boundaries of the system. One analysis that emphasized the provision of material support to needy workers before welfare reform was Christopher Jencks's *Rethinking Social Policy*.[6] Jencks identified two target groups for work supports: single mothers who work and parents with low-wage jobs. He proposed a series of measures to assist single mothers, including job training, minimum wage rates, child support enforcement, and the provision of cash assistance welfare to all eligible working mothers (though he viewed this last idea as politically impossible). He proposed to assist low-wage parents by increasing EITC benefits, providing tax credits for child care expenses, allowing low-wage workers to purchase Medicaid coverage, providing housing tax credits (as a form of rental assistance), and providing mortgage assistance.

More recently, Isabel Sawhill and Ron Haskins have analyzed work supports as an issue related to welfare reform.[7] Their list of work supports includes the minimum wage, state and federal EITC programs, the child tax credit, TANF earned income disregards, food stamps, Medicaid and CHIP, child care assistance, child support enforcement, and education and training.[8] Our program list overlaps significantly with theirs, although we include school meals and rental assistance and exclude child support and human capital programs. We include school meals and rental assistance in order to provide a more comprehensive list of the means-tested benefits available to working families. However, our decisions to exclude child support enforcement and human capital programs warrant further explanation.

Child support payments can be a valuable income source for struggling working mothers.[9] There are currently two parallel child support enforcement systems operating in the United States. One is an administrative system composed of state IV-D agencies (created under section 4, subsection D, when the Social Security Act was amended in 1974) that provide legal assistance, paternity determination, and collection services.[10] The other is the remnant

6. Jencks (1992).
7. Sawhill and Haskins (2002a, 2002b).
8. Sawhill and Haskins (2002b).
9. Sawhill and Haskins (2002b).
10. Garfinkel (2001).

of the local judicial system that requires private legal counsel and relies on courts to create and enforce support orders.[11]

Several features of the child support system make it inappropriate as a work support program for the purposes of our analysis. First, although TANF recipients are required to cooperate with state IV-D agencies and must assign their support payments to the state as an offset to their welfare grant, these agencies also serve people who do not receive welfare but use the IV-D system as an alternative to the private legal system.[12] Consequently, it is difficult to specify which aspects of the child support enforcement system serve needy workers and which serve the public in general. The requirement that TANF recipients participate in the child support system has resulted in a marked increase in the proportion of welfare recipients who receive child support payments. Irwin Garfinkel notes that between 1978 and 1998, the proportion of welfare recipients who received child support roughly doubled, from 13 to 25 percent.[13] However, Robert Lerman and Elaine Sorensen conclude that the effect of child support enforcement on poverty and welfare dependency is slight, because the government retains most of the child support payments made to welfare recipients.[14] In sum, we do not consider child support enforcement to be a work support because it does not target needy workers and because the material benefits for needy workers who do participate are often elusive, depending on their history of welfare participation and the ability of a private party (the noncustodial parent) to pay.

Although education and training programs can help low-wage workers to advance in the labor market, we exclude such programs from the work support system.[15] Federal human capital development programs provide basic education, skill development, on-the-job training, work experience, job readiness, and job placement services to assist displaced workers, disadvantaged adults, welfare recipients, youths in low-income families, and disabled people. The variety of programs and the many different categories of people targeted raise questions for defining the boundaries of the work support system. We do not include education or training programs that target specific groups, such as youths or disabled people, because these programs do not broadly target needy workers. However, our decision to exclude those programs that target disadvantaged adults and welfare recipients requires further explanation.

11. Crowley (2003).
12. Roberts (1994).
13. Garfinkel (2001).
14. Lerman and Sorensen (2003).
15. Sawhill and Haskins (2002b).

Education and training programs that serve welfare clients and disadvantaged adults have been the target of several recent reform efforts. In 1997 special welfare-to-work education and training grants were created to assist "hard cases" among TANF recipients. The 1998 Workforce Investment Act (WIA) overhauled federally sponsored education and training programs by requiring all states to integrate their training and employment services into one-stop career centers.[16] Although WIA participants need not be low-income people, local officials are supposed to give priority to people who are trying to make the transition from welfare to work. The WIA did not change the services that were offered by education and training programs, though it did reorganize the implementation of those services. Local officials were directed to create Workforce Investment Boards through which local business, labor, community, and government leaders could help to design and coordinate policy.

For several reasons we do not count the various education and training programs implemented under the WIA (including such innovations as individual development accounts) as work supports for the purposes of our analysis. First, although welfare clients are a priority target group for some human capital development programs, education and training services are not specifically targeted to needy workers and many of the program participants are displaced rather than disadvantaged workers. Second, employment and training programs are not intended as income supplements for needy workers but are attempts to enhance the human capital of low-wage workers so that they can become higher-wage workers. In that sense, they have a different, though related, purpose: education and training programs are intended to transform participants so that they can succeed in the labor market; work support programs enhance the material rewards available to needy workers who are stuck at the bottom of the labor market.

Our analysis of the work support system focuses on workers who are trapped at the bottom of the labor market—people who are expected to be low earners for extended periods of time. We are concerned with the material supports available to these workers and their dependents. We have defined the scope of the work support system to reflect that concern. However, as this discussion has demonstrated, other analysts have identified different objectives, and this has resulted in the creation of different program lists. Although there is substantial overlap between the program list we analyze and those proposed by others, reasonable people can disagree about the purpose, and therefore the scope, of the work support system.

16. Bell (2000).

In the following sections we briefly describe the policies and programs we have included as components of the work support system. The programs histories are not comprehensive; rather, they emphasize recent changes that help to explain the current status of work support programs and benefits.

Minimum Wage

The federal minimum wage is an hourly wage floor that governs conditions in U.S. labor markets. In contrast to the other work supports described in this chapter, the minimum wage does not involve direct government expenditures or sacrifice of tax revenues; it is a legal condition that affects labor costs for employers and the wages and employment prospects of workers at the bottom of the wage distribution. This is significant because the minimum wage shifts the costs of redistribution from the public to employers and (possibly) to low-wage workers who find their opportunities in the job market diminished when the minimum wage is increased.

The federal minimum wage originated in 1938 as a provision of the Fair Labor Standards Act and required employers who were engaged directly or indirectly in interstate commerce to pay a minimum of 25 cents per hour. Since that time, the federal minimum wage has been increased eight times, and more and more employers have been subjected to its requirements. During the 1990s it was raised three times: in 1991, from $3.80 to $4.25; in 1996, to $4.75; and in 1997, to the current level of $5.15. Recent proposals to increase the minimum wage have died in Congress. Despite the increases, the purchasing power of the minimum wage, adjusted to reflect changes in the cost of living over time, is lower than it was in the 1960s and 1970s.

Although the federal minimum wage establishes a national standard, fifteen states—Alaska, California, Connecticut, Delaware, Florida, Hawaii, Illinois, Maine, Massachusetts, New York, Oregon, Rhode Island, Vermont, Washington, and Wisconsin—and the District of Columbia have minimum wage rates in 2005 that exceed the federal requirement. The highest rates are those of Washington ($7.35), Oregon ($7.25), Alaska ($7.15), and Connecticut ($7.10).

An important distinction between the minimum wage and other work supports is that employers, not governments, pay the costs of the wage increases. Certainly, the minimum wage targets low-wage workers and provides a work incentive by increasing the hourly wage gained from employment. However, increasing the minimum wage may also reduce demand for low-wage labor, dimming the job prospects of low-skill workers.[17]

17. Neumark and Wascher (1997).

If so, it is possible that minimum wage increases are detrimental to some low-wage workers.

The effects of increasing the minimum wage on earned income, poverty, and unemployment are controversial. David Neumark, Mark Schweitzer, and William Wascher argue that increasing the minimum wage diminishes earned income among low-wage earners by reducing work hours and dimming employment prospects, especially for nonunion workers.[18] Other critics claim that minimum wage increases do little to relieve family poverty because many minimum wage workers are secondary earners in relatively affluent families.[19] Beyond this, some critics suggest that few workers earn the minimum for long periods before they move up to better-paying jobs.[20] These claims are disputed. Proponents claim that many minimum wage workers provide a significant share of total family income, and some empirical research suggests that although the predictions about reduced demand for labor are accurate, the effects of recent minimum wage increases on demand have been slight and are relevant primarily to the employment prospects of teenagers.[21] Beyond this, longitudinal research suggests that although most workers do earn more than the minimum wage shortly after starting their careers, a substantial portion of workers earn the minimum for significant periods of time. People with low educational achievement, women with children, blacks, and people working outside urban centers are likely to earn the minimum wage for longer periods of time.[22]

We include the minimum wage as a work support because it enhances the material rewards gained from work for those at the bottom of the labor market. However, the minimum wage may be a less effective work support than other programs because it is poorly targeted; many beneficiaries of minimum wage increases are secondary earners in higher-income families.[23] In addition, in many local labor markets the minimum wage may be inconsequential, because it is set below the prevailing market wage. Despite these limitations, a minimum wage increase can provide a substantial material gain for workers at or near the bottom of the labor market.[24]

18. Neumark, Schweitzer, and Wascher (2000).
19. Burkhauser and Finegan (1989).
20. Schiller (1994); Smith and Vavrichek (1992).
21. Sawhill and Thomas (2001); Bernstein and Schmitt (2000); Card and Krueger (1995).
22. Carrington and Fallick (2001).
23. Sawhill and Haskins (2002b); Burkhauser and Finegan (1989).
24. Sawhill and Thomas (2001).

Federal and State Income Taxes

During the 1990s the federal and several state income tax systems were transformed into significant work supports through the expansion of the EITC program and the creation of parallel state programs, along with the reduction of income tax burdens. In 2001 the generosity of the child tax credit, a provision of the personal income tax that had previously provided few benefits to low-income workers, was enhanced and made conditionally refundable.[25] As a consequence of these changes, needy workers are able to retain more of their earnings and the tax system has been transformed into a significant antipoverty tool.[26]

Federal Tax Credits and Personal Income Taxes

The federal government provides tax credits to low-income working families. The credit that provides the greatest amount of assistance to needy workers is the earned income tax credit, which is a refundable personal income tax credit. The federal EITC was initiated in 1975 as a means to stimulate employment, combat welfare dependency, and compensate low-income workers for the expenses of Social Security payroll taxes.[27] Between 1975 and 2000, tax expenditures associated with the EITC grew from $3.9 billion to $31.5 billion.[28] The EITC is currently the largest income supplement program in the United States and is widely praised as an effective tool against poverty.[29] As an "earnings credit," it pays benefits to workers based on family size and earned income. In their phase-in range, EITC benefits increase with earned income, creating a positive work incentive for some recipients. Those who qualify may use the credit to offset federal tax liabilities, receive a lump sum payment as a tax refund, or apply to receive advance EITC payments in their paycheck (though few recipients choose this option).

The EITC was conceived as an alternative to negative income tax proposals that had gained popularity in the early 1970s.[30] President Reagan later

25. On the paucity of benefits, see Sawhill and Haskins (2002b).

26. One tax credit we do not discuss as a work support is the dependent care tax credit. This is a means-tested program that provides a credit for child care expenses as an offset to tax liability. The credit is not refundable, and because few low-income workers have a federal tax liability, it provides scant benefits to assist needy workers. Blau (2003) reports that only 0.7 percent of the payments were provided to families with adjusted gross incomes of less than $15,000 in 1999.

27. Ventry (2000); Scholz (1994).

28. Hotz and Scholz (2003).

29. Blank, Card, and Robins (2000); Scholz (1994); Hoffman and Seidman (1990).

30. Hotz and Scholz (2003).

embraced the EITC as an alternative to welfare; the 1986 Tax Reform Act expanded EITC benefits and indexed them to inflation.[31] The EITC was expanded again in 1990, when more generous benefits were provided for families with two or more children. President Clinton viewed the EITC as a way to "make work pay" and engineered a significant expansion of the program.[32] In 1993 benefits were extended to childless workers. Between 1993 and 1998 the value of EITC benefits "rose 120 percent for a single mother with two children (and 40 percent for a single mother with one child)."[33]

For the purposes of qualifying for the EITC, earned income includes wages, salaries, and tips; net earnings from self-employment; some nontaxable income, such as salary deferrals and reductions, employer-provided lodging and meals, and housing allowances; and disability benefits received from an employer's disability retirement plan in advance of the minimum retirement age.[34] Among the many types of income that do not count as earned income are welfare benefits, workfare benefits, and Social Security retirement benefits.[35]

Other conditions restrict eligibility. These conditions differ, depending upon whether the claimant has a "qualifying child," and there are three different benefit schedules. More generous benefits are paid to those with a qualifying child; that is, a son, daughter, grandchild, adopted child, stepchild, or foster child under the age of 19, or under the age of 24 if a full-time student. A disabled child is a qualifying child regardless of age. Qualifying children must have lived with the EITC claimant in the United States for six months or more during the year for which the claim is made.[36] Those without a qualifying child are paid according to a less generous benefit schedule and must meet other eligibility tests: they must be between the ages of 25 and 65; cannot be the dependent of another person (whether or not that person makes the claim of dependency); and must have lived in the United States for at least six months during the year for which the EITC is claimed.

Only workers with modified adjusted gross incomes below specified thresholds qualify for the EITC; thresholds vary depending upon marital status, tax-filing status, and the number of qualifying children claimed. In 2002, for those with two or more qualifying children, the income limit for married couples filing jointly was $34,178. For those with one qualifying child, the

31. Ventry (2000).
32. Browning (1996).
33. Blank, Card, and Robbins (2000, p. 408).
34. Internal Revenue Service (1999).
35. *Green Book* (2000).
36. Internal Revenue Service (1999).

income limit for married couples filing jointly was $30,201. For those with no qualifying children, the income limit for married couples filing jointly was $12,060. Income thresholds are adjusted annually to reflect changes in the cost of living. There are also limits on investment income. In 2002 the investment income threshold for EITC eligibility was $2,550.

EITC benefits are phased in at a fixed rate from the first dollar of income earned. Since 1999 the phase-in rate for families with two or more children (the most generous benefit schedule) has been 0.40; that is, benefits increase 40 cents for each dollar of earned income until the top of the phase-in range is reached. The benefit payment is then stable across a fixed income range before the phase-out begins. The phase-out rate since 1999 has been .2106; that is, for each additional dollar earned above the phase-out threshold, EITC benefits decline by a little more than 21 cents.

Although its effects on the behavior of low-income workers are complex, the EITC is viewed as an effective antipoverty program. A report by the Center on Budget and Policy Priorities credits the EITC with lifting 4.6 million people out of poverty in 1996; 2.4 million of these were children.[37] The report concludes that the anti-poverty effectiveness of the EITC has been increasing, in part because of declines in the effectiveness of other programs. It is now lifts more children out of poverty than any other government program.

A report by the Congressional Budget Office notes that the EITC reduced the federal tax burden on low-income individuals, increasing their after-tax income.[38] Comparing the effective federal tax burdens in 1979 and 1997, the report notes that although tax rates declined for all household income levels, the decline was greatest in low-income households, where the EITC made effective tax rates negative, offsetting increases in social insurance and excise taxes. The report states that expansion of the EITC in the 1990s reduced effective tax rates by almost one-third and made the federal income tax system more progressive.

Although the federal EITC is celebrated as a means of assisting low-income working families, it has not escaped criticism.[39] One contention is that the EITC depresses the wages of some low-income workers. Because the program compensates different low-income workers at different rates, based on family structure and size, a net wage differential is created. EITC participants with children enjoy a higher net wage (the market wage plus their more generous EITC benefit), while low-income workers without children receive a lower net

37. Center on Budget and Policy Priorities (1998).
38. Congressional Budget Office (2001).
39. Ventry (2000).

wage.[40] Another criticism is that more generous EITC payments may have reduced work incentives for some beneficiaries. Based on a review of the existing literature, Joseph Hotz and John Scholz drew four conclusions about the effects of the EITC on labor market participation: (1) the EITC increases labor market participation among single-parent households; (2) these increases are significant; (3) the EITC has modest negative effects on labor market participation among two-parent families; and (4) the EITC slightly reduces the hours worked by labor force participants.[41]

Aspects of the administration of the EITC have been targets of criticism. Program administration has been criticized because it is linked to the tax system.[42] Although this link provides a convenient and inexpensive way to distribute benefits, some eligible people fail to receive benefits because they do not file income tax returns.[43] Also, there is evidence of fraud in benefit claims.[44] Inaccurate self-reporting by taxpayers about family structure can lead to overpayment of EITC benefits.

The federal tax credits available to low-income working families were further enhanced by recent changes in the child tax credit. Prior to these changes, the credit benefited very few low-income workers because it was not refundable.[45] The Economic Growth and Tax Relief Reconciliation Act of 2001 increased the child tax credit to $1,000 per qualifying child, effective in 2003, and made it conditionally refundable. The credit is limited to those with modified adjusted gross incomes below specific thresholds. However, these thresholds qualify low- and middle-income workers for benefits. In 2003, couples (married filing jointly) with modified adjusted gross incomes below $110,000 and single taxpayers with incomes below $75,000 qualified to receive the full credit. However, the credit is refundable only to compensate workers for the amount of Social Security taxes they paid and only if they have three or more qualifying children. Thus, to some extent, the child tax credit complements the EITC by providing refundable benefits to low-income workers with more than two qualifying children (recall that although this group qualifies for the maximum EITC benefits, benefits do not increase when there are more than two children in the family). However, many low-income workers (especially those with children) receive EITC payments that eliminate their tax liability and provide refunds. These workers will not receive assistance from

40. Browning (1996); Phelps (1994).
41. Hotz and Scholz (2003).
42. Hotz and Scholz (2003).
43. Dickert-Conlin and Holtz-Eakin (2000); Hoffman and Seidman (1990).
44. Ventry (2000); General Accounting Office (2001a).
45. Sawhill and Haskins (2002a).

Table 2-1. State EITC Programs, 2003

State	Percent of federal EITC	Refundable?
Colorado[a]	10	Yes
District of Columbia	25	Yes
Illinois	5	No
Indiana	6	Yes
Iowa	6.5	No
Kansas	15	Yes
Maine	5	No
Maryland[b]	18, 50	Yes, No
Massachusetts	15	Yes
Minnesota[c]	25–45	Yes
New Jersey[c]	20	Yes
New York	30	Yes
Oklahoma	5	Yes
Oregon	5	No
Rhode Island	25	No
Vermont	32	Yes
Wisconsin[c]	4–43	Yes

Sources: Johnson (2001); Johnson, Llobrera, and Zahradnik (2003).

a. Colorado suspended payment of state EITC benefits in 2002, due to fiscal constraints.

b. Recipients select either the refundable or the nonrefundable credit.

c. Benefit levels vary according to family size or income. New Jersey figure is for income levels below $20,000.

the child tax credit, unless they have three or more children. This suggests that its beneficiaries are more likely to be middle-income workers who have a tax liability or lower-income workers who qualify for EITC benefits that are insufficient to eliminate their tax liability.

State Income Taxes and EITC Programs

During the 1990s several states initiated tax credit programs related to the federal EITC. As of April 2003, seventeen states had EITC programs; twelve provided refundable credits and six provided nonrefundable credits (Maryland offered both types of credits, though workers could claim only one).[46] Table 2-1 reports the states offering EITC programs, the benefit rates expressed as a proportion of federal EITC payments, and whether the credit is refundable. The table shows that the generosity of the few state EITC programs varies significantly, from a low of 4 percent of the federal EITC for one-child families in Wisconsin to a high of 50 percent in Maryland.

46. Center on Budget and Policy Priorities (2003); Johnson, Llobrera, and Zahradnik (2003).

Other recent changes in state income tax policy also have reduced the tax burden facing low-income working families. The Center on Budget and Policy Priorities has studied the "tax threshold" (the level at which states begin to tax income) and reports that a "growing number of states exempt poor families from the income tax."[47] Between 1991 and 2000, most of the forty-two states that collect an income tax raised their tax threshold; Alabama and Connecticut were the exceptions. Between 1996 and 2000, a number of states raised their tax threshold enough to effectively eliminate the income tax for low-income workers. Only ten states tax the income of a minimum wage worker supporting a family of three (which is below the federal poverty standard). Twenty-three states have tax thresholds that eliminate taxes on a family of four with poverty-level earnings. Twenty-six states have tax thresholds that eliminate taxes on a family of three with poverty-level earnings. States are more likely to tax the near poor. Of the forty-two states with income taxes, thirty-one tax three- or four-person families with incomes at 125 percent of the federal poverty standard.

Food Stamp Program

The Food Stamp Program is a means-tested transfer program that increases the purchasing power of low-income households to help them enjoy a nutritionally adequate diet.[48] R. Shep Melnick has called food stamps a "rare bird" in the collection of U.S. safety net programs and describes the program as

> a nationally uniform, noncategorical, means-tested income maintenance program. Aid is available to all low-income households regardless of family composition. Consequently, food stamps provide assistance to several groups that fall between the cracks of categorical welfare programs: two-parent families, single adults, and childless couples. The low benefit-reduction rate—about 30 percent—allows the working poor to receive income support.[49]

Eligible households receive food stamp benefits in the form of electronic balances and use these funds to purchase approved foods at participating retail stores. Food stamp benefits vary according to household size and income (and are higher in Alaska and Hawaii). They are intended to make up the difference between the household's expected outlay on food purchases and the

47. Center on Budget and Policy Priorities (2001, p. 1).
48. Department of Agriculture (2000a).
49. Melnick (1994, p. 183).

government's standard of the expenditure required to purchase a "nutritionally adequate low-cost diet."[50] The Thrifty Food Plan developed by the Department of Agriculture (USDA) is the basis for the government's standard of an adequate low-cost diet.[51]

The Food Stamp Program was initiated as a pilot program in 1961 and made permanent in 1964; national eligibility standards were created in 1971.[52] In 1974 Congress initiated a significant expansion in program participation by mandating that states offer food stamp services. The program is an individual entitlement; qualified households have a legal right to receive benefits, and federal funds to provide food stamps are not subject to budgetary limitations.[53] Funding for the program is mostly a federal responsibility, although states do pay for administrative costs, for special program options, and penalties for erroneous benefits. States administer the program; local social service departments determine eligibility, calculate benefits, and issue food stamps within federal rules.

During fiscal year 2002, approximately 19.1 million people received food stamps; the average monthly household benefit was $79.60 per person; the total federal expenditure for food stamps in 2002 was $21,657,000,000.[54] Following declines from 1994 to 2000, program participation started increasing in 2001. Although several factors influenced the decline in the 1990s, more than 50 percent of it has been attributed to the fact that fewer eligible people received program benefits.[55] The recent increase in participation is probably due to the economic recession, as food stamp participation closely tracks macroeconomic trends.

Most food stamp benefits are distributed to poor families: 89 percent of food stamp households had incomes below the federal poverty standard; 34 percent of food stamp households had incomes below 50 percent of the poverty standard, and these households received 55 percent of all program benefits. Most of the low-income households served by the program included children.[56] The program served an average of 4 million households with children a month; 85 percent of food stamp households with earned income were households with children.[57]

50. *Green Book* (2000).
51. Department of Agriculture (1999a).
52. Currie (2003).
53. King (2000); Melnick (1994).
54. *Green Book* (2004).
55. Rosso (2003).
56. Department of Agriculture (2000b).
57. Rosso (2003).

Although only 23.1 percent of food stamp households received TANF benefits in fiscal year 2001, there is a close association between receipt of cash assistance welfare and food stamps.[58] In most states, the programs are jointly administered by state social service agencies; receipt of cash assistance makes one categorically eligible to receive food stamps, but many people who are eligible for food stamps do not receive cash assistance. There is also a state program option to provide "transitional food stamps" to people leaving cash assistance (including those making the transition from welfare to work). These former TANF recipients can receive up to five months of benefits at the level of their last month of TANF participation.[59] One consequence of the close relationship between receipt of cash assistance and food stamps is that food stamp participation among eligible households is higher among cash assistance recipients.

Some food stamp recipients are low-income workers. In 2001, 27 percent of food stamp households had earned income.[60] However, the USDA has acknowledged that the program has difficulties serving eligible working households. In 1994 it estimated that 2.7 million eligible households among the working poor (54 percent) did not participate in the Food Stamp Program.[61] A follow-up study identified five reasons for lack of participation: (1) some did not know they were eligible; (2) some perceived they did not need such assistance; (3) some thought the benefits would be too low to bother with; (4) some expected administrative hassles and disrespectful treatment from the social service department employees who determine eligibility; and (5) some cited the stigma of participation.[62]

Eligibility for food stamps is determined at the household level. A household may be a person living alone or several people (related or not) who live together, if they usually have meals together. To receive food stamps, households must pass financial, categorical, or work-related eligibility tests.[63] Household members must have combined financial assets and monthly income below the standards established for the program. The amount of the benefit varies inversely with the income of the household and directly with the number of people. Eligibility also depends on other considerations. TANF and Supplemental Security Income (SSI) households are automatically eligible to

58. Figure is from Rosso (2003).
59. *Green Book* (2004).
60. Rosso (2003).
61. Department of Agriculture (1994).
62. Department of Agriculture (1999b).
63. Currie (2003).

receive food stamps. And households with an elderly or disabled member enjoy more liberal eligibility standards.

A key concern in establishing eligibility is the value of assets possessed by the members of the household, because asset limits are more stringent than income limits in terms of limiting participation by needy working families. Household assets generally cannot exceed $2,000, unless there is an elderly or disabled person in the household, in which case the limit is $3,000. Automobiles are an exception. The general rule is that automobiles are counted at their fair market value less $4,650. However, many states have taken advantage of an option in the Food Stamp Program that allows TANF vehicle eligibility standards to be used. This has the effect of extending eligibility to families with more valuable vehicles.[64]

Work requirements have long been an element of Food Stamp Program eligibility. The Food Stamp Act of 1977 created several new bases for disqualification from the program, including lack of cooperation with work requirements. To receive food stamps, physically and mentally fit household members between the ages of 18 and 60 were required to register for and accept employment. People subject to Title IV of the Social Security Act, working thirty hours per week, with dependent children under 12 years of age, or in drug or alcohol rehabilitation were exempted from these requirements.[65]

The work requirements related to the Food Stamp Program have increased over time. In 1985 the Food Security Act required that states develop and implement employment and training programs for food stamp recipients. Currently, work requirements apply to physically and mentally fit people between the ages of 15 and 60, although exceptions are made for those aged 16 to 18 who are in school or an approved training program. Those subject to the requirements must register for employment, participate in employment and training programs, and accept employment offers. Provisions of the 1996 Personal Responsibility and Work Opportunity Reconciliation Act (PRWORA) have made selected groups responsible for their work and Food Stamp Program participation history. Fit individuals between 18 and 50 years of age who have no dependent children and are not pregnant are ineligible for food stamps if, during the past thirty-six months, they received food stamp benefits for three months while not working or participating in an approved work program for at least twenty hours per week.[66]

64. *Green Book* (2004).
65. *Green Book* (2002).
66. *Green Book* (2000).

The Food Stamp Program currently enforces the following work requirements for household heads who are fit and aged from 16 to 59 (with exceptions):

1. They must register for employment (with state welfare or employment offices);

2. They must accept a job if offered;

3. They must participate in any job search or training activities required by the welfare agency;

4. They must cooperate with the welfare agency by providing information to determine job availability; and

5. They may not quit a job without good cause or reduce their work hours to less than thirty per week.[67]

The PRWORA influenced eligibility and work requirements for food stamp recipients in other ways as well. Previously, food stamp benefits went up when cash benefits were reduced. The PRWORA changed that practice: those who lose cash assistance for noncompliance with TANF rules are prohibited from receiving an increase in food stamp assistance to compensate. Beyond this, as the work requirements for receipt of cash assistance have changed under state waivers or TANF plans, states have been permitted to extend these requirements to food stamp participants. Sixteen states have decided to include food stamp sanctions for noncompliance with TANF program requirements in their plans, potentially reducing food stamp benefits by as much as 25 percent.[68]

The connection between welfare reform and food stamp participation has also raised concerns because the implementation of the PRWORA was occasioned by a reduction in food stamp participation. According to a survey of state administrators conducted by the General Accounting Office (GAO), three factors were responsible for declines in food stamp participation in the mid-1990s: the strength of the U.S. economy, provisions of the PRWORA that changed eligibility rules and limited participation, and state and local initiatives designed to reduce cash welfare participation.[69] A subsequent GAO report explained the ways in which program quality control issues interact with welfare reform to reduce food stamp participation.[70] The federal government monitors state performance under the auspices of its quality control program, an aspect of Food Stamp Program administration (implemented by the USDA) that checks state compliance with federal eligibility and benefit guidelines.

67. *Green Book* (2004).

68. Zedlewski and Brauner (1999).

69. General Accounting Office (1999). GAO interviewed officials from forty-nine of the fifty states and from the District of Columbia; Rhode Island did not respond.

70. General Accounting Office (2002a).

States are held accountable for errors, including overpayments. From the perspective of the states, the cases of low-income workers are the most likely to generate erroneous food stamp payments, because their work hours (and hence their incomes) fluctuate more from month to month. As a result, many states grant food stamps to low-income workers for only a short period, requiring frequent reassessments of eligibility. This requires additional visits to the local social services department, increasing the "hassle factor" that many eligible low-income workers cite as a barrier to participation.

A study aimed at reforming the Food Stamp Program to better serve the working poor called attention to the joint administration of TANF and food stamps as a potential problem. On the basis of site visits and interviews with social services administrators in several states, the authors concluded that joint administration confuses the "narrative of assistance."[71] The confusion stems from the association between cash assistance and food stamp eligibility. Because cash assistance is a common road to food stamps, clients may wrongly conclude that ineligibility for cash assistance also disqualifies them from food stamps. Federal rules that have sought to make eligibility standards for TANF and food stamps compatible (and to liberalize food stamp eligibility standards) contribute to this confusion.

The federal government has recently taken steps to increase food stamp access among low-income workers. Specific proposals have been compiled in a report of state best practices distributed by the Department of Agriculture.[72] Best practices include (1) enhancing client convenience by extending office hours, establishing satellite offices, and accepting information through drop boxes; (2) providing additional resources (such as advocates, transportation, or interpreters) for clients; (3) providing clients with better program information; and (4) simplifying the application process. The Farm Security and Rural Investment Act of 2002 (FSRIA) also took several significant steps to reform the Food Stamp Program and encourage participation among low-income workers. One needed reform was the liberalization or elimination of vehicle asset tests for food stamp eligibility. The FSRIA allowed states to make food stamp income and asset tests conform to their TANF and Medicaid asset and income tests. Beyond this, the FSRIA eased the threat of sanctions resulting from overpayments to food stamp recipients with earned income and also provided a number of state options to reduce administrative burdens on applicants, in order to make food stamp benefits more accessible.[73] Whether

71. Lerman and Wiseman (2002, p. 49).
72. Department of Agriculture (2000c).
73. *Green Book* (2004)

these changes will redress the problems the program has experienced in serving low-income working families remains to be seen.

School Lunch and Breakfast Programs

The school lunch and breakfast programs provide subsidized meals to millions of school children daily. In fiscal year 2001, on an average day 25.4 million children received lunch and 7.8 million children received breakfast. The programs subsidize all of the meals served at participating schools and child care institutions with cash payments and commodities and provide additional subsidies for low-income children. Those with incomes below 130 percent of the federal poverty standard are entitled to receive free lunch and breakfast at participating schools. Those with incomes between 130 percent and 185 percent of the poverty standard are entitled to reduced-price meals.

The school lunch program was created in 1946, when the National School Lunch Act consolidated numerous existing child nutrition programs into a comprehensive national initiative and established an administrative framework for program operations.[74] The school lunch program is an individual entitlement; students who attend participating schools and qualify on the basis of income eligibility guidelines are entitled to receive program benefits without regard to budget constraints.[75] The program is operated by state education agencies in all fifty states and the District of Columbia, under agreements with the USDA. Local schools operate the program in cooperation with state education agencies and in compliance with federal guidelines that regulate competing food services, lunch content, and eligibility determination. Approximately 83 percent of all schools (both public and private) offer lunch program services, and 92 percent of students attend schools that offer such services.[76] These schools are reimbursed on a per meal basis; common reimbursement rates are established for the forty-eight contiguous states and District of Columbia, and higher rates are set for Alaska and Hawaii. Schools that serve a large proportion of low-income children are entitled to receive an additional cash payment. Schools also receive commodities (foods or food products); some commodities are provided as an entitlement to the schools to underwrite the costs of the program, and others are provided when in surplus.

The school breakfast program was initiated as a pilot program in 1966 and made permanent in 1975.[77] Currently, more than 75,000 schools and institu-

---

74. Currie (2003); Stoker (1991).
75. Melnick (1994); Stoker (1991).
76. Currie (2003).
77. Currie (2003).

tions participate. The program is administered in a manner similar to the school lunch program. Local schools provide the services, operating their programs in cooperation with state education agencies and within federal guidelines. Eligibility standards for free and reduced-price breakfasts are the same as for free and reduced-price lunches. Schools receive lower reimbursements for providing breakfast, but rates are higher in Alaska and Hawaii, and special assistance is available for schools that serve a large proportion of breakfasts to low-income children (about 65 percent of breakfasts served receive this additional support). In fiscal year 2002, more than 8.2 million children received school breakfast benefits, and more than 6.8 million of them received free or reduced-price breakfasts.

We consider some benefits of the school lunch and breakfast programs to be work supports. The federal government provides a general subsidy to all program participants regardless of income. However, there are also special subsidies to underwrite the costs of providing free and reduced-price meals and we consider these to be work supports because eligibility to receive assistance is targeted to children in low-income working families.

Medical Assistance

Medical assistance provides needy people with access to health care. Changes in eligibility for medical assistance programs, in particular the decisions to decouple medical assistance from cash assistance welfare programs and to establish more liberal income eligibility guidelines, have increased access to medical assistance among low-income workers. However, the gains have been uneven: Access to medical assistance for children and pregnant women has improved significantly, but limited parental eligibility and low levels of participation among those who are eligible indicate that significant gaps in medical assistance coverage persist.[78]

Two major programs that provide medical assistance to low-income workers and their families are Medicaid and the Children's Health Insurance Program (CHIP is sometimes implemented as an extension of state Medicaid programs, at the state's discretion). Title XIX of the Social Security Act established Medicaid to provide medical assistance to the "categorically needy" and the "medically needy."[79] The federal government and the states jointly finance Medicaid. The federal government provides grants to states in inverse relation to their per capita income, to finance program benefits. States pay the

78. Broaddus and others (2002).
79. *Green Book* (2000).

balance of program costs, and the state role in financing may influence the scope of Medicaid coverage or services. Although, as an individual entitlement, Medicaid benefits are not limited by budget constraints, states may be inclined to limit services or eligibility in order to control costs. State eligibility and benefit standards do vary.

Jonathan Gruber observes that Medicaid is actually composed of four different programs. One program provides access to health care for low-income people, especially children. The other three programs serve the elderly and the disabled, providing insurance coverage to supplement Medicare, health care access for the disabled, and long-term care for the indigent elderly. The services provided to the elderly and the disabled consume three-fourths of Medicaid's budget.[80] Yet because the indigent elderly and disabled people are special categories of beneficiaries and their benefits are not linked to work, we do not consider their Medicaid benefits to be work supports. We are concerned with those aspects of Medicaid that target low-income people.

Medicaid eligibility requirements are complicated, and because states are empowered to design and operate their own programs within federal guidelines, there is substantial variation among states in terms of coverage, benefits, and reimbursement rates. Recent policy changes have expanded state authority. States are permitted to provide Medicaid benefits to children who meet the income guidelines but not the definition of a "dependent child" of Aid to Families with Dependent Children. States may disqualify adults (except pregnant women) who refuse to comply with TANF work requirements, but may not disqualify their children. States may provide Medicaid benefits for pregnant women and children less than 1 year old whose family income is no more than 185 percent of the federal poverty standard (forty-one states and the District of Columbia provide such benefits). States also may extend Medicaid coverage for children even if they no longer meet income eligibility tests and may provide services to children while eligibility is being determined.[81]

State influence on Medicaid eligibility is limited by federal guidelines that require states to serve populations designated as eligible on the basis of income guidelines. Federally mandated extensions of Medicaid benefits were enacted in the late 1980s and early 1990s. In 1988 Medicaid coverage was mandated for pregnant women and infants (up to age 1) if family income was less than 100 percent of the federal poverty standard. In 1989 Medicaid

80. Gruber (2003).

81. The states have enjoyed the option of "presumptive eligibility" (the extension of Medicaid services while eligibility was being determined) for pregnant women since 1986. The details of Medicaid eligibility for low-income children and pregnant women are discussed on pages 894 and 895 of the *Green Book* (2000).

coverage was expanded to include children under age 6 and pregnant women in families with incomes below 133 percent of the poverty standard. In 1990 a phase-in began that mandated coverage of children aged 6–18 in families with incomes below 100 percent of the federal poverty standard.[82] As a result of these mandates, states are now required to provide Medicaid coverage to pregnant women and children under age 6 whose family incomes are below 133 percent of the poverty standard, and to cover all children under age 19 in families with incomes below the federal poverty standard.[83]

The mandatory extensions of Medicaid benefits resulted in an increase in the number of people served, especially pregnant women and children. Although the number of persons served by Medicaid varied little from 1977 to 1989, between 1989 and 1995 the number grew from about 23.5 million to more than 36.3 million.[84] In 1998 Medicaid covered 10.2 percent of the total population and 40.3 percent of the population below the poverty standard.[85] Although most Medicaid recipients were poor children or adults in families with poor children, most benefits went to the elderly and the disabled.[86]

Medicaid benefits also have been extended to some low-income workers through a linkage with the cash assistance welfare system. Subject to limiting conditions, states are required to extend Medicaid benefits for as long as one year to people who are making the transition from welfare to work, to remove loss of medical assistance as a barrier to employment; though time limited, the extension of transitional medical assistance is significant.[87]

Access to medical assistance for low-income children increased further as a result of the creation of CHIP.[88] According to the Balanced Budget Act of 1997, the purpose of CHIP is to "initiate and expand child health assistance to uninsured, low-income children." CHIP is a matching federal grant program to the states. States establish eligibility standards within federal guidelines and may choose three different mechanisms to implement their programs: they may expand Medicaid eligibility, they may create a separate program within federal guidelines, or they may use a combination of both strategies. The federal government makes matching grants to states to finance the program with payments that are more generous than Medicaid reimbursement rates. However, unlike Medicaid, the federal contribution to CHIP

82. Health Care Financing Administration (2000).
83. *Green Book* (1998).
84. Health Care Financing Administration (2000).
85. *Green Book* (2000).
86. Gruber (2003).
87. *Green Book* (2003).
88. Broaddus and others (2002).

funding is a capped block grant.[89] Funding for CHIP was first provided in October 1997.[90]

In 1999 a total of 1,979,450 children were enrolled in CHIP nationwide. These were newly insured children, as states are forbidden from using CHIP funds to insure children who were Medicaid eligible by the standards of March 1997. Although coverage standards vary from one state to another, in all states the top Medicaid eligibility standard is the lower limit of CHIP eligibility. Thus CHIP extends medical assistance to children whose family incomes had made them ineligible for Medicaid. Upper-level eligibility guidelines range from 100 percent to 350 percent of the federal poverty standard.[91]

CHIP is an important extension of medical benefits to low-income workers. Eligibility for CHIP, in contrast to TMA, is not linked to the transition from welfare to work. And CHIP eligibility is based on more liberal income guidelines than for Medicaid. However, the program targets children exclusively. While CHIP is a significant benefit to children in low-income working families, it provides no coverage for parents and does not benefit low-income workers without children. In addition, a recent evaluation of CHIP indicates that there are significant barriers to participation, including ignorance of benefits and eligibility criteria as well as limited information about how to enroll in the program. These barriers appear to be less important to those with previous experience of Medicaid.[92]

Although the opportunities of access to medical assistance for low-income workers and their children have multiplied in recent years, access remains a problem, especially for low-income working parents. According to Broaddus and coauthors, "poor parents who work are more likely to be uninsured than poor parents who do not work."[93] A recent report by the Census Bureau indicates that the situation is not improving.[94] The proportion of the population without medical insurance increased between 2000 and 2001: in 2001, 41.2 million people lacked medical insurance; that is, 14.6 percent of the population and 1.4 million more than in 2000.

89. Dubay, Hill, and Kenney (2002).
90. *Green Book* (2000).
91. Department of Health and Human Services (1999b).
92. Woolridge and others (2003).
93. Broaddus and others (2002, p. 3).
94. Census Bureau (2002a).

Temporary Assistance for Needy Families

TANF is the primary cash assistance program to provide income support to poor families with children; only families with a minor child or a pregnant person may receive TANF benefits. Created by the PRWORA in 1996 to replace Aid to Families with Dependent Children, TANF has four stated purposes:

1. To assist needy families, so that children may be cared for in their homes or the homes of relatives;

2. To end dependence on government benefits by promoting job preparation, work, and marriage among needy parents;

3. To prevent and reduce the incidence of out-of-wedlock pregnancies; and

4. To encourage the formation and maintenance of two-parent families.

Although states are empowered to use TANF funds to promote these goals, states are also permitted to divert funds for a variety of purposes other than funding cash welfare.[95] This power is significant, because it creates opportunities for financing other programs (such as child care grants) that benefit needy workers.

TANF was a major shift in federal welfare policy that changed the legal and financial foundations of means-tested cash assistance; the program created new eligibility requirements for individuals and created new opportunities and requirements for the states. Benefits provided to individuals under AFDC were individual entitlements; TANF provides no individual entitlement to benefits. Under AFDC, unlimited matching funds were provided to the states to make payments to eligible individuals; TANF provides a fixed block grant to the states ($16.5 billion annually) and subjects the states to maintenance-of-effort requirements. TANF gives states the authority to decide which families to assist, including the power to establish income and asset disregards. But individuals must satisfy new federal requirements to maintain eligibility for cash assistance: beneficiaries must meet the state work requirements and lifetime eligibility is limited to five years (though 20 percent of a state's caseload is exempted from this time limit). In addition, families must assign child support rights to the state, and unwed mothers under age 18 must live in an "adult-supervised arrangement" and stay in school to maintain TANF eligibility.

States are required to achieve minimum rates of work participation for TANF participants or face financial penalties. States must require TANF

95. *Green Book* (2000).

recipients to work after 24 months but may require earlier work efforts; more than a dozen states require work immediately.[96] However, states may achieve these work requirement goals either by placing recipients in specific work activities or by reducing their cash assistance caseloads. Given the significant reductions in welfare caseloads that occurred between 1994 and 2000, states have had little difficulty satisfying the work requirements.

Welfare participation grew significantly between 1970 and 1975. Although growth continued after 1975, it slowed considerably between 1975 and 1990. The rate of cash assistance participation began to grow significantly in 1990 and peaked in 1994. Since then, caseloads have declined. Among families, the decline between 1994 and 2002 is estimated at more than 58 percent. By 1999 the number of cash assistance recipients was lower than it was in 1970.[97]

The value of cash payments made through the AFDC or TANF programs has declined over time. Since 1970 the real value of cash assistance payments has declined in all fifty states and the District of Columbia.[98] The largest decline was in Texas, where the value of cash welfare payments decreased by 69 percent between 1970 and 2000; in Idaho and New Jersey, it decreased by 68 percent. The smallest declines, at 21 percent, were in Maine and Wisconsin; in California, the decline was 22 percent. The median decline in the real value of state welfare benefits was 47 percent over this period. To some extent this decline in cash assistance was offset by increases in food stamp benefits, though the magnitude of this offset varied from state to state.[99]

Recent changes in cash assistance welfare payments and eligibility requirements influence the well-being of needy workers because many TANF recipients work, and state-level TANF programs encourage them to do so. However, changes enacted under the PRWORA have made the relationship between the receipt of welfare and work more complex. An Urban Institute report examined whether recent changes in welfare programs in twelve states have made it more attractive for welfare clients to enter the paid labor force.[100] The income gain a family receives when moving from welfare to part-time work at minimum wage is quite significant; although it varies from state to state, it averages 51 percent. A family that moves from part-time to full-time work has an average income gain of 20 percent. The EITC is responsible for a large part of this gain.

96. *Green Book* (2000).
97. Moffitt (2003).
98. *Green Book* (2000, pp. 389–90).
99. King (2000).
100. Acs and others (1998).

When families emerging from the cash welfare system are compared to low-income working families outside the welfare system, an equity concern arises. Many states have elected to provide "earnings disregards" for TANF recipients who go to work. This means that TANF participants retain a portion of their benefit (the amount varies from state to state) for some time, even while earning income. This encourages work by reducing the implicit benefit tax (the loss of benefits when income is earned), but it also creates an inequity between those moving from welfare to work and low-income workers outside the cash welfare system.

Recent changes in cash assistance welfare programs are important to the well-being of needy workers in two ways. Needy workers emerging from the cash welfare system benefit from changes that allow them to combine TANF benefits with earned income (though it is important to keep in mind that this transition period counts toward the overall five-year limit on TANF eligibility). However, state TANF plans that aim to induce welfare recipients to work with earnings disregards significantly disadvantage low-income workers who are not TANF participants. As a result of welfare reform, states are striving to reduce cash assistance caseloads, and this makes it more difficult for people to enter the welfare system, and hence enjoy the special rewards that are available when leaving it.

Child Care Grants

With a majority of mothers participating in the paid labor force in the United States, the quality and affordability of child care is a significant concern. In addition, child care subsidies are important for helping people make the transition from welfare to work.[101] The Family Support Act (adopted in 1988) and the Omnibus Budget Reconciliation Act of 1990 resulted in the creation of four federally funded child care programs that targeted AFDC families, families that once received AFDC, low-income working families at risk of becoming eligible to participate in AFDC, and other low-income families.[102] These programs were consolidated and expanded by the PRWORA into the Child Care and Development Block Grant (CCDBG). The CCDBG is supported by a combination of discretionary and entitlement funding (though the entitlement is to the states, not to individual recipients). Together, these sources constitute the Child Care and Development Fund (CCDF).

101. Blau (2003).
102. *Green Book* (2000).

According to the Department of Health and Human Services, the purpose of the CCDF is "to help subsidize the child care expenses of low- and moderate-income families so they can work or attend education or training programs."[103] Potentially, the CCDF could be a significant source of benefits to low-income workers. However, restrictive eligibility standards in many states, funding limitations, and the federally required preference for families that are making the transition from welfare to work effectively limit the child care benefits available.

There has been a substantial increase in the funds devoted to the CCDF. From 1992 to 1998, total funding increased almost 300 percent. The monies are divided among the states according to a formula that includes the number of children under age 5, the number of children receiving free or reduced-price lunches (a common indicator of poverty), and per capita income.[104] In fiscal year 2000, the states expended a total of $8 billion for child care assistance, including $2.0 billion of TANF funds that were transferred to the CCDF.[105]

Although federal guidelines allow states to provide child care services to families with incomes at or below 85 percent of the state median level, forty-one states have adopted more restrictive eligibility guidelines. New Jersey has the most stringent standard, providing CCDF benefits only to those families with income at or below 37 percent of the state median level. In addition, the availability of services is influenced by budgetary concerns. Since individuals are not entitled to child care services, even if they meet state eligibility requirements there is no guarantee they will receive benefits. Families connected to the cash welfare system receive priority. Federal law requires that at least 70 percent of state child care funds are devoted to the needs of families that are making the transition from welfare to work or families that are at risk of cash welfare participation. Federal law also requires that states give priority to families that are identified in state plans as "very low income."[106] Finally, states generally restrict eligibility to families in which both parents are working and in which there are children under age 13, though some exceptions exist.[107]

Benefits are usually distributed in the form of certificates or vouchers that participants use to reduce the out-of-pocket costs of child care. Although states establish reimbursement rates for providers, in twenty-four states,

103. Department of Health and Human Service (1999a).

104. *Green Book* (2000).

105. Department of Health and Human Service (2001).

106. *Green Book* (2000).

107. Department of Health and Human Services (1999a).

providers may charge parents an additional amount if their provider's rates exceed the state's reimbursement level. States also develop a fee schedule, based upon family income and size, to determine the copayment families are required to make. There is significant variation in copayment rates across the states, but the median monthly copayment for a two-person family with an income of $10,000 was $37. In most states, families with an income of $20,000 are required to pay the full market rate for child care.[108]

Despite the additional resources the PRWORA has provided for child care assistance and the fact that states have transferred TANF funds to provide additional funding, the need has not been met. The Department of Health and Human Services estimated that only about 15 percent of eligible children received assistance from the CCDF in fiscal year 1998; of the 9.9 million children eligible under state guidelines, only 1.5 million received assistance. The unmet need would be even greater if states had adopted eligibility guidelines allowed by federal standards. Under federal law, children in families with incomes at or below 85 percent of the state median level are eligible for assistance, but only nine states have adopted this standard. Using the federal standard, 14.7 million children were eligible for assistance in 1998, and the program served only about 10 percent of these children.[109] In addition, in a report to Congress on the status of welfare reform in 2000, the Department of Health and Human Services stated that there were "extensive waiting lists" for child care services and that of the 50 to 70 percent of former welfare recipients who had left the rolls and were working, only about 30 percent were receiving child care assistance.[110]

Rental Assistance

An array of federal programs provides housing assistance to people in many different circumstances. Working with local public housing authorities (PHAs), housing nonprofits, and commercial real estate interests, the federal government subsidizes housing construction, ownership, and rental. Two federal agencies have primary responsibility for housing programs: the Department of Housing and Urban Development (HUD) and the Department of Agriculture. The Internal Revenue Service also is indirectly involved in housing assistance programs, because tax incentives are used to encourage homeownership and to influence commercial construction plans. Finally,

---

108. Department of Health and Human Services (1999a).
109. Department of Health and Human Services (1999a).
110. Department of Health and Human Services (2000).

federally sponsored enterprises (quasi-government entities, such as Fannie Mae and Freddie Mac) organize and participate in mortgage markets.[111]

We are concerned with federal housing programs that assist needy workers: programs that target people making the transition from welfare to work, and those that target low-income households for rental subsidies and mortgage interest subsidies.[112] Housing assistance can be "an important support for working families" because the material benefit of the subsidy may be enhanced by asset ownership, mobility, and residential choice.[113] However, as explained above, we do not consider mortgage interest subsidies to be work supports, because a minimum income is required to qualify.

Rental subsidies are relevant to the work support system. Rental assistance reduces the expenses recipients pay for rent and regulates housing quality. The programs are redistributive in two senses: they have upper-income eligibility limits and the amount of the subsidy varies inversely with income.[114] Unlike mortgage subsidies, rental subsidies do not provide the benefit of asset ownership, and not all forms of rental subsidy provide mobility and residential choice. Although some rental assistance programs allow participants to select the location and unit they prefer in the private rental market, not all rental assistance programs are so flexible.

Rental assistance was initiated with the Housing Act of 1937. The most common form of assistance provided at that time was financial support to underwrite the construction of housing projects owned and operated by local PHAs. State governments chartered local PHAs to receive intergovernmental grants and manage housing programs; the agencies were typically organized at the county or municipal levels; currently, more than 3,400 operate in the United States.[115]

The nature of rental assistance changed as new missions, participants, and policy tools were introduced. In 1954 the federal government first contracted with private parties (initially nonprofits, but later for-profit firms also) to provide low-income housing. In 1965 Congress created the Section 23 program that allowed local public housing authorities to lease existing apartments in unsubsidized housing. In 1974 Section 23 was replaced by the Section 8 "certificate program," and in 1983 the Section 8 "voucher program"

111. Koppell (2003).

112. *Green Book* (2003).

113. Schwartz and Miller (2002, p. 197); Department of Housing and Urban Development (2000).

114. Olsen (2003).

115. On organization, see Schwartz and Miller (2002); the figure is from Olsen (2003).

was created.[116] The certificate program was a significant change in rental assistance policy because it allowed individual recipients to seek housing in the private rental market. The voucher program was more flexible than the certificate program because it allowed participants to rent more expensive units (if they paid the difference) and to use their vouchers outside the jurisdiction of origin, a feature known as portability.[117] The two Section 8 programs were consolidated in 1998, making the more flexible practices of the voucher program applicable to certificate program participants.[118] In 1999 the Welfare-to-Work voucher program was created to provide housing assistance for families making the transition from welfare to work.[119] Over time, federal rental assistance programs turned away from the production of housing projects to emphasize placing participants in existing rental units, and shifted management responsibilities from the public to the private sector.

Two broad categories of rental assistance currently serve low-income households: project-based subsidies for construction or rehabilitation of specific rental units and household-based subsidies that permit participants to select rental units in the existing market.[120] The ability to select the rental unit is important, because recipients may elect to live in a neighborhood that is relatively safe and offers better educational or economic opportunities.[121] Household-based subsidies typically are provided in the form of housing vouchers that are the basis of contractual agreements between landlords and local PHAs. If the landlord accepts the voucher, the PHA makes subsidy payments directly to the landlord to reduce the tenant's out-of-pocket rental expense. By contrast, project-based rental assistance is linked to particular units in particular locations and may expose recipients to problems that are associated with concentrated poverty, such as crime, poor public services, and limited economic opportunities. This type of assistance is provided directly to the local entity (public or private) that owns the rental facility, for

---

116. Olsen (2003).

117. Department of Housing and Urban Development (2000).

118. Department of Housing and Urban Development (2000); Sard and Lubell (2000).

119. Department of Housing and Urban Development (2000).

120. *Green Book* (2000); Sard and Lubell (2000). We should not exaggerate the choice that is available to recipients of rental subsidies. They are constrained by discrimination, income, and the reluctance of landlords to rent to them. One factor that influences a landlord's decision is the competence of the local PHA. Turner (2003). Prior to the consolidation of the Section 8 program in 1998, regulation also constrained choice. The constraints are likely to be especially severe in tight rental markets. Cunningham (2004); Turner (2003).

121. Burton (2004); Turner (2003); Schwartz and Miller (2002).

its construction or rehabilitation. The assistance indirectly benefits the target group by providing below-market rents.

In some instances, project- and household-based assistance is closely linked. The federal HOPE VI project provides grants to demolish distressed public housing projects. The housing projects are often replaced with mixed-income housing, displacing some public housing tenants. Displaced tenants are a priority target group for housing assistance. Although displaced tenants may be assigned to units in other housing projects, rental assistance is most frequently provided through vouchers.[122] Displaced tenants who were given vouchers tended to move to neighborhoods with lower poverty, more racial diversity, and less crime than residents who remained in public housing. However, such improvements are relative: even after relocating, most voucher recipients still lived in segregated neighborhoods with high poverty and crime rates.[123]

Federal rent subsidies must be rationed because demand for assistance far exceeds supply. Rental assistance has never been an entitlement, and so many eligible people do not receive benefits.[124] Many of the eligible people who do not receive rent subsidies would like to receive them; there are long waiting lists in most localities, and in some localities the waiting lists are closed from time to time because of excessive demand.[125] Nevertheless, the number of participanting households has increased: between 1977 and 2000, the number of renters grew from 2.07 million to 5.06 million.[126]

Although local PHAs enjoy substantial discretion, eligibility for housing assistance is based upon federal standards that define income thresholds in relation to local median income; there are no asset tests.[127] This is an unusual basis for eligibility compared to other means-tested programs in the United States, which either have national income standards (for example, the EITC or the Food Stamp Program) or state-level standards (for example, medical assistance, child care assistance, or TANF). Although it is unusual, this approach allows the distribution of housing program benefits to reflect local housing market conditions.

To qualify for assistance, a family of four must have an adjusted income below 80 percent of the local median income. This basic standard is modified

122. Cunningham (2004).
123. Burton (2004).
124. Olsen (2003); Turner (2003); Schwartz and Miller (2002); *Green Book* (2000).
125. Olsen (2003); Schwartz and Miller (2002).
126. *Green Book* (2000).
127. Olsen (2003).

to reflect differences in family size.[128] Because local median income varies substantially, the family income thresholds vary from one locality to the next. Rebecca Schwartz and Brian Miller illustrate the possible extent of variation: in 2001 the national area median income was $52,500; in Starr County, Texas, it was $16,300; in Fairfield County, Connecticut, it was $109,800.[129] Thus, unlike in most other means-tested programs, people with vastly different incomes are eligible to receive housing assistance, depending upon where they live.

The federal government does require local authorities to give priority consideration to lower-income families. Beginning in 1975, Congress directed PHAs to provide a growing share of housing assistance to "very low-income households," those with incomes below 50 percent of local median income.[130] In the Quality Housing and Work Responsibility Act of 1998, Congress created a new priority category for housing assistance: "extremely low-income families" are those with incomes below 30 percent of local median income. Current federal guidelines direct local authorities to provide 75 percent of newly available vouchers and 40 percent of newly available public housing units to extremely low-income families.[131] However, changes in federal targeting requirements have not altered the local basis for income eligibility.

Several matters aside from income are linked to eligibility to receive or to continue to receive rental assistance. There is a "community work requirement" for nonworking public housing residents, who must perform eight hours of community service a week; those in compliance with TANF work requirements are exempt. Although there are no additional work requirements currently associated with rental assistance, local authorities have the option to create such a link.[132] Some other aspects of personal responsibility are also linked to eligibility for housing assistance. When Congress consolidated the Section 8 programs in 1998, local PHAs were empowered to conduct background investigations to screen tenants, and to terminate assistance for criminal behavior and drug or alcohol abuse.[133]

The size of the rental subsidy depends upon a number of different factors. First, the subsidy reflects local rental market conditions. Locales that have higher rents provide higher subsidies, other things being equal. Second,

128. See Olsen (2003) for details.
129. Schwartz and Miller (2002).
130. Olsen (2003).
131. Sard and Lubell (2000).
132. Sard and Lubell (2000).
133. Department of Housing and Urban Development (2001).

family size and composition are important. Larger families qualify for larger (and higher cost) units. And families with same sex children may be expected to have the children share a single bedroom, whereas families with different sex children may be permitted to have separate bedrooms (the ages of the children also may weigh in this decision). Finally, the subsidy varies inversely with income. Rental subsidy participants usually pay a fixed share of their income for rent. Thus families with higher incomes receive a lower subsidy.

The primary voucher program that assists low-income families is the Housing Choice voucher program. HUD allocates vouchers to local PHAs, which in turn issue vouchers to families that rise to the top of their waitlists, considering also federal targeting priorities. The family is responsible for finding a suitable housing unit (it must be decent, safe, and sanitary) to rent from a landlord who is willing to accept the voucher. There is a time limit on the search; if the family cannot find a satisfactory unit within that period, it must forfeit the voucher.[134] Although most voucher recipients (about seven in ten) are successful in finding a suitable unit before the time expires, some are not.[135]

The Housing Choice voucher program provides a subsidy that is the lesser of the payment standard or the rent on the unit minus 30 percent of the family's adjusted monthly income.[136] For a family with adjusted monthly income of $1,000 and eligible for a two-bedroom unit, for example, if the local payment standard for a two-bedroom apartment is $400 and the family selects a unit that rents for $420 per month, the subsidy is the payment standard minus 30 percent of adjusted monthly income ($400 − [0.3 * $1,000]), or $100 per month. The family's net rent payment is thus $320.

HUD guidelines state what types of income should be included and what types should be excluded when calculating a participant's adjusted income. The full amount of pre-tax earnings, net business income, benefits paid in place of earnings (such as unemployment or disability compensation), cash welfare assistance, income from assets, and regular cash contributions (such as alimony and child support payments) are all included. However, benefits from food stamps and the EITC, child care grants provided by the Child Care and Development Block Grant, earnings from family members under the age of 18, and earnings and benefits from HUD-sponsored employment and training programs are excluded.[137]

134. Department of Housing and Urban Development (2004).
135. Turner (2003).
136. Department of Housing and Urban Development (2004).
137. Department of Housing and Urban Development (2001).

A consequence of the localized income eligibility standard and the ability of participants to receive assistance indefinitely (so long as the local payment standard continues to be higher than 30 percent of their adjusted income) is that housing assistance is enjoyed by a significant number of households that are not poor, as defined by the federal poverty standard. Because the income eligibility standard for housing assistance is linked to local median income and the federal poverty standard is a uniform national standard, there are many locales where people with incomes far in excess of the poverty standard are eligible for housing assistance. Edgar Olsen observes: "Forty-three percent of the households served by HUD's programs are above the poverty line . . . while 70 percent of the renters below the poverty level are not served."[138]

Some aspects of rental voucher programs have been criticized.[139] The discretionary budget status of rental assistance programs means that many eligible people do not receive benefits. This is a significant equity concern, as similarly situated people do not enjoy equal access to benefits. Transforming the program into an entitlement is one means proposed to end this problem. Although it is difficult to measure the extent to which housing assistance is a disincentive to work, the effect appears to be small. Finally, housing assistance does appear to create an efficiency loss compared to cash. The subsidy ratio is estimated to be about 80 percent for rental vouchers: $1 of rental assistance in the form of a voucher has a cash value of about 80 cents to recipients. To increase program efficiency, cash could be provided instead of vouchers.

The portability feature of the rental voucher program has been criticized because of administrative problems and discrimination in housing markets. Although housing advocates celebrate the freedom of choice that vouchers offer, portability has been described as "a bureaucratic nightmare" for families and housing authorities.[140] When families want to use a voucher issued in one jurisdiction to move to another, the issuing agency must transfer the family to the agency that serves the relocation area or make regular payments to offset administrative expenses. To avoid the hassles of billing and paying expenses, many PHAs have reached agreements to "absorb" families that wish to transfer their vouchers from one jurisdiction to another. However, this practice limits the ability of localities that receive a net in-flow of voucher-holders to serve the people on their waitlists.[141] Finally, discrimination in

138. Olsen (2003, p. 394).
139. Olsen (2003).
140. Turner (2003, p. 3).
141. Turner (2003).

rental markets, possibly reflecting concerns about crime or the social service needs of voucher participants, further impedes portability.[142]

Conclusion

This chapter has identified and described the programs that compose the work support system. Recent policy changes have expanded the opportunities for needy workers to supplement earned income with a variety of means-tested tax and transfer benefits. These benefits, in concert with minimum wage increases, have enhanced the material rewards for workers at the bottom of the labor market. The expansion of the federal EITC and the creation of state EITC programs have made the tax system a significant source of support for low-income workers, especially those with children. Needy workers and their families are also more likely to enjoy access to medical assistance as a result of recent policy changes. The mandatory extension of Medicaid benefits to children in families with incomes below the poverty level and the creation of CHIP has expanded access to health care among low-income children.

The review of programs also clarifies the three different types of relationships that exist between the work support system and the welfare system. First, some work support programs extend the welfare system by allowing welfare clients to retain some benefits as they make the transition from welfare to work; examples are TANF earned income disregards and transitional medical assistance. These programs are distinctive in that all the benefits they provide are time limited and available only to people emerging from the cash welfare system.

Second, some work support programs expand the welfare system by allowing needy workers access to means-tested benefits that are also provided to people with no earned income. This is the largest group of programs and includes food stamps, school meals, rental assistance, and child care assistance. It is arguable whether Medicaid should be included in this category, since eligibility for TMA is an extension of Medicaid eligibility. However, Medicaid itself is offered to low-income working adults as a state option, and states are required to offer Medicaid to the children of low-income workers, a clear extension of medical assistance benefits. These programs serve needy workers who are outside the cash assistance welfare system and people making the transition from welfare to work, and so it seems appropriate to include Medicaid in this category.

142. Turner (2003).

Finally, a few work support programs are entirely separate from the welfare system because only people with earned income can qualify to receive benefits. The state and federal minimum wage rates and state and federal EITC programs are examples. CHIP is an ambiguous case. Because CHIP was specifically designed to complement and extend medical assistance benefits to children who are not eligible for Medicaid, it could be considered an extension of the welfare system. However, where states have implemented it as a separate program, it may be more appropriate to consider it an exclusive work support benefit.

The review of programs in this chapter also suggests which classes of needy workers are best served by the work support system. Our definition of the work support system identified three classes of needy workers: low-wage workers, low-income workers, and people making the transition from welfare to work. Of these three groups, the system provides the most generous support to people making the transition from welfare to work. These people are eligible for several special support programs during the transition and are a priority target group for many other work support services. Low-income workers fall in a middle ground in terms of the scope and generosity of services; they are eligible for many work support programs, and their opportunities for work support benefits are impressive when they have dependent children. Finally, low-wage workers are the group least well served by the work support system; only the minimum wage directly targets this group. Only those low-wage workers who are also members of the other classes of needy workers are likely to enjoy substantial access to work support benefits.

The work support system offers needy workers an impressive array of material supports that includes cash, food, health care, child care, and housing. However, many constraints limit the ability of needy workers to receive these supports. Some of these limitations appear to be intentional, as they are related to program design (such as budget constraints), while others appear to be unintended consequences (such as the reduction in food stamp participation following the implementation of welfare reform). The significance of program design to the potential and limitations of the work support system is discussed in chapter 3.

3

Program Design

This chapter describes and analyzes the design of work support programs. The work support system distributes benefits to needy workers and regulates their behavior by directing consumption and encouraging or requiring work. There is a tension between these goals that reflects a concern that has long been central to social policy debates in the United States: how can government assist the needy without undermining personal responsibility and creating dependency?

Most work support programs use a small set of policy tools to distribute benefits and regulate behavior. Lester Salamon defines a policy tool as "an identifiable method through which collective action is structured to address a public problem."[1] A single policy tool can be used in many different programs, and a single program may use several different policy tools. Six policy tools are components of the work support system:

(1) *Direct government*: actions taken by government employees to distribute work support benefits or regulate behavior;

(2) *Grants*: federal funds provided to state and local intermediaries to finance work support programs;

(3) *Vouchers*: certificates that needy workers can exchange for goods or services;

(4) *Tax expenditures*: financial benefits distributed through the tax system that offset tax obligations or increase after-tax income;

(5) *Social regulation*: behavioral standards linked to receipt of benefits (limited here to work requirements); and

1. Salamon (2002a, p. 19).

(6) *Economic regulation*: formal rules that govern activities and relationships in the marketplace.

The program descriptions we have presented in chapter 2 suggest several additional design features that also must be considered in order to understand the operation of the work support system. A key design issue is federalism, more specifically, the role of states and localities in the development of eligibility and benefit standards for work support programs. Some work support programs feature national benefit and eligibility standards, while in others standards vary from state to state or even within states. The source of eligibility and benefit standards has distributive consequences for work support benefits: programs that are governed by national standards tend to homogenize benefits across states and localities, whereas programs that are governed by state or local standards provide opportunities for benefits to vary from place to place.

Budget constraints are another design concern, related to federalism. Some work support programs are subject to direct budget constraints (annual appropriation limits), others are subject only to indirect constraints (state benefit and eligibility restrictions that reflect cost concerns), and others still are not subject to budget constraints at all (individual entitlements with national eligibility and benefit standards). Such constraints influence the distribution of program benefits by establishing the extent to which the implementation of work support programs is hampered by scarcity. The means used to adjust the value of benefits over time is another design concern. Although in a few work support programs benefit and eligibility standards are automatically adjusted to reflect changes in living costs over time, in most programs they do not change unless policymakers intervene. This affects the value of work support benefits over time; programs that are not adjusted automatically are likely to decline in real value.

The symbolic aspects of policy are also key design considerations, and the welfare system is an important source of symbols for the work support system. Anne Schneider and Helen Ingram argue that policy designs cannot be understood simply in instrumental terms; designs "contain symbolic and interpretive dimensions that are as important as the instrumental aspects."[2] The standards and practices of the welfare system are especially significant, because many work support programs serve needy workers and welfare recipients alike. Two policy tools, social regulation and vouchers, have symbolic connections to the welfare system, but there are other connections as well. The concerns of the welfare system are evident in the selection of the target groups

2. Schneider and Ingram (1997, p. 2).

served by work support programs and those specifically excluded from receiving benefits; many work support programs target or favor low-income families with children.[3] In addition, noncitizens' eligibility for work support programs is often related to immigration status (except for the minimum wage and school meal programs). Beyond this, some work supports have time-limited benefits, reflecting the emphasis on temporary assistance that was institutionalized by the 1996 Personal Responsibility and Work Opportunity Reconciliation Act (PRWORA). Finally, access to work support benefits is related to cash assistance welfare participation in two ways: (1) those within the cash welfare system are eligible for work supports that those outside the welfare system cannot receive; and (2) some work support programs give preferential treatment to people making the transition from welfare to work.

Policy Tools

The work support system distributes cash and in-kind benefits to materially improve the lot of needy workers and their families. Five of the six policy tools are used to distribute benefits: direct government, grants, vouchers, tax expenditures, and economic regulation. However, these benefits often come with strings attached. Two of the six policy tools (vouchers and social regulation) are used to regulate behavior. Although the primary purpose of vouchers is to distribute benefits, they also limit the consumption options of needy workers, and thereby regulate their behavior. The work support system also strives to influence the behavior of needy workers by encouraging work; social regulation, the primary tool for that purpose, is a feature of many work support programs.

Table 3-1 shows the work support programs described in chapter 2 and the six policy tools that operate in the work support system. Several tools are common features of work support programs. Direct government is the only tool used by all of them. Grants are frequently used by the federal government to provide assistance to state or local governments.[4] In fact, income tax cred-

---

3. Schneider and Ingram (1997).

4. Our claim that several work support programs combine direct government and grants may be controversial. To some extent, these tools are described as alternatives rather than complements. Leman (2002) implies that direct government means program implementation through a coherent hierarchy. By contrast, to Beam and Conlan (2002), grants introduce intergovernmental relations into the implementation process, calling the hierarchical model into question. Our view is that the distinction between direct government and grants is partly a matter of perspective. The federal government provides grants to states in order to finance (to varying degrees) program expenses. However, government employees deliver benefits directly

Table 3-1. Tools Used by Work Support Programs

Program	Direct government	Grants	Vouchers	Social regulation	Tax expenditure	Economic regulation
Minimum wage	X			n.a.		X
Income tax credits	X			n.a.	X	
Food stamps	X	X	X	X		
Child care	X	X	X	X		
School meals	X	X	X			
TANF	X	X		X		
Medical assistance	X	X	X			
Rental assistance	X	X	X	X		

n.a. = Not applicable.

its and the minimum wage are the only work support benefits that are not financed by intergovernmental grants. Although work support grants mostly provide cash to state or local governments, many work support benefits are distributed to needy families in the form of vouchers; for example, food stamps, child care, school meals, medical assistance, and rental assistance. Although states now provide food stamp benefits in the form of an electronic debit card, this practice does not alter the essential character of food stamps as vouchers, because use of the benefit card is still restricted to the purchase of approved items.[5] Table 3-1 also shows that several work support programs feature social regulations to enforce work requirements.

Some of the unusual characteristics of work support programs are also evident from table 3-1. The minimum wage is a distinctive work support because its requirements are not organized as a government program that distributes benefits; the minimum wage is a form of economic regulation that benefits needy workers by changing conditions in the labor market. State and federal earned income tax credit (EITC) programs and the child tax credit use an unusual tool to distribute work support benefits: tax expenditures. In addition, although people must work to benefit from the minimum wage and tax credit programs, work requirements are not enforced by social regulation; work requirements are implicit in the organization of the benefit. You

to needy workers. In this sense, beneficiaries experience direct government. Especially important in this regard is Leman's emphasis on the coercive power of direct government. Our view is that coercion is a common feature of work support programs.

5. The conversion of food stamp benefits from coupons to electronic benefit cards was completed in 2004. However, the significance of the conversion to our discussion is only that it may limit stigma and encourage participation. The electronic benefit cards are essentially reusable vouchers.

must be a worker to gain benefits from minimum wage increases and you must be a worker to have the earned income that is necessary to get EITC benefits or the child tax credit. School meals and some forms of medical assistance are the only work support benefits that can be enjoyed without some sort of implicit or explicit work requirement. All other work supports use program benefits as a carrot to influence the behavior of recipients by encouraging (or requiring) them to work.

Direct Government

Direct government action is part of the effort to distribute all work support benefits. "Direct government is the delivery or withholding of a good or service by government employees."[6] Federal and state governments establish and enforce minimum wage legislation through their departments of labor. The Internal Revenue Service (IRS) distributes EITC payments and child tax credits; state tax officials distribute state EITC payments. State social service employees distribute Temporary Assistance for Needy Families (TANF) benefits. Local school officials distribute school meals; since both public and private schools participate in school meal programs, in some cases school meals are not provided directly by government employees but rather by employees under contract to the government.

Other work support programs require direct government action but the government does not distribute benefits directly—government employees distribute the means for needy workers to purchase benefits in the marketplace. State social services employees distribute food stamps, medical assistance cards, and child care coupons. Needy workers use food stamps to purchase approved foods at retail outlets; medical assistance cards to gain access to medical treatment at hospitals, health clinics, and participating private practitioners; and child care coupons to pay a share of the cost of purchasing care from providers.

Direct government is a tool that is particularly well suited for coercion—defined as threat or use of punishment—to gain compliance with program rules.[7] Public employees deliver goods or services in a manner consistent with bureaucratic rules that limit the discretion of workers who come into contact with the public and structure the experiences of those who seek benefits. The primary way that government bureaus coerce applicants to comply with their rules is by withholding benefits until the rules are satisfied (though there are a limited number of exceptions to this practice for medical assistance).

6. Leman (2002, p. 49).
7. Leman (2002).

Typically, the burden of proof for eligibility is placed on the applicant. The bureau's rules contain standards of proof that must be satisfied before benefits are provided and a method of calculating those benefits based upon information provided by the applicant.

The coercive authority of direct government is also used to enforce the work requirements that are often a condition of initial or continuing eligibility to receive work support benefits. The threat of withholding benefits provides the initial power to enforce work requirements. Once the applicant begins to receive benefits, the threat of withdrawing or reducing benefits is used to coerce continuing compliance with work requirements. TANF, food stamps, child care grants, and housing assistance all have work regulations. Although rules and the vigor of enforcement vary from one program to another, in all cases satisfying work rules is a condition of continuing eligibility.

Although all of the programs implemented by direct government have the potential for coercion, simply classifying all work support programs together under the heading of direct government can obscure as much about their operation as it reveals. To most workers, government enforcement of minimum wage laws is invisible. They experience the minimum wage as a term of employment, and except in cases where government must intervene to enforce the requirement on reluctant employers, no contact with government occurs. Even among the work support benefits that must be obtained from specific government bureaus, there are important differences in the experiences. Although IRS employees distribute EITC and child tax credit benefits (and their equivalents at the state level distribute state EITC benefits), only in rare circumstances do people seeking these benefits come into direct contact with government employees. Usually, the transaction is handled through the mail so that the actions of IRS workers are largely invisible to the beneficiary. The lack of face-to-face contact reduces hassle and stigma, which is likely to encourage people to claim benefits.

Direct government provides work support benefits without hassle and stigma in only one other case: school meals. School employees are reluctant to police benefits, are inclined to use their knowledge about children's circumstances to augment official sources of information, and view beneficiaries sympathetically (though forms must be completed and eligibility must be documented). Beyond this, because the direct beneficiaries of school meals are children, federal regulations require that needy children who receive a free or reduced-price meal should not be singled out and stigmatized.[8]

8. Stoker (1991).

All of the other work support programs require face-to-face contact between government employees and beneficiaries in an organizational environment that can create hassle and stigma. TANF, food stamps, child care grants, medical assistance (even when implemented in cooperation with state public health agencies), and rental assistance are typically distributed by public employees who enforce work requirements, use intrusive processes to determine eligibility, and require periodic reassessment of eligibility. These transactions are anything but invisible, creating a "hassle factor" and reducing program participation.

Grants

According to David Beam and Timothy Conlan, "grants are payments from a donor government to a recipient organization (typically public or nonprofit) or an individual . . . they are a gift that has the aim of either 'stimulating' or 'supporting' some sort of service or activity by the recipient."[9] Intergovernmental grants are provided for food stamps, child care, school meals, medical assistance (both Medicaid and the Children's Health Insurance Program, CHIP), TANF, and rental assistance. A common financing arrangement is that the federal government provides cash grants to states, which are passed on to provide benefits to needy working families. Work supports such as Medicaid, TANF, school meals, CHIP, and rental assistance are among the largest federal cash grants provided to the states; together, these programs account for more than half of all intergovernmental grant expenditures.[10] Medicaid is by far the largest such grant.[11]

Work support grants have several common features. They are all categorical grants—designed to serve particular, narrow purposes—and they are all formula grants—allocated on the basis of calculations that represent program needs.[12] Some work support grants are individual entitlements (food stamps, Medicaid, and school meals are examples); in such cases there is no upper limit to the funds provided to support these programs and receipt of benefits is an enforceable individual right.[13] Other work support grants are "capped," meaning that the amount of funding is fixed by Congress (TANF is an example).

9. Beam and Conlan (2002, p. 341).

10. Beam and Conlan (2002).

11. However, it is important to remember that only a small share of total Medicaid benefits is provided to needy workers and their families. Most Medicaid benefits are paid for services to the disabled and the elderly poor. See Gruber (2003).

12. Some readers may object to the inclusion of TANF in this generalization. The TANF block grant may be a reflection more of historic program expenditures than of existing need.

13. King (2000).

Although categorical formula grants allow the federal government and state governments to cooperate in the pursuit of common objectives, the federal government uses a variety of techniques to monitor and control the use of grant funds. States are required to complete detailed applications that explain how they intend to use grant funds. A lead agency is designated in each state, and a variety of certifications are offered to assure the federal government that the grant will be used for the stated purpose and will be operated in a manner consistent with federal requirements. Depending on the program, the grant may require matching state funds (normally state matches are inversely related to state need) or "maintenance of effort," that is, proof that the state has not reduced spending by substituting the federal grant for past state funding.

Once the grant is awarded, the federal government monitors state actions through audits and periodic reports.[14] Some grant programs have provisions that hold states responsible for expenditures that are inconsistent with federal rules; for example, states are required to refund overpayments of food stamp benefits. Others have periodic audits to check state and local compliance with federal guidelines and to assess whether the use of program funds is consistent with federal rules. For example, the Department of Agriculture (USDA) audits local schools to ensure that only eligible students receive free and reduced-price lunches.[15]

The flexibility of states and localities is constrained by federal requirements and varies considerably from one work support grant to another. State flexibility is especially important to TANF, child care, and medical assistance programs. States establish TANF and child care eligibility requirements and benefit generosity; needy workers eligible to receive benefits in one state may be ineligible in another, while eligible workers may qualify for different amounts of support in different states. States also influence medical assistance grants both by establishing eligibility standards and by defining the scope of covered services. Needy workers eligible for medical assistance in one state may be ineligible in another, and medical services provided in one state may not be provided in another. Local housing authorities establish eligibility guidelines for the distribution of rental assistance. Rental assistance is distinctive from other work support grants because the grants empower local housing authorities rather than states to establish eligibility and benefit standards.

14. Beam and Conlan (2002).
15. Stoker (1991).

Vouchers

Eugene Steuerle and Eric Twombly define a voucher as "a subsidy that grants limited purchasing power to an individual to choose among a restricted set of goods and services."[16] Many work support grants are presented to recipients in the form of vouchers. Vouchers are unlike cash because they specify and restrict what recipients may consume. They allow government to control the use of grants by needy working families by limiting their choices, thus influencing the value and distribution of work support benefits.

Vouchers encourage efficiency in the production of goods and services but may reduce the value of benefits a program provides. In comparison to direct government, vouchers empower beneficiaries as consumers, creating opportunities for them to exercise limited choice and giving them more control over the goods and services they consume. Vouchers are often favorably compared to direct government because they introduce choice and competition into the production of goods and services. This is expected to create efficiency gains. The voucher empowers the beneficiary to shop among a limited set of options. Because beneficiaries are shoppers rather than a captive audience, producers of the goods and services are expected to be more responsive to their concerns and to produce higher value goods or services. Consequently, vouchers are associated with symbolic benefits: efficiency and choice.[17]

However, another issue regarding the efficiency of vouchers is their association with in-kind rather than cash benefits. As Robert Moffitt has observed: "the value of an in-kind transfer cannot be more than, and may be less than, the value of an equal-dollar cash transfer."[18] In-kind subsidies (such as means-tested program benefits) are expected to distort consumption patterns; vouchers result in "overconsumption" of the good or service they provide if the amount of the voucher is more than recipients would otherwise be inclined to spend on them.[19] Consequently, from the perspective of consumer benefit, vouchers are less efficient than cash.

Although all vouchers, by design, limit choice, the extent to which choice is restricted varies from one work support program to another. The Food Stamp Program and child care grants allow needy families significant freedom of choice to select the retail outlets and product characteristics they prefer. Medical assistance programs and school meals are much more restrictive. Although to a limited extent recipients of medical assistance can select serv-

16. Steuerle and Twombly (2002, p. 446).
17. Steuerle and Twombly (2002, p. 446).
18. Moffitt (1989, p. 385).
19. Smeeding (1984).

ice locations and practitioners, these choices may be severely restricted due to reimbursement rates that limit the number of participating providers or administrative arrangements (often designed as cost control strategies) that assign recipients to specific health care organizations. School meals limit consumption options even more. Although the richness of meal choices varies from one school to another, the lunch ticket provided is valid only in the school cafeteria. Eligible participants can choose to accept the meals offered by their school or must fend for themselves.

Vouchers have important political implications because they broaden support for redistribution and deflect criticism of abuse. Producer groups favor vouchers over cash because the vouchers can only be used to acquire particular goods and services, thus ensuring that producers of those goods and services benefit from redistributive programs.[20] This can broaden the coalition to support programs that target low-income families.[21] In addition, the provision of in-kind benefits may have significant political implications by helping to control costs and reduce abuse. Charles Blackorby and David Donaldson have suggested that the distribution of in-kind services instead of cash ensures that only those with real need will seek benefits.[22] If, for example, medical assistance was provided as cash rather than a card, every eligible person would have an incentive to seek the benefit, whether or not he or she needed medical treatment. By providing in-kind services through vouchers, the government limits costs (only those in need of medical treatment actually use the benefit) and abuse (benefits are provided to the target population for the intended purpose). Finally, policymakers favor vouchers for in-kind goods and services because they limit the potential that government support will be used to underwrite consumption of which the public may disapprove; cash benefits can be spent on vice or trivial desires, vouchers cannot. Beyond this, vouchers for in-kind benefits offer the opportunity for policymakers and the public to express their disapproval of specific goods and services. It is no accident that food stamps cannot be used to purchase cigarettes or alcohol, or that the Hyde Amendment prevents Medicaid funds from being used for most abortion services.

Tax Expenditures

Tax expenditures are another means of providing benefits to needy workers. According to Christopher Howard, "a tax expenditure is a provision in tax law

---

20. Steuerle and Twombly (2002).
21. Moffitt (2000).
22. Blackorby and Donaldson (1988).

that usually encourages certain behavior by individuals or corporations by deferring, reducing, or eliminating their tax obligation."[23] The federal government and several states offer refundable EITC programs to support low-income workers, and the federal government has a child tax credit; these programs sacrifice tax revenue and encourage work by providing a cash benefit. Howard observes that although the majority of tax expenditures are devoted to purposes related to social welfare (housing, health, employment, training, education, and income security) the distribution of benefits is typically skewed to the relatively affluent. The EITC is an exception to this rule.

The EITC benefits low-income workers. As a refundable credit, it provides benefits even to those with no tax liability, and because benefits can often be claimed without direct contact with government employees, there is little stigma associated with participation.[24] The EITC is distinctive among tax expenditure programs for several reasons. First, unlike most tax expenditures, it targets low-income people, making the tax system more progressive. Second, the EITC is a fully refundable tax credit that reduces tax liability or creates a cash refund. Although Howard sees room for simplification, he describes the EITC as "in several respects a model tax expenditure."[25] It targets low-income workers but gives no preference to specific occupations or industries, it is refundable, it does not confer windfall benefits on employers, and its benefits flow directly to workers.

The claim that employers do not receive a windfall benefit should not be taken to imply that they do not benefit from programs like the EITC. Whether benefits are provided directly to low-income workers or to the firms that hire them, it is expected that the employment tax credits will be advantageous to the firms.[26] An employment tax credit for workers is expected to increase labor supply, depressing market wages (if wages are not constrained by other factors, such as the minimum wage). Although the net wage (the market wage plus the benefit payment) that workers receive is higher than the original market wage, employers pay a lower market wage. However, because the EITC is paid directly to low-income workers, its benefit to employers is concealed.

Social Regulation

Social regulation is meant to influence the behavior of needy workers who receive work support benefits. Peter May defines regulation as "rules that identify permissible and impermissible activity on the part of individuals,

23. Howard (2002, p. 411).
24. Howard (2002).
25. Howard (2002, p. 437).
26. Dickert-Conlin and Holtz-Eakin (2000).

firms, or government agencies, along with accompanying sanctions or rewards, or both"; social regulation, in particular, targets behavior that threatens "public health, safety, welfare, or well being."[27] Social regulations in the work support system enforce work requirements. Regulation is a coercive tool because those subject to the regulatory requirements are thought to be in conflict with them. Because social regulation creates conflict between regulators and regulated parties, it is usually implemented by direct government action. Food stamps, TANF, child care grants, and rental assistance have work requirements that must be satisfied in order to gain or maintain eligibility for work support benefits.

To enforce social regulations, an administrative system must develop rules, standards to gauge compliance with the rules, and a set of penalties or rewards. The behavior of those subject to the rules must be monitored to ensure compliance.[28] Typically, compliance with the requirements is established prior to the provision of benefits and checked periodically for as long as benefits are received. The frequency with which compliance is checked is an important consideration, not only because it influences program integrity, but also because it contributes to the "hassle factor" that discourages participation among eligible needy workers. An investigation by the General Accounting Office of the relationship between the food stamp quality control system and participation rates suggests such a link; low-income workers are more likely to have incomes that fluctuate due to irregular work schedules and temporary employment. States are concerned that such cases may create eligibility errors and so require frequent reassessments. This increases the hassle factor and reduces participation.[29]

The "work requirements" that are enforced by social regulation do not necessarily require beneficiaries to work. The behaviors that count toward compliance with work rules are defined by regulatory standards, which vary from program to program and (for some programs) from place to place. For example, a variety of different types of activity can satisfy TANF work requirements. TANF recipients may engage in education or training programs, participate in job search or soft-skill seminars, or even receive substance abuse treatment in order to comply with federal and state work requirements.

Social regulation is important to the political support of the work support system because it allows benefits to be provided (potentially undermining work incentives, or at least creating concern about work incentives) while

27. May (2002, p. 157).
28. May (2002).
29. General Accounting Office (2002a).

affirming the expectation that people will work. If the public develops the impression that work support benefits undermine work incentives, political support will be more difficult to sustain. Social regulation reassures the public. Policy analysts, however, disagree. It is a common concern among economists that means-tested benefits undermine work incentives.[30] By constraining the ability of low-income workers to reduce their work effort, social regulation reduces concerns about the work support system's influence on personal responsibility.

Economic Regulation

Economic regulation, the formal rules made by public agencies that govern activities in the marketplace, is described by Lester Salamon as "a special bureaucratic process that combines aspects of both courts and legislatures to control prices, output, and/or the entry and exit of firms in an industry."[31] Regulation is an indirect way for government to benefit needy working families. Although it is coercive and direct for the regulated parties, an important political characteristic is that the costs of regulatory compliance do not show up in government budgets and are imposed in "subtle and indirect ways" that "are shifted to private businesses, to consumers, or to the economy." In this way the costs of economic regulation "are conveniently hidden from popular view, which makes them far more palatable politically."[32]

The minimum wage is a rule that governs most labor market transactions.[33] By establishing a wage floor for most employment relationships, it structures the expectations of both employers and potential employees; employers expect to pay at least the minimum and potential employees expect their wage offer to be at least at the minimum. Thus the minimum wage is a regulatory price control for the exchange of labor. By creating a minimum hourly price for labor it removes competition in the labor market below that price. This restricts the liberty of employers and employees; most legitimate

30. Browning (1973, 1996).

31. Salamon (2002b, p. 118).

32. Salamon (2002b, p. 145).

33. While discussing the concept of economic regulation, Salamon draws a distinction between rules that are specified in legislation and rules that are developed by government agencies (2002b, pp. 118–19). If this were the case, the minimum wage might be seen as a statutory requirement rather than as a form of economic regulation. Our view is that Salamon's distinction is too cut and dried. Even legislation that contains relatively clear standards (for example, the amount of national minimum wage) also contains ambiguities (such as what classes of employment are subject to the requirement) that must be resolved through agency rule making. While we agree that the clarity of legislative standards is an important consideration, we see the matter more as a difference of degree than as a difference in type.

Table 3-2. Program Characteristics

Program	Eligibility and benefit schedule	Cost-of-living adjusted over time?	Budget constrained?
Minimum wage	National[a]	No	n.a.
EITC	National	Yes	No
Food stamps	National	Yes	No
Child care	State	No	Yes
School meals	National	No	No
TANF	State	No	Yes
Medical assistance	State	No	Depends on design
Rental assistance	Local	Limited	Yes

n.a. = Not applicable.
a. Minimum national standards may be exceeded by the states.

employers are required to offer to pay the minimum wage, and most legitimate employees cannot offer to accept employment for less than the minimum wage.

Federalism is an important but limited element of minimum wage requirements. The federal minimum wage is an example of partial preemption of state regulatory authority by the federal government.[34] Federal law requires that states enforce the federal minimum wage unless a state elects to enforce a higher state minimum wage. Many states continue to have minimum wage rates below the federal requirement "on the books," but these rates are merely symbolic because states are prevented from enforcing them.

Standards in the Work Support System

Program characteristics also influence the performance of work support programs; see table 3-2. One key consideration is the source of standards for eligibility and benefits. Although state officials implement most work support programs within the broad requirements of federal policy, there is an important distinction between programs that feature national eligibility and benefit standards and those whose standards vary from state to state. In addition, one work support program (rental assistance) is governed by standards that vary from locale to locale. Another consideration is whether benefits and eligibility standards are automatically adjusted for changes in living costs over time. The decision to make eligibility and benefit standards adjustable automatically ensures that the real value of work support benefits will be

34. Reagan (1987).

maintained over time. A final consideration is budget constraints. Access to some work support programs is limited by budget constraints that create the need to restrict eligibility or ration benefits. Programs without budget constraints are more reliable sources of support for needy working families.

Table 3-2 suggests that for the majority of work support programs, states are influential participants in the policymaking process. States influence the eligibility for benefits and the generosity of benefits for child care grants, TANF, and medical assistance (Medicaid, transitional medical assistance, and CHIP). Local officials typically work within the program frameworks of their state, except in the case of rental assistance, for which standards are local. Only the federal tax credits (the EITC and the child tax credit) and food programs (food stamps and school meals) feature national eligibility and benefit standards that are largely consistent across the nation.[35]

Table 3-2 also indicates that work support benefits are typically not adjusted automatically to account for changes in living costs over time; only the EITC program and food stamps are exceptions. For the EITC program, both the income level for eligibility for benefits (the benefit thresholds) and the amount of the payment provided at different levels of earned income are automatically adjusted annually. The income eligibility standards and benefit levels for food stamps are also adjusted annually. To some extent, rental assistance is adjusted automatically over time, because eligibility is based on local median income and benefit payments are based on estimates of local rents. The value of other work support benefits gradually will be eroded unless policymakers intervene.

Table 3-2 also indicates the budgetary status of work support programs. As a tax expenditure program, the federal EITC is not budget constrained. Under normal circumstances, the same would be true for state programs. However, some states have linked their EITC payments to their fiscal health—if the fiscal condition of the state is poor, payments may be suspended. TANF, child care grants, and CHIP programs (when CHIP is not implemented as a Medicaid extension) are budget constrained. There are two ways for those implementing policy to deal with budget constraints: they can act as gatekeepers, who restrict access to benefits by keeping people out of the program, or they can ration assistance by creating a waitlist of people who are eligible to receive benefits. The other programs are individual entitlements.

Although entitlement status is a key consideration in terms of federal budget constraints, federalism can create indirect constraints even for individual

35. As noted in chapter 2, benefits for these programs are uniform in the forty-eight contiguous states and higher in Alaska and Hawaii. However, benefit levels are established by Congress, not at the discretion of the state.

entitlements. At the federal level, the key issue is whether the program is an individual entitlement. Programs that are individual entitlements circumvent the normal congressional appropriations process. Qualified applicants enjoy benefits as a matter of individual right, and the federal government is obliged to spend the funds required to finance the benefits, regardless of the costs.[36] Work support programs that are individual entitlements include Medicaid, food stamps, and school meals. At the state level, however, some of these individual entitlements are subject to subtle and indirect constraints.

If federal entitlement programs feature state eligibility and benefit standards, states can engage in indirect cost control by manipulating those standards. Medicaid is an example. Motivated by the fact that they are responsible for a share of Medicaid costs, states establish eligibility standards and the scope of benefits provided to exercise indirect controls over state costs. Thus although Medicaid is an individual entitlement, and as such is not budget constrained at the federal level, state participation in financing the benefits and state authority to influence eligibility and benefit standards can be a significant indirect constraint on access and the services participants receive. Only those work support programs that are individual entitlements with national eligibility and benefit standards, such as food stamps and school nutrition programs, are completely free of budget constraints.

Budget constraints are likely to create a gap between supply and demand for benefits. This gap has been most evident in the large demand for child care grants and rental assistance. Studies by the Department of Health and Human Services indicate that a large part of the demand for child care services remains unmet by current funding; this is true even among those making the transition from welfare to work, a priority target population.[37] This shortfall exists despite funding increases and the fact that many states have reprogrammed TANF funds to expand access to child care.[38] Rental assistance is also in short supply. Local housing authorities have long waiting lists of people seeking rental assistance, and from time to time the lists grow so long that local officials stop adding names.

The Influence of the Welfare System

There is significant overlap between the work support system and the welfare system, and consequently, the welfare system is an important design influence for several work support programs. Many programs that serve as work supports

36. King (2000).
37. Department of Health and Human Services (1999a, 2000).
38. General Accounting Office (2002b).

Table 3-3. Welfare Program Characteristics of Work Support Programs

Program	Available within or outside the welfare system?	Time-limited benefits?	Child required for benefits?	Special standards for immigrants?
Minimum wage	Both	No	No	No
EITC	Both	No	No[a]	Yes
Food stamps	Both	No	No	Yes
Child care	Both[b]	No	Yes	Yes
School meals	Both	No	Yes	No
TANF	Within	Yes	Yes	Yes
Medical assistance	Both[b]	Varies[c]	Varies[c]	Yes
Rental assistance	Both[b]	No	No	Yes

a. More generous benefits are provided to families or households with children.

b. Those within the cash welfare system get priority or preferential treatment.

c. Standards vary from state to state and program to program, and also depend on whether the beneficiary is a child or an adult.

provide benefits to three different target groups: low-income workers; people making the transition from the welfare system to work; and welfare recipients. Three work support programs—TANF, medical assistance, and food stamps—also compose the traditional core package of welfare benefits. Table 3-3 reports the extent to which work support programs reflect the concerns of the welfare system, in particular, the values evident in the PRWORA. The table indicates whether program benefits are available to needy workers within or outside the cash assistance welfare system. TANF benefits are reserved for those within the cash assistance system and those who are making the transition from welfare to work. These two groups also receive priority treatment for child care grants and special opportunities to receive medical assistance (that is, TMA). This indicates that some aspects of the work support system are designed to encourage welfare recipients to enter the labor market, and that to some extent inequality among needy workers is tolerated to accomplish that objective.

The PRWORA sets lifetime time limits on eligibility to receive cash assistance. Table 3-3 indicates that two work support programs are similarly time limited. TANF benefits are subject to a lifetime limit of five years (with some exceptions). In addition, TANF earned income disregards, the TANF benefit that those making the transition from welfare to work can enjoy along with earned income, is time limited. Standards vary from one state to another, but in most states earned income disregards are exhausted after one year of full-time minimum wage employment. In addition, *some* medical assistance benefits are time limited. TMA, the program that extends Medicaid eligibility to those making the transition from welfare to work, is typically limited to one year, though state-level standards vary.

Table 3-3 also indicates whether immigration status is considered in determining eligibility for program benefits; specifically, are U.S. citizens and legal immigrants treated differently? We link this matter to provisions of the PRWORA, because the 1996 welfare reform made significant changes in immigrants' eligibility for most means-tested benefits (though some of these restrictions were later relaxed). To understand the implications of the PRWORA on program eligibility, it is necessary to distinguish citizens from noncitizens and legal resident aliens from people who are in the U.S. illegally. U.S. citizens, regardless of whether they are native born or naturalized, have never faced eligibility restrictions related to their immigration status when applying for means-tested federal benefits. The restrictions affect eligibility among those who are not citizens.

Prior to 1996, eligibility standards for means-tested federal programs were based on a distinction between those who were in the U.S. legally (lawful permanent residents and refugees) and those who were in the U.S. illegally, that is, people who entered the country without inspection or who had overstayed their nonimmigrant (such as tourist or student) visas.[39] Immigrants who were in the country legally enjoyed the same access to means-tested federal benefits as U.S. citizens did. However, illegal immigrants were not eligible to receive most forms of means-tested assistance (emergency Medicaid benefits were an exception). The PRWORA changed the eligibility standards for means-tested federal benefits that legal immigrants had enjoyed.

The PRWORA restricted the eligibility of legal immigrants for a variety of means-tested federal programs by one of two methods: "deeming," in which the income and assets of the immigrant's sponsor are considered in determining eligibility; and "barring," whereby specific legislative standards prohibit immigrant eligibility categorically. The act imposed a permanent bar on food stamp eligibility for legal permanent residents who entered the United States after August 22, 1996. This bar was later lifted for legal permanent resident children, regardless of entry date, and for qualified aliens who have resided in the United States for five years or more. TANF and Medicaid had different restrictions. States were permitted to ban participation among legal immigrants who entered the United States before the enactment of the PRWORA. However, legal immigrants who entered after the PRWORA

39. The following discussion is based on U.S. House of Representative, Committee on Ways and Means (2004).

became law were barred for a five-year period from receipt of TANF or Medicaid (except for emergency treatment).

The ban on the provision of federal benefits to legal immigrants goes beyond these core welfare programs to affect many other work supports. In fact, as indicated by table 3-3, only two forms of work supports are available to legal immigrants during their first five years in the United States: the minimum wage and school meal programs. The PRWORA specifically exempted school meals from the ban. The minimum wage, as a regulatory condition governing the labor market, also affects the material well-being of low-wage immigrant workers. However, given the employment prospects and patterns of some immigrant workers, it is possible that the benefits of minimum wage legislation are also elusive. The minimum wage can only be enforced among workers in legitimate, "on the books" employment. Unscrupulous employers or their intermediaries may exploit people who work in the cash economy by paying a subminimum wage. In addition, legal immigrants (among others) who work in restaurants or in agriculture may be exempt from minimum wage standards.

Finally, table 3-3 shows that many work support programs provide benefits exclusively to families or households with children, and that some are more generous when children are present or when low-income workers must support more than one child. Child care grants, school meals, and TANF limit benefits only to families with children. State and federal EITC programs provide more generous benefits to families with children, and the federal EITC provides its most generous benefits to families with two or more children. The child tax credit clearly is limited to families with children. Medical assistance is more complicated. Many children in low-income families qualify for medical assistance through CHIP, though state eligibility standards vary. Medicaid also provides access to medical assistance for many low-income children. Although it is not necessary to have children in order to receive medical assistance, children are a preferred target population and are more likely than adults to receive medical assistance benefits.

Conclusion

The analysis suggests that the performance of many work support programs is subject to serious constraints. Medical assistance benefits are not a reliable source of support for many needy workers, and several characteristics of the programs (Medicaid and CHIP) explain why this is so. First, the cost controls put in place by many states restrict eligibility, especially among low-income working adults. TMA is a limited, temporary solution to this problem, because it applies only to those making the transition from welfare to work and its duration is time limited. Although there have been marked improvements in access to health care for low-income children, gaps in medical assistance for low-income adults are a serious limitation of the work support system. As a result, low-income workers are more likely than welfare clients to lack health insurance.[40]

The work support system has developed its current form in part because of the imperatives of the welfare system, and this may have significant consequences for its performance. The welfare system is presently oriented toward reducing cash assistance participation, not toward supplementing earned income with means-tested benefits. That orientation may undermine the ability of needy workers to gain access to work support benefits, even when those benefits are individual entitlements. The Food Stamp Program and Medicaid are compromised as work supports because many low-income working families do not receive benefits they are entitled to. This is likely a result of local administration and the emphasis placed in social service departments on reducing cash assistance welfare participation. In addition, concerns about food stamp quality control may be reducing food stamp participation among qualified low-income workers, though the USDA has recently been taking steps to rectify that situation.

Another way in which the benefits received by needy working families are influenced by the welfare system is the preference that several work support programs give to families making the transition from welfare to work. These families enjoy access to TANF earned income disregards, TMA, and priority treatment for child care grants and rental assistance. Child care benefits are insufficient to meet the needs even of the favored population that is making the transition from welfare to work.[41] In addition, most states have adopted eligibility guidelines for child care benefits more restrictive than federal regulations, and this precludes many low-income working families from receiving benefits. These guidelines and resource limitations create a significant unmet need for child care among needy working families.

If the purpose of the work support system is to provide material support for needy working families, two programs stand out in this review. Because they are available nationwide, are not budget or time constrained, and are automatically adjusted for changes in living costs over time, the EITC program and the Food Stamp Program provide the most reliable support to needy

40. Broaddus and others (2002).
41. Department of Health and Human Services (2000).

workers in the United States. In addition, these benefits are available both within and outside the welfare system, and it is not necessary to have children in order to qualify for benefits (though food stamps benefits do vary with household size, and needy workers with children receive more generous EITC benefits).

Part 2
The Generosity of
Work Support Programs

4

State-Level Benefits

Needy working families can realize significant material gains by participating in work support programs. Work support benefits vary from place to place, they vary according to family size and structure, they vary according to participation in Temporary Assistance for Needy Families (TANF), and they vary according to work effort, earned income, and length of employment. The number of work support programs in which one participates is also a crucial factor. In this chapter we estimate the nominal income and benefits that can be gained from participating in the work support system in the fifty states and the District of Columbia. We assume a single mother with two children has emerged from the cash assistance welfare system and is in month thirteen of employment. Estimates of state benefit generosity are presented for full-time and half-time year-round minimum wage workers. In general, estimates are based on benefit rates in 2000. They represent the nominal value of work support benefits because they are not adjusted to reflect differences in living costs (which we consider in chapter 5).

Our analysis focuses exclusively on minimum wage workers. There are several good reasons for this. First, basing the earned income estimates on minimum wage rates makes them policy relevant, because minimum wage rates are discretionary policies for states. By focusing on minimum wage earners our estimates capture important differences in state-level compensation for work and the effects such differences have on eligibility for and generosity of means-tested benefits at the state level. Second, minimum wage workers are at the bottom of the labor market. Consequently, they are the workers with the greatest need of work supports. Finally, the annual earnings of full-time minimum wage workers are a good basis on which to assess the prospects of people making the transition from welfare to work (a topic we discuss in more detail in chapter 6).

People moving from welfare to work often earn $7 or $8 per hour. However, they rarely find full-time, year-round employment. That means that rather than $14,000 to $16,000 per year, they typically earn between 70 and 95 percent of the federal poverty standard, or between $9,700 and $13,200 annually.[1] Our full-time, year-round minimum wage worker earns $10,700. People qualify for work support benefits on the basis of income, not hourly wage rates. Consequently, the estimates we present are a fair representation of the typical low-end outcome achieved by people moving from welfare to work.

The notion of the generosity of state benefits requires some clarification. As previously explained, the work support system is composed of programs that feature national eligibility and benefit standards and programs that allow state discretion in these matters. We use the concept of "state benefit generosity" to indicate the relative generosity of this combination of nationally defined and state-discretionary benefits available in each state and the District of Columbia. As a consequence, the generosity of state-level benefits is a function of policy decisions at both the state and the national levels.

Our estimate of total income and benefits is the sum of nine different sources of material support available to needy workers: earned income from a minimum wage job, less federal and state income taxes and federal payroll taxes; federal earned income tax credit (EITC) benefits; TANF earned income disregards; the face value of food stamps; the maximum face value of state child care grants; the estimated market value of Medicaid benefits; the government cost of means-tested components of school meal programs; the face value of rental assistance; and refundable state EITC benefits. Appendix A explains the estimation method used for each work support component. Our estimates of total income and benefits are based upon the assumption that needy workers participate fully in the work support system and receive all possible benefits. As such, the estimates presented in this chapter represent the maximum possible benefits the work support system may provide in each state and the District of Columbia but do not necessarily indicate how the system actually performs.

The work support system has significant potential to reduce poverty among needy working families. In all fifty states and the District of Columbia, the combination of minimum wage work and work supports provides an income and benefit total that exceeds the federal poverty standard by a wide margin. However, only some work support benefits are provided in cash

1. The federal poverty standard figure is from McMurrer and Sawhill (1998).

(TANF and federal or state EITC payments), and it may not be appropriate to treat all benefits as equivalent to cash income. One cannot directly translate the costs or face value of in-kind benefits into a cash income equivalent if the needy working family would not have spent at least that amount in cash to purchase the benefit provided.[2] However, even if work support participation is limited to receipt of benefits that can plausibly be treated as cash, in all fifty states and the District of Columbia, one full-time minimum wage worker supporting a family of three can receive an income that exceeds the federal poverty standard.

Analysis of state-level benefit estimates shows that state discretionary policy decisions influence the nominal generosity of benefits. States that have TANF earned income disregards, parental eligibility for medical assistance, generous child care grants, substantial rent subsidies, and refundable state EITC benefits offer larger total benefit packages for work support participants. In addition, state minimum wage rates that exceed the federal rate increase earned income for minimum wage workers.

However, work support programs are subject to a number of constraints, such as limited workforce participation, budget constraints, and administrative practices that limit or discourage participation. To consider the effects of these constraints on state benefit generosity, we analyze six different scenarios for work hours and program participation. When opportunities to participate in work support programs are constrained, the system provides a porous safety net for needy workers who experience reduced employment opportunities. By linking means-tested benefits to work, policymakers have created a fragile support system.

Work Support Benefit Estimates

The benefits the work support system provides can result in significant material gains for needy working families. Figure 4-1 presents estimates of the total income and benefits that minimum wage work and the work support system provide in the fifty states and the District of Columbia as the sum of earned income, cash benefits, and in-kind benefits. These estimates are based on an optimistic scenario: the worker in our family of three moved from the cash assistance welfare system to work a little more than one year ago and is participating in all possible work support programs and receiving the maximum benefits the state provides. Under these circumstances, the work support system provides impressive material gains. The median estimated annual total

2. Smeeding (1984).

Figure 4-1. Nominal Work Support Income and Benefit Estimates

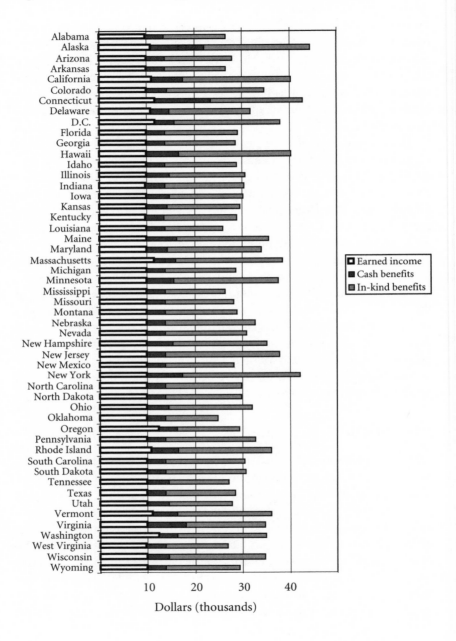

Dollars (thousands)

of income and benefits is $30,506 and the mean is $32,033; Alaska provides the largest total ($44,329), and Oklahoma provides the smallest ($24,679).

Although the work support system provides income and benefits from a number of different sources, earned income is the largest single component, constituting $10,187 in the average state (after income and federal payroll taxes) and 31.8 percent of the income and benefit total.[3] Two state discretionary policies influence earned income: minimum wage rates and income taxes. Eleven states had minimum wage rates that exceeded federal requirements in 2000, and ten states charged full-time minimum wage workers an income tax. State income taxes were generally modest. The highest estimated annual tax was $218 (in Alabama), and the average for the ten states that charged an income tax for full-time minimum wage workers was only about $100. The coefficient of variation (indicating the amount of variation in the distribution relative to a variable's scale) for the distribution of earned income at the state level is equal to 0.07.[4] Compared to most other components of work support, interstate variation in earned income is slight.

The work support system provides three cash benefits to complement earned income: federal EITC payments, state EITC payments, and TANF. Federal EITC benefits average $3,880, 12.1 percent of the estimated income and benefit total in the average state. These benefits vary little from place to place (the coefficient of variation for their distribution is 0.01). The federal EITC is governed by national eligibility and benefit standards, and consequently benefits are uniform across the nation. However, in a handful of places (such as Connecticut, the District of Columbia, Oregon, and Washington) minimum wage rates are high enough that a full-time minimum wage worker receives slightly less than the maximum possible EITC benefit; the higher earnings that result from the higher minimum wage rate place full-time, year-round minimum wage workers in the phase-out range for the federal EITC. The largest benefit losses are in Oregon and Washington, where they amount to about $150 annually.

3. The "average state" refers to the unweighted average of all fifty states and the District of Columbia. The average is unweighted because it does not account for differences in population. However, since we are interested in comparing state policies, not reconstructing national averages on the basis of weighted state income and benefit levels, unweighted averages are more appropriate.

4. To assess variation among the states and across the different programs that compose the work support system, we calculate the coefficient of variation: the standard deviation of a variable's distribution divided by its mean, with a range from zero to infinity. Paul Peterson (1995) has used this statistic to indicate whether or not interstate variation in welfare generosity was increasing or decreasing over time. We use the statistic in a slightly different way: to make cross-sectional comparisons of different benefit distributions.

State EITC programs provide an annual benefit of only $107 and compose only 0.3 percent of the income and benefit total in the average state. However, this average is somewhat misleading because few states have a refundable EITC. Among the eight states that did offer such a program in 2000, benefits averaged $685 annually for a full-time minimum wage worker. The most generous states were Vermont, which paid a state EITC benefit of $1,244, and Minnesota and New York, both of which paid $972. Compared to other work supports, the distribution of state EITC benefits varies a great deal (the coefficient of variation is 2.6). State EITC programs are distinctive because they are the only work support programs implemented by the states that lack federal revenue sharing. Thus few states have a refundable EITC, and those that do are acting entirely within their own discretion.

Cash from TANF constitutes only a small portion of the income and benefit total, even for someone emerging from the cash welfare system and receiving the maximum possible payments; benefits in the average state are $735, or 2.3 percent of the total. However, thirty-five states and the District of Columbia provide no TANF benefits whatsoever in the thirteenth month of full-time minimum wage employment. Of those that do, Connecticut provides the highest benefit, at $7,632 annually; Alaska is a close second, with $7,440; and a total of nine states provide TANF payments in excess of $1,500 annually. (Of course, eligibility to receive such payments is time limited in all jurisdictions; even the generous benefits in Connecticut and Alaska will eventually expire.) The coefficient of variation for the distribution of TANF earned income disregards is 2.28, indicating that there is significant interstate variation in TANF benefits compared to other work supports. This is not surprising, because the program was specifically designed to devolve policymaking authority to the states, and state policymakers may have different views on earned income disregards, in terms of both the magnitude and the duration of benefits.

The combination of earned income and cash benefits constitutes less than half of the income and benefit total in the average state; the majority of work supports are in-kind benefits. In the average state, child care grants provide $6,808, or 21.3 percent of the total; medical assistance amounts to $4,236 (13.2 percent); rental assistance provides $3,755 (11.7 percent); the Food Stamp Program provides $1,762 (5.5 percent); and school meals contribute $561 (1.8 percent). Four of these in-kind benefits exhibit moderate amounts of interstate variation: for child care benefits, the coefficients of variation is 0.33; for medical assistance, 0.39; for rental assistance, 0.29; and for food stamps, 0.28. School meal programs are exceptional, because interstate variation in the distribution of school meal benefits is slight. This reflects the fact that the only differences in school meal benefits are the two specifically created by Congress: the slightly higher reimbursement rates for Alaska and Hawaii.

State Policy Decisions

The extent of states' generosity in providing nominal work support benefits reflects the policy decisions they make. Table 4-1 compares the income and benefit total provided by work support programs in the ten most and ten least generous states and summarizes states' decisions on discretionary policies. The table indicates that the policy choices of more generous states tend to be different from those of less generous ones. The more generous states are likely to provide earned income disregards that allow full-time minimum wage workers to receive TANF benefits (seven of ten do); by contrast, only two of the ten less generous states provide earned income disregards. The more generous states are also more likely to provide Medicaid coverage for low-income working parents (all ten do) than less generous states (only three of ten do).[5] The more generous states are likely to provide higher child care benefits; seven of ten provide annual payments in excess of $8,000. Child care payments are lower in the less generous states; none provides annual payments in excess of $6,000. In addition, earned income is higher in the more generous states, six of which have a minimum wage that exceeds the federal minimum, while none of the less generous states does. Although three of the ten more generous states have a refundable state EITC programs, none of the less generous states does. Finally, four of the ten most generous states provide rental subsidies in excess of $4,800 annually, but none of the less generous states does so.

It is also clear from table 4-1 that states at the extremes of the distribution of state benefit generosity tend to use their discretion consistently. Among the ten most generous states, most have made several discretionary decisions that enhance work support generosity. Eight of the ten most generous states made affirmative decisions on four or more of the six discretionary work support design issues. Conversely, seven of the ten least generous states did nothing to enhance work support generosity, and the others made affirmative decisions on two or fewer work support design issues.

---

5. All states provide Medicaid eligibility for the children in a full-time minimum wage worker's family as required by federal mandate.

Table 4-1. Work Support Policies of the Most and Least Generous States, Nominal Benefits

State	Total annual work support (dollars)	TANF disregards	Parental Medicaid	Child care assistance over $8,000	Minimum wage	State EITC	Rental assistance over $4,800
Most generous							
Alaska	44,329	Yes	Yes	Yes	Yes	No	No
Connecticut	42,689	Yes	Yes	Yes	Yes	No	No
New York	42,223	Yes	Yes	Yes	No	Yes	No
California	40,357	Yes	Yes	Yes	Yes	No	No
Hawaii	40,245	Yes	Yes	No	Yes	No	Yes
Massachusetts	38,413	No	Yes	Yes	Yes	Yes	Yes
D.C.	37,976	No	Yes	No	Yes	No	Yes
New Jersey	37,868	No	Yes	No	No	No	Yes
Minnesota	37,548	Yes	Yes	Yes	No	Yes	No
Rhode Island	36,075	Yes	Yes	Yes	No	No	No
Least generous							
New Mexico	28,108	No	No	No	No	No	No
Arizona	28,010	No	Yes	No	No	No	No
Utah	27,591	Yes	Yes	No	No	No	No
Tennessee	27,005	Yes	Yes	No	No	No	No
West Virginia	26,763	No	No	No	No	No	No
Arkansas	26,636	No	No	No	No	No	No
Alabama	26,528	No	No	No	No	No	No
Mississippi	26,356	No	No	No	No	No	No
Louisiana	25,928	No	No	No	No	No	No
Oklahoma	24,679	No	No	No	No	No	No

Source: Authors' analysis.

An End to Poverty as We Know It?

The income and benefit total provided by the work support system compares favorably to the federal poverty standard. In the year 2000, the poverty standard for a family of three, including two children, was $13,874. The median and mean work support income and benefit totals are more than double the federal poverty standard. In Oklahoma, the state with the lowest nominal income and benefit total, the sum of income and benefits exceeds the federal poverty standard by 77.9 percent. However, the federal poverty standard is a cash income standard, whereas these income and benefit estimates are a mixture of in-kind and cash benefits. As noted above, it is not always appropriate to treat work support benefits as equivalent to cash.

This begs the question of which work support benefits (aside from cash benefits, such as TANF and EITC programs) can be considered equivalent to cash income for recipients. Few in-kind benefits can be treated as cash. However, it is likely that the face value of food stamps is roughly equivalent to cash income. A study of the substitution of cash for food stamps in Puerto Rico showed little impact on food expenditures.[6] A subsequent study by Robert Moffitt suggested that substituting cash for food stamps made little difference because "most [recipient] households were inframarginal—that is, most consumed more food than the benefit when on the program."[7] Moffitt suggests that the same effects are likely in the mainland United States, where incomes are higher but food stamp benefit levels are the same. Janet Currie has reviewed several food stamp "cash out" demonstrations and concludes that although there is some evidence that participants who received the cash out reduced expenditures on food, these were households in which the benefit was greater than or equal to the food budget.[8] Because most recipients are inclined to spend as much or more cash than the food stamp benefit to purchase food, the face value of food stamps can be treated as cash. However, school meals, medical assistance, child care, and rental assistance are unlikely to be equivalent to cash. Although needy working families value these benefits (and loss of medical assistance or child care benefits may reduce labor force participation), it is unlikely that the face value of benefits or government costs indicate cash income gains, because beneficiaries would be unlikely to spend equivalent sums to purchase these services if the benefits were provided in cash.[9]

However, if only earned income, cash benefits, and food stamps are considered—combining full-time minimum wage work, federal and state EITC

6. Devaney and Fraker (1986).

7. Moffitt (1989, p. 406).

8. Currie (2003).

9. If in-kind benefits are to be discounted, what discount rate is appropriate? A recent review of the literature on child care programs stated that there is "no research on the implicit cash value of in-kind child care subsidies." Blau (2003, p. 467). Jonathan Gruber's (2003, p. 43) analysis of medical assistance programs reports that estimation of the cash value of medical assistance benefits is "a daunting challenge" and that there is "no consensus at this point on the value of Medicaid to recipients in dollar terms." He reports that Smeeding estimated such benefit at less than half their market value. Janet Currie (2003) reports little research about the cash value of school nutrition program benefits, although she argues that the expected effect of the school lunch and breakfast programs is not to increase the amount of food consumed, but to alter the composition of participants' diets. Thus the appropriate discount rates to apply to the various in-kind work support benefits are largely unknown.

benefits, TANF earned income disregards, and the face value of food stamps—work support participants in all fifty states and the District of Columbia still enjoy an income that exceeds the federal poverty standard. In Alabama, the state with the smallest total, this measure of work support income is $15,483 ($9,675 from earnings net of taxes, $3,888 from the federal EITC, zero for the state EITC, zero from TANF, and $1,920 from food stamps). Alabama does nothing to enhance work support generosity and charges full-time minimum wage workers the highest income tax of any state. However, even Alabama's work support income level is approximately 12 percent above the federal poverty standard for a family of three. In Connecticut, the state with the greatest total income from the cash components, work support income totals $25,520 ($11,813 from earnings net of taxes, $3,867 from the federal EITC, $7,632 from TANF earned income disregards, zero from the state EITC, and $2,208 from food stamps), exceeding the federal poverty standard by almost 84 percent.

The fact that cash income totals exceed the federal poverty standard even in the least generous state has two important implications. First, state discretionary programs that provide cash benefits (TANF earned income disregards and state EITC benefits) are not necessary to boost the incomes of needy working families above the poverty standard. Our family of three will have an income above the poverty standard, regardless of state policy choices, on the basis of the federal minimum wage, federal EITC benefits, and food stamp benefits only. All of these policies and programs are governed by national standards; policy decisions made in Alabama do not affect the value of benefits that the state's residents can receive. Second, comprehensive participation in work support programs is not necessary to secure an income that exceeds the poverty standard. Full-time minimum wage work and receipt of the federal EITC and food stamps is sufficient to escape poverty as defined by the federal government, regardless of state of residence.

Limitations and Constraints

How is work support generosity affected by work opportunity and factors that constrain program participation? In chapters 2 and 3 we suggested that the benefits provided by some work support programs are subject to a number of constraints, including budget constraints and administrative practices that may limit or discourage participation. In addition, the linkage of work to means-tested benefits makes employment opportunities an important constraint.

To consider the implications of these constraints for the material well-being of needy workers, table 4-2 presents information about the generosity of work support benefits in the average state, based upon six different scenarios for work hours and program participation. Work hours are divided into two categories: full time and half time. This distinction helps to gauge the effects of limited work opportunities, because work hours influence earned income, and that in turn influences work support generosity. Program participation is divided into three categories: full participation in all work support programs, participation in tax and individual entitlements programs only, and participation only in programs that are free of budget constraints and administrative practices that may limit participation (only federal and state EITC programs and school meal programs satisfy these conditions).

The program participation categories represent different assumptions about the effects of constraints on access to work support benefits. The first program participation category is consistent with the analysis presented thus far and shows the maximum possible income and benefits that the work support system can provide; implicitly, this scenario downplays the significance of budget and administrative constraints. However, as we have noted, it is possible that needy workers will not be able to participate fully in work support programs if budgets are constrained or administrative practices discourage receipt of benefits. The second participation category assumes that needy workers benefit only from individual entitlements and tax programs, because these programs are not budget constrained, or are constrained only indirectly by state eligibility and benefit standards; this scenario ignores administrative barriers to participation. The third category assumes that no benefits, not even individual entitlements, are received when administrative practices are in place to discourage participation (for example, the "work first" strategies used by many local social service departments to implement welfare reform, or the practice of closing waitlists for rental assistance used by local housing authorities). We assume that the needy worker either did not approach the agency to request assistance or did so and was rebuffed. This is a plausible scenario, given that participation in entitlement programs administered by local social service departments declined as welfare reform that emphasized moving recipients into the workforce was implemented, and that many local housing authorities regularly close their waiting lists.[10]

10. This scenario allows participation in child nutrition and tax programs. It is not necessarily the most limited scenario for participation in the work support system. Although school lunch service is almost universal in the United States, the same is not true for school breakfast. Fewer schools offer this service, and if breakfast is not available, the estimated benefit total will be lower. Beyond this, some studies contend that potential EITC beneficiaries fail to

Table 4-2. Work Support Program Benefits by Work Hours and Participation Scenario

Dollars

Work hours and level of participation	Earned income	Federal EITC	TANF	Food stamps	Child care	Medical assistance	School meals	Rental assistance	State EITC	Total
Full time										
Full participation	10,187	3,880	735	1,762	6,808	4,236	561	3,755	107	32,031
Tax and entitlements	10,187	3,880	0	1,983	0	4,236	561	0	107	20,954
No benefits with constraints	10,187	3,880	0	0	0	0	561	0	107	14,735
Half time										
Full participation	5,103	2,210	2,462	2,555	3,247	4,236	561	4,896	62	25,332
Tax and entitlements	5,103	2,210	0	3,294	0	4,236	561	0	62	15,466
No benefits with constraints	5,103	2,210	0	0	0	0	561	0	62	7,936

Source: Authors' calculations.

The table shows that full-time work in conjunction with all work support benefits provides an average income and benefit total of $32,031. Full-time work and participation in only entitlement and tax programs yields an estimated total of $20,954. This suggests that budget constraints are a serious brake on work support generosity; compared to the total for full participation, the income and benefit loss due to budget constraints is approximately 35 percent.[11] Full-time work and participation in only tax and school meal programs yields an estimated total of $14,735. This suggests that the combination of budget constraints and administrative bars to participation can compromise work support generosity; compared to the total for full participation, the income and benefit loss is approximately 54 percent.

Half-time workers who participate fully in the work support system receive an estimated income and benefit total of $25,332 in the average state. Generally, half-time workers get more benefits than full-time workers do from resource-constrained programs such as TANF, child care, and rental assistance. Participation in only entitlement and tax programs provides an income and benefit total for half-time workers of $15,466, a loss of approximately 39 percent compared to full work support participation. Half-time workers who receive only tax and school meal benefits receive an estimated total of $7,936, a benefit loss in excess of 69 percent compared to full work support participation. This shows that budget constraints and administrative bars to participation are even more serious for part-time workers than for full-time workers, because a larger share of the material support they enjoy comes from budget-constrained programs and programs that may be subject to participation limits.

The steep benefit losses experienced by full- and half-time workers under the different scenarios of participation in work support programs suggest that the constraints that reduce work support participation are significant. Although full work support participation provides an income and benefit total that exceeds the federal poverty standard by a wide margin, these constraints reduce a full-time worker's total work support benefit to the poverty level; the income and benefit total for a full-time minimum wage worker who

---

receive benefits because they do not file tax returns. On this point see Dickert-Conlin and Holtz-Eakin (2000) and Hoffman and Seidman (1990).

11. Table 4-2 shows that as TANF income is lost there is an increase in food stamp benefits that equals 30 percent of the loss. However, this may underestimate the increase in food stamp benefits that will be provided because loss of child care support can increase out-of-pocket child care costs, reducing net income and further increasing food stamp benefit payments. Given the complexity of various state child care programs, this possibility is not included in the benefit adjustments.

receives only tax and school meal benefits is approximately 106 percent of the poverty standard for a family of three. Beyond this, when work opportunities are limited, access to entitlement benefits is critical to keep needy working families above the poverty line. Half-time minimum wage workers who receive only tax and school meal benefits—the most pessimistic scenario for work support system generosity we consider—have an income and benefit total that is only 57.3 percent of the federal poverty standard. For their income to rise above the poverty line, these workers must receive tax and entitlement benefits. Unfortunately, the pessimistic scenario may be the most realistic. People making the transition from welfare to work often become part-time workers because they are unable to find full-time, year-round employment.[12] The work support system can help, but evidence suggests that although the EITC is widely used, participation in other programs, such as TANF, food stamps, and Medicaid, is less likely.[13]

Table 4-2 also demonstrates that some work support programs compensate for earned income loss while others compound it. This has implications for the effectiveness of the work support system as a safety net when work opportunities are constricted. On average, the estimated income and benefit total of half-time workers who participate fully in the work support system is 79 percent of that received by full-time workers, because earned income and tax losses are offset by gains in TANF, food stamp, and rental assistance benefits. Because federal and state EITC payments are positively related to work hours for most minimum wage workers, an income loss due to a reduction in work hours is compounded by a loss of tax benefits. However, half-time workers receive more than half the amount of EITC benefits received by full-time workers, because of the benefit structure.[14] Child care grants are also reduced, but this loss reflects lower need for child care due to fewer hours worked. On balance, the system more than compensates for tax benefit losses; the income gained from TANF, food stamps, and rental assistance is greater than the income lost due to the state and federal EITC programs. (If child care grants are also considered income lost, the losses outweigh the gains, but that stretches the meaning of the term.) Thus the analysis suggests that if needy

12. McMurrer and Sawhill (1998).

13. Loprest (2002); Zedlewski (2002).

14. Readers will recall from the discussion in chapter 2 that the EITC benefit structure is complex. It has a benefit phase-in range, a stable benefit range, and a benefit phase-out range. Most full-time, year-round minimum wage workers are at the cusp of the phase-out range (this explains why slightly higher minimum wage rates in some states reduce EITC benefits). If work hours are halved, EITC benefits are not cut in half because much of the income loss occurs over the stable benefit range.

workers find their work opportunities diminished, the work support system can operate as a safety net that compensates for lost income.

This result is crucially influenced by our assumption that people participate fully in the work support system. In that context, when work hours are reduced (as might be the case during an economic recession), the work support system does help to compensate for the loss of earned income that needy workers suffer, by providing more generous benefits. However, if budget constraints or administrative bars limit program participation, the work support system is likely to provide material assistance that helps to make work pay only when employment opportunities are not constrained. For needy workers whose work hours are reduced (from full time to half time) and who receive tax and entitlement benefits only, the gains in food stamp benefits are insufficient to overcome the loss of EITC benefits. If these same needy workers receive only tax and school meal benefits (because of administrative bars to participation), the work support system does nothing to compensate for their lost earned income. When work opportunities and program participation are constrained, the work support system provides no safety net for needy workers.

Conclusion

This chapter has presented estimates of the material gains that can be realized by combining minimum wage work with work support benefits. These benefits can be quite significant and have the potential to lift many needy working families out of poverty, even when program participation is limited. The analysis also indicates that states are important participants in the work support system in two ways. First, states influence the nominal generosity of work support benefits by making policy design decisions. Second, states (in particular, social service department personnel) are important gatekeepers of the work support system, influencing the generosity of work support benefits through program implementation. Access to work supports that are controlled by social services departments is important because it provides a safety net of benefits for needy working families. Without access to TANF and food stamps, needy workers can rely on the work support system only in good economic times. When times get bad, needy workers are working without a safety net.

5

The Cost of Living

The analysis of nominal work support benefit generosity presented in chapter 4 neglects three important considerations: (1) there are differences in living costs across the fifty states and the District of Columbia; (2) the federal poverty standard is a single national standard and does not reflect subnational and substate variation in living costs; and (3) the federal poverty standard is not adequate as a measure of self-sufficiency. To address these concerns, in this chapter estimates of state benefit generosity are adjusted according to the cost of housing in the fifty states and the District of Columbia, and nominal income and benefit estimates are compared to basic family budgets to assess the extent to which the work support system allows needy working families to become self-sufficient.[1]

This approach raises an important question, discussed briefly in chapter 1: what is the meaning of self-sufficiency when the work support system links receipt of means-tested benefits to work? One possible standard is that people are self-sufficient when they accept the responsibility of working to support themselves and their family. Certainly, all the combinations of earned income and work support benefits that we consider allow an individual to meet this standard, because the benefit estimates are conditioned on work. Another possible standard is that means-tested benefits should constitute less than 50 percent of total income.[2] Whether the needy working family we consider meets this standard depends on the extent to which it par-

---

1. For basic family budgets, see Bernstein, Brocht, and Spade-Aguilar (2000); Boushey and others (2001).

2. Department of Health and Human Services (1997).

ticipates in the work support system. Full participation implies that the majority of the family's material support comes from means-tested program benefits. However, if needy workers only receive tax and school meal benefits, the majority of the family's material support is earned income. A third possible standard is the absence of participation in cash assistance welfare. All of the scenarios we consider assume that the head of a family of three emerged from the cash assistance welfare system more than one year ago. If she is a full-time minimum wage worker, she is self-sufficient by this standard in all but fifteen states because she is no longer TANF eligible, and she will eventually exhaust her eligibility for TANF benefits in all fifty states and the District of Columbia. If she works half time at minimum wage, she is self-sufficient by this standard in only ten states in month thirteen of employment. Of course, if she receives only tax and entitlement benefits or tax and school meal benefits, she is self-sufficient by this standard regardless of work effort. Our view of self-sufficiency is related to need: the family is minimally self-sufficient when the income and benefit total provided by the work support system meets the family's needs. In this chapter basic family budgets serve as the standard of need.

Cost-adjusted estimates of work support benefits more accurately reflect the real value of the material support the system provides. The same nominal benefits do not provide the same purchasing power or an equivalent lifestyle in every state and locality across the United States. Without cost-of-living adjustments, state generosity may be misunderstood. In fact, analysis of the adjusted estimates affects one's understanding of the relationship between states' discretionary policy decisions and state generosity. Although the association between states' decisions and nominal work support generosity is clear, the association between state discretionary policy choices and cost-adjusted generosity is more ambiguous, because the states that enhance generosity also tend to have high costs of living. Our evidence suggests that these more generous benefits only partially compensate residents for higher living costs.

Comparisons of nominal work support benefits with basic family budgets reveal that although most states provide sufficient support for a minimal lifestyle in low-cost areas, typically they do not provide enough in high-cost areas. This suggests that the limitations of the work support system are more serious in large metropolitan areas, where living costs tend to be higher. The District of Columbia, as an exclusively urban area, makes this point clearly: Although it is among the ten most generous states in nominal terms (see table 4-1), the analysis we will present in this chapter shows that the District of

Columbia performs very poorly when work support generosity is compared to basic family budgets. In addition, constraints on employment or program participation make it impossible for needy workers to be minimally self-sufficient even if they live in low-cost areas of low-cost states.

Housing Cost Adjustments

We adjusted the nominal estimates of total work support system income and benefits to reflect differences in median housing costs in the fifty states and the District of Columbia in 2000.[3] The housing adjustment factor was calculated by dividing the median housing price in each of the fifty states and the District of Columbia by the average of median housing prices.[4] All of the nominal estimates of the value of work support program benefits were divided by this adjustment factor and then summed to calculate the total value of housing-adjusted income and benefits. Hawaii, California, Massachusetts, and New Jersey had the highest housing costs; Arkansas, Mississippi, Oklahoma, and West Virginia had the lowest. The median housing-adjusted income and benefit total provided by the work support system was $34,233, and mean was $34,035. North Dakota provided the largest housing-adjusted total: $47,346; and Hawaii provided the smallest: $17,498.

Adjusting for cost-of-living differences increased the variation in the distribution of total income and benefits; differences in state benefit generosity were exaggerated rather than reduced by the adjustment. The distribution of nominal benefits has a range of $19,650 (with a coefficient of variation of 0.15), while the the distribution of cost-adjusted benefits has a range of $29,848 (with a coefficient of variation of 0.21). This is a curious result. Accounting for differences in living costs might be expected to reduce the variation in the distribution as high-cost, high-benefit states and low-cost, low-benefit states are pulled toward the middle of the distribution. That the variation increased is a clue that something else has happened by cost-adjusting the benefit estimates.

There is a negative relationship between the estimated nominal income and benefit totals for the fifty states and the District of Columbia and the housing-adjusted totals.[5] This means that adjusting for differences in living costs

3. Median housing costs at the state level and in the District of Columbia were taken from data on the median value of owner-occupied units in the 2000 census.

4. The average of median housing values in the fifty states and the District of Columbia in 2000 was $118,759.

5. The correlation coefficient is −.35, indicating that states with relatively generous nominal benefits tended to be less generous when benefits were cost adjusted.

changed significantly the analysis of which states are generous and which states are not. The negative relationship implies that the order of state generosity has been reversed: states that were generous in terms of nominal benefits are not so in terms of cost-adjusted benefits, and vice versa. The effect of controlling for living costs was not to condense the distribution by pulling the outlying cases back toward the middle; rather, controlling for living costs reversed the order of the states, moving what once were more generous states toward the bottom of the distribution and vice versa.

Table 5-1 shows how the housing-cost adjustment affects the relationship between state generosity and state discretionary policy choices. There is little resemblance between the lists of most and least generous states based upon housing-adjusted benefits and the lists based upon nominal benefits (see table 4-1). None of the ten most generous states in terms of housing-adjusted benefits is included among the ten most generous states for nominal benefits. Only two states, Arizona and Utah, were among the ten least generous states for both nominal and cost-adjusted benefits. However, several states moved from the bottom ten to the top ten, and vice versa. Arkansas, Mississippi, and West Virginia are among the ten least generous states for nominal benefits, but among the ten most generous for cost-adjusted benefits. California, Hawaii, Massachusetts, and New Jersey are among the ten most generous states in terms of nominal benefits, but among the ten least generous when benefits are cost-adjusted.

When benefits are adjusted for housing costs, state discretionary policies are no longer a clear basis for predicting state benefit generosity. If anything, state policy choices that enhance work support generosity are inversely related to housing-cost-adjusted income and benefit estimates. The ten most generous states do little to increase work support benefits; five of them do nothing to enhance work support generosity. Only two of the ten most generous states provide TANF earned income disregards; only four offer parental Medicaid eligibility; only one provides child care grants in excess of $8,000; and one other provides state EITC payments. None of the most generous states has a minimum wage rate in excess of the federal minimum wage, and none provides rental assistance in excess of $4,800. Paradoxically, the ten least generous states are more likely to have used their discretion to increase the generosity of work support benefits: all ten of them did something, and several made multiple discretionary decisions to enhance work support generosity. Three of the ten least generous states provide TANF earned income disregards; nine provide parental Medicaid assistance; four provide child care grants in excess of $8,000; five have state minimum wage rates; two have

Table 5-1. Work Support Policies of the Most and Least Generous States, Housing-Cost-Adjusted Benefits

State	Total annual work support (dollars)	TANF disregards	Parental Medicaid	Child care assistance over $8,000	Minimum wage	State EITC	Rental assistance over $4,800
Most generous							
North Dakota	47,346	No	Yes	No	No	No	No
South Dakota	45,627	No	No	No	No	No	No
Nebraska	44,168	No	Yes	No	No	No	No
Mississippi	43,927	No	No	No	No	No	No
West Virginia	43,874	No	No	No	No	No	No
Iowa	43,838	Yes	Yes	No	No	No	No
Arkansas	43,666	No	No	No	No	No	No
Maine	42,741	Yes	Yes	Yes	No	No	No
Kansas	42,033	No	No	No	No	Yes	No
Texas	41,194	No	No	No	No	No	No
Least generous							
Arizona	27,461	No	Yes	No	No	No	No
New Jersey	26,297	No	Yes	No	No	No	Yes
Nevada	25,624	No	Yes	No	No	No	Yes
Colorado	24,703	No	No	Yes	No	Yes	No
Massachusetts	24,624	No	Yes	Yes	Yes	Yes	Yes
Washington	24,598	No	Yes	Yes	Yes	No	No
Oregon	22,937	No	Yes	No	Yes	No	No
California	22,672	Yes	Yes	Yes	Yes	No	No
Utah	22,432	Yes	Yes	No	No	No	No
Hawaii	17,498	Yes	Yes	No	Yes	No	Yes

Source: Authors' analysis.

state EITC programs; and four provide annual rental assistance in excess of $4,800.

The analysis of housing-cost-adjusted benefits has turned the analysis of nominal benefits presented in chapter 4 on its head. Many states with high costs of living used state discretionary policies to provide additional work support benefits. However, when these benefits are adjusted to reflect differences in living costs, states that initially appear to be generous are seen in a different light: state discretionary policies often do not provide sufficient additional benefits to compensate for higher living costs. Ironically, states that have done nothing to provide additional work support benefits are often more generous. However, the generosity of these "do nothing" states is a function of work support programs that feature national eligibility and benefit standards in conjunction with low living costs, not of state discretionary policy choices.

Basic Family Budgets

The second cost-of-living adjustment we present is based upon basic family budgets and assesses the extent to which the work support system provides an income and benefit total that makes needy working families minimally self-sufficient.[6] "Basic family budgets measure the income a family requires to afford basic needs for a safe and decent standard of living."[7] Budgets have been estimated for a variety of family sizes and structures in numerous locations in the fifty states and the District of Columbia for 1996. The components of the budgets are food, housing, health care, transportation, child care, other necessities, and taxes. There are two advantages to using basic family budgets for cost-of-living adjustments: (1) they are estimates of the income families actually need to have a minimal, decent style of life; and (2) they are constructed to reflect the costs of various localities, allowing one to consider substate variation in living costs.

We created ratios by dividing the nominal income and benefit totals by financial need, as measured by minimum and maximum basic family budgets for a family of three with two children in each state. These ratios measure the proportion of the basic family budget that is provided by earned income and the work support system and indicate the extent to which the system provides an income for self-sufficiency. In some states there are significant differences in budget estimates among localities (only one budget was estimated for the District of Columbia). For example, in California the maximum budget is $41,196 for San Francisco, and the minimum budget is $29,069 in Yuba City.[8] To account for such differences, we used the minimum basic family budgets in each state to construct "low-cost" ratios and the maximum budgets to construct "high-cost" ratios of self-sufficiency in relation to need.

In order to construct the ratios, we revised the basic family budgets and work support program benefit estimates to make them compatible. Basic family budgets do not account for whether states provide the services included as basic needs (such as medical assistance or child care grants). The adjustments we make depend on our assumptions about work support participation

6. Bernstein, Brocht, and Spade-Aguilar (2000); Boushey and others (2001).
7. Boushey and others (2001, p. 7).
8. Boushey and others (2001).

and are explained in detail in appendix B. We compared the revised work support system income and benefit totals to the revised basic family budgets for the three work support program participation scenarios introduced in chapter 4: a full-time minimum wage worker participates in all available work supports (full participation); only in tax and entitlement programs; or only in tax and school meal programs that have no direct budget constraints or bars to participation.

Table 5-2 presents the eleven most and ten least generous state-level jurisdictions in terms of the proportion of need fulfilled by earned income and work support system benefits provided to full participants in low-cost areas.[9] The results indicate that in most cases the work support system provides an adequate income to meet the basic needs for families that live in low cost areas and participate fully in the work support system. Full participation in the work support system by a full-time minimum wage worker provides 112 percent of the basic family budget in a low-cost-of-living area in the average state. Work support income and benefit totals are 100 percent or more of basic family budgets in low-cost areas in forty-four states. The highest self-sufficiency ratio was 151 percent in Nebraska, and the lowest was 73 percent in the District of Columbia. States did not perform nearly as well in high-cost-of-living areas; even when needy working families enjoy full-time, year-round employment and participate fully in work support programs, the self-sufficiency ratio in the average state was only 89 percent. Only eight states provided an adequate income and benefit total in high-cost areas. Nebraska had the highest self-sufficiency ratio in high-cost-of-living areas: 117 percent; New York and West Virginia had the lowest: 69 percent. In high-cost areas in most states, full participation in the work support system fails to provide an adequate income for a full-time minimum wage worker to enjoy a minimally decent life style.

Table 5-2 also demonstrates the importance of work support program participation. When full-time minimum wage workers are not able to participate fully in the work support system, self-sufficiency ratios decline quickly in all fifty states and the District of Columbia. When the needy working family receives benefits from tax and entitlement programs only, in the average state the self-sufficiency ratio is 67.6 percent in low-cost areas and 56.7 percent in high-cost areas. Once again, Nebraska is the most generous state, with a self-

9. We include twenty-one states in this table rather than twenty because of a tie on the selection criterion. For this table, we selected states on the basis of their self-sufficiency ratios in low-cost areas. Iowa, Connecticut, and Illinois tied for ninth place. Consequently, all three were included.

Table 5-2. Self-Sufficiency Ratios by Participation Scenario and
Local Cost of Living

Percent

State	Full participation		Tax and entitlements only		Tax benefits and school meals only	
	Low cost	High cost	Low cost	High cost	Low cost	High cost
Most generous						
Nebraska	151.0	117.0	85.0	71.0	66.9	57.0
California	143.0	76.0	64.6	41.2	56.4	37.1
Massachusetts	131.0	92.0	70.4	54.9	57.1	45.7
Ohio	128.0	98.0	72.1	59.3	59.0	49.3
Washington	128.0	100.0	71.7	60.2	60.3	51.5
North Carolina	127.0	101.0	83.8	69.6	65.1	55.2
New York	126.0	69.0	57.6	38.1	48.5	33.2
South Dakota	123.0	106.0	72.8	65.1	61.3	55.1
Iowa	121.0	96.0	71.9	60.5	58.2	49.7
Connecticut	121.0	85.0	58.4	44.2	48.0	37.0
Illinois	121.0	85.0	67.4	51.8	54.4	42.9
Least generous						
Montana	102.0	100.0	67.1	66.0	52.4	51.7
Georgia	102.0	76.0	70.5	55.5	55.7	44.9
Nevada	101.0	96.0	61.5	59.4	49.3	47.7
Colorado	99.0	80.0	56.8	48.5	48.3	41.5
Maryland	98.0	70.0	57.8	44.8	49.2	38.5
Rhode Island	98.0	84.0	51.9	46.3	43.6	39.3
Hawaii	98.0	89.0	54.2	50.2	41.7	38.8
Delaware	96.0	91.0	63.2	60.2	51.1	48.9
New Hampshire	90.0	77.0	48.6	42.8	42.1	37.3
D.C.	73.0	73.0	44.6	44.6	37.7	37.7

Source: Authors' calculations, as described in text.

sufficiency ratio of 85.0 percent in low-cost areas. However, Nebraska provides benefits for only 71.0 percent of needs to tax and entitlement participants in high-cost areas. The District of Columbia is the least generous, with a self-sufficiency ratio of only 44.6 percent for tax and entitlement participants.

When the needy working family receives tax and school meal benefits only, the self-sufficiency ratio in the average state drops to 55.8 percent in low-cost areas and to 47.4 percent in high-cost areas. Mississippi replaces Nebraska as the most generous state; in low-cost areas of Mississippi the self-sufficiency ratio is 68.9 percent, but in high-cost areas the self-sufficiency ratio is only

59.9 percent. The District of Columbia remains the least generous low-cost location when only tax and school meal benefits are received, with a self-sufficiency ratio of 37.7 percent. However, the District of Columbia stands out in this analysis because the states are composed of rural areas, small towns, and cities, whereas the District is exclusively a high-cost urban area. If the District of Columbia were compared to other large urban areas, its performance would not be so unusual. For example, in New York City (the highest-cost locale in New York State) the self-sufficiency ratio is only 33.2 percent; tax and school meals benefits in conjunction with full-time minimum wage work only provide about one-third of the income required for a minimal basic living standard.

In sum, when variation in living costs within states is considered, most states, including many with high costs of living (California, Connecticut, New York, and Massachusetts) have polices that can provide sufficient incomes for residents of low-cost areas. But these policies do not provide an adequate income in their high-cost-of-living areas. Beyond this, work support program participation must be comprehensive in order for a minimum wage worker to have an adequate income. When budget constraints or bars to participation limit access to work support benefits, states uniformly perform poorly in terms of providing needy working families the income required for a minimally decent living standard. Depending upon how restricted work support program participation is, needy families supported by a full-time minimum wage worker and residing in high cost areas may receive as little as one-third of what is required for minimal self-sufficiency.

Conclusion

This chapter has presented adjusted estimates of work support benefit generosity in the fifty states and the District of Columbia. When nominal estimates of work support benefits are adjusted for living costs, a significant change in the relative generosity of the states is evident. The relationship reported in chapter 4 between nominal work support income and state discretionary policy choices follows a simple logic. States that use their discretion to provide additional work support benefits provide a higher income and benefit total. However, when benefits are cost adjusted, this simple logic breaks down.

When state benefits are compared to basic family budgets, it is apparent that the work support system provides less than many needy working families require. Only full participation combined with residence in a low-cost area was enough to gain minimal self-sufficiency. It also is apparent that living costs within states affect work support generosity; states did a better job of providing an adequate budget for self-sufficiency in low-cost areas than in high-cost areas. In addition, our analysis demonstrates the importance of comprehensive work support program participation. When participation was restricted, none of the states did an adequate job of providing for needy working families.

Our analysis of work support benefit estimates adjusted for housing costs suggests a different (and ironic) conclusion. Although the generosity of the work support system depends to a great extent upon where you live, state policy decisions are not of primary importance. Generous states are less likely to have made policy decisions to enhance the generosity of their work support benefits. The factor that unites generous states is low living costs; low living costs increase the value and purchasing power of income and benefit totals that are driven by policy decisions made at the national level. This suggests that the upper bounds of work support system generosity are largely determined in Washington, D.C., not in state capitals.

6

From Welfare to Work Supports

One objective of the work support system is to encourage work.[1] The work support system enhances the material well-being of needy workers by allowing them to combine means-tested tax and transfer benefits with earned income. We demonstrated in chapter 4 that the material rewards of work alone pale in comparison to the rewards of work in conjunction with work supports. We now consider, further, whether work supports encourage people to leave the welfare system to enter the workforce.

To answer this question, we compare the benefits of welfare participation to the rewards that the work support system provides. There are two dimensions to this exercise. First, we consider the necessary sacrifice of means-tested benefits as earned income increases. This benefit loss amounts to a tax on earned income (what economists call an "implicit benefit tax") and is expected to discourage work. We measure this negative incentive by comparing the means-tested benefits received by nonworking welfare clients to those received by half-time and full-time minimum wage workers. Second, we consider the work support system's potential to encourage work by allowing needy workers to combine tax and transfer benefits with earned income.[2] We measure this positive incentive by comparing the same welfare package to the income and benefit totals that the work support system offers to half-time and full-time minimum wage workers.

1. Sawhill and Haskins (2002a, 2002b).
2. We do not explicitly consider the complexity that may be introduced to this decision when there is more than one low-income worker in a family. However, the discussion presented in chapter 2 noted that in such circumstances, receipt of work support benefits might induce some secondary earners to reduce work effort.

The effects of the work support system on work incentives are important because work incentives are related to welfare dependency. Explanations of welfare dependency often focus on the economic incentives created by means-tested benefits.[3] From this perspective, welfare participation is a rational response: when the welfare system provides greater material rewards than the labor market, people are attracted to welfare and stay with it for as long as they can.

Chapter 1 linked concerns about the rewards of the labor market relative to the welfare system to three influential ideas that have shaped U.S. social policy: the less eligibility principle, the doctrine of laissez-faire, and the distinction between the deserving and the undeserving poor. The work support system challenges these ideas by providing means-tested benefits that complement rather than compete with work. If needy workers can gain access to the same or similar benefits as welfare recipients enjoy, redistributive programs need not be seen as a source of welfare dependency. If minimum wage work and work support benefits provide a standard of living that exceeds what is possible from welfare participation alone, a generous work support system can be part of the solution to welfare dependency.

As noted previously, the work support system and the welfare system include many of the same programs: TANF, food stamps, and medical assistance are examples of the overlap. If employment is required to receive benefits or if benefits can be received in conjunction with work, the dichotomy between welfare and work (and between the undeserving and the deserving poor) that is the basis of concerns about welfare dependency is undermined. Abandoning this dichotomy makes sense because it is an unrealistic description of the lives and experiences of most welfare recipients, who cycle in and out of the labor market for a variety of reasons.[4] It also offers a new possibility for thinking about redistribution in relation to work: the rewards of work need not be determined primarily by what the market provides. Therefore, the lowest material rewards available to workers in the labor market need not define or constrain redistributive generosity in the welfare system because a generous and effective work support system elevates the material condition of workers at the bottom of the labor market. This suggests that the work support system can reconcile redistributive public policies with the work ethic.

Although contemporary analysts are more attuned to the work support system, past analysis of welfare dependency has sometimes overlooked its significance. For example, Michael Tanner, Stephen Moore, and David Hartman

3. Murray (1984); Tanner, Moore, and Hartman (1995); Besharov (2003).
4. Handler (1995).

toted up the dollar value of the benefits that various means-tested programs provide to welfare participants and calculated the "wage equivalent" that a worker would have to earn to get a similar income.[5] They concluded that in seven states and the District of Columbia, welfare participation is more lucrative than a job paying $25,000 per year. Leaving aside the criticism that their analysis describes possibilities for welfare participation that are not often realized (rather than the system's actual performance), our main objection is that they do not consider the tax and transfer programs that benefit needy workers. In other words, they ignore the work support system. Under this system, work and means-tested benefits are not alternatives but complements.

The Implicit Benefit Tax

To examine what happens to a family's eligibility for means-tested benefits once the head of the household makes the transition from welfare to work, we estimated the maximum benefits that welfare recipients can receive in the fifty states and the District of Columbia and compared these totals to the benefits offered to half- and full-time minimum wage workers. As in our earlier analyses of work support generosity, our calculations of welfare benefits are based upon a family of three with two children and include the maximum state TANF payment, the value of Medicaid benefits for all three family members, the face value of food stamps, the value of means-tested school meal benefits for one child, and rental assistance.[6] We compare these welfare benefits to work support benefits in month thirteen of employment to avoid counting benefits that are lost shortly after the transition from welfare to work. (Work support benefits are more generous the more recently one has left the welfare system.) The value of work support benefits is also based upon a family of three with two children and includes TANF earned income disregards, federal and state EITC programs, the value of Medicaid benefits, the face value of food stamps, the value of means-tested school meal benefits for one child, and rental assistance. (Child care grants are not included in this analysis.)[7] All of the income and benefit totals presented in this chapter have been cost adjusted using the housing cost adjustment factor described in chapter 5.

5. Tanner, Moore, and Hartman (1995).

6. TANF payments and the face value of food stamps are from the U.S. House of Representatives, Committee on Ways and Means (2000). The other benefits are estimated as explained in appendix A.

7. For the purposes of this comparison, we have chosen not to treat child care grants as work supports. Child care benefits for needy workers amount to thousands of dollars annually per household in even the least generous state. But such grants are also available to welfare

In the average state, nonworking welfare clients are eligible to receive $21,187 in benefits annually. If these individuals were to take up half-time minimum work, they would be eligible for benefits worth $17,965; and with full-time minimum wage work, $15,907. Moreover, the composition of the benefit package changes once welfare recipients begin to work.

As table 6-1 shows, for nonworking welfare recipients, the largest benefit ($5,855 in the average state) is provided by rental assistance. TANF provides $5,033 in cash. Medical assistance benefits are worth $5,250 in the average state. (Average medical assistance benefits are generally greater for welfare participants than for needy workers because under welfare, all three family members are eligible to receive benefits in all fifty states and the District of Columbia.) Food stamp benefits provide $4,437. The remaining $612 represents school meals.

At $5,167 in the average state, rental assistance is also the largest benefit available to half-time minimum wage workers, representing 28.8 percent of the benefit total.[8] But TANF benefits decline sharply when people work half time, even though many states provide TANF earned income disregards. Half-time minimum wage workers receive a TANF benefit of $2,369 in cash, which is 13.2 percent of the benefit total in the average state. The value of medical assistance also declines, because in twenty states half-time minimum wage workers are no longer eligible for medical assistance in month thirteen of employment. Medical assistance benefits are valued at $4,484, or 25 percent of the benefit total. The face value of food stamps falls to $2,878, constituting 16 percent of total benefits. The value of school meals ($612) is not affected by the transition from welfare to work. Finally, half-time minimum wage workers enjoy an average federal EITC benefit of $2,398 in cash and an average state EITC benefit of $58 in cash. Together these tax programs provide 13.7 percent of the benefit total and help compensate for the loss of TANF and other benefits.

---

recipients without earned income; eligibility is typically contingent on participation in a "work-related" activity, which need not be paid labor. Moreover, child care benefits are compensation for a specific expense that is incurred when making the transition from welfare to work or participating in a work-related activity; in that sense, they do not represent an income gain per se. If child care benefits had been included in the calculation of work support benefits, in the average state half-time minimum wage workers would have gained approximately $3,500 and full-time minimum wage workers would have gained an additional $7,250.

8. Rental assistance is only slightly lower for half-time minimum wage workers than for welfare participants because TANF benefits count as income for the purposes of calculating the rental subsidy benefit. On average, welfare participants receive higher TANF benefits than half-time minimum wage workers. In calculating the rental subsidy for half-time minimum wage workers, earned income is offset by the loss of TANF benefits.

Table 6-1. Means-Tested Benefits in the Transition from Welfare to Work

Income source	Income and benefit total (dollars)			As percentage of total			As percentage of benefits		
	Welfare	Half-time work	Full-time work	Welfare	Half-time Work	Full-time Work	Welfare	Half-time work	Full-time work
Earned income	0	5,536	11,051	0	23.6	41.0	...	...	...
Benefit total	21,187	17,965	15,907	100	76.4	59.0	...	...	...
Rental assistance	5,855	5,167	3,897	27.6	22.0	14.5	27.6	28.8	24.5
TANF	5,033	2,369	609	23.8	10.1	2.3	23.8	13.2	3.8
Medical assistance	5,250	4,484	4,484	24.8	19.1	16.6	24.8	25.0	28.2
Food stamps	4,437	2,878	1,958	20.9	12.2	7.3	20.9	16.0	12.3
School meals	612	612	612	2.9	2.6	2.3	2.9	3.4	3.8
Total EITC	...	2,456	4,355	...	10.5	16.2	...	13.7	27.4
Federal	...	2,398	4,254	...	10.2	15.8	...	13.3	26.7
State	...	58	101	...	0.2	0.4	...	0.3	0.6

Source: Authors' calculations, as described in text.

EITC benefits are even greater for full-time minimum wage workers. In the average state, refundable tax benefits amount to $4,354 (that is, the sum of $4,253 from the federal EITC and $101 from state EITC programs)—or 27.4 percent of the total benefits available to this group. In contrast, TANF benefits are reduced significantly when work hours increase from half- to full-time, to the quite modest average of $609 in cash. Rental assistance also declines as earnings increase; full-time minimum wage workers receive $3,897 in the average state, 24.5 percent of total benefits. Similarly, as earned income increases, the value of food stamps falls to $1,958 in the average state, 12.3 percent of the benefit total. The values of medical assistance and school meals do not change.

The extent to which benefits decline as earned income grows is captured by the implicit benefit tax rate. Positive implicit benefit tax rates are thought to discourage work by reducing the gain in material well-being that is associated with each additional dollar of income. Figure 6-1 displays the implicit benefit tax rates for full-time workers and for half-time workers in all fifty states and the District of Columbia

In all jurisdictions, the implicit benefit tax rate increases as earned income rises. The average implicit benefit tax rate is 24.8 percent for full-time workers, and 15.0 percent for half-time workers. This means that moving out of the welfare system to full-time, year-round minimum wage work results in a loss of about one-fourth of the estimated value of means-tested benefits received as a nonworking welfare client. Connecticut has the lowest tax rate for both full-time and half-time workers: 6.2 and 3.7 percent, respectively. This is primarily a consequence of generous TANF earned income disregards and the fact that even a full-time minimum wage worker is eligible for medical assistance in Connecticut. The highest implicit benefit tax rate for full-time workers is 35.2 percent, in Oregon, which has a high state minimum wage rate and does not provide TANF earned income disregards to such workers in month thirteen of employment. The higher earnings that result from the higher state minimum wage reduce food stamp and rental assistance benefits. South Dakota has the highest implicit benefit tax rate for half-time workers, at 23.3 percent.

Work Supports and Incentives to Work

The existence of positive implicit benefit tax rates suggests that the work support system in conjunction with the welfare system functions as a negative income tax (NIT)—that is, it distributes benefits in an inverse relationship to household or family income. Many contemporary means-tested transfer

Figure 6-1. Implicit Benefit Tax Rates

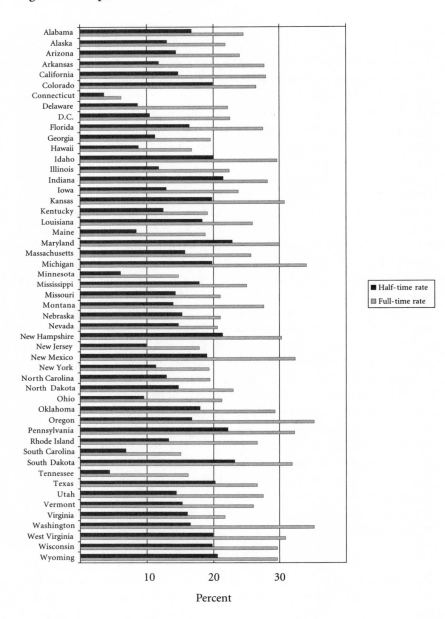

programs in the United States are designed on this basis.[9] The income transfer (T) provided by an NIT program is a function of r, the marginal tax rate
(the implicit benefit tax rate); B, the break-even point at which the transfer
payment is zero; and income (Y). The income guarantee (also called the security wage) is the benefit provided when the participant's income is zero. (An
important characteristic of NIT plans is that they provide benefits to participants with and without earned income.) In this context, the security wage is
the benefit total provided by the welfare system to nonworkers in each state.
The implicit benefit tax rate, r, varies from state to state. The relationship of
these parameters is specified by[10]

$$T = r\,(B - Y).$$

Economists expect those affected by an NIT to reduce work hours for two
reasons: the income effect and the substitution effect. The income effect,
which grows with the size of the income transfer (or in this case, the magnitude of the means-tested benefit provided by the program), is that individuals
increase consumption because they are more affluent as a result of the income
the NIT program provides. In particular, they consume more leisure time by
electing to work less. The substitution effect, which is related to the implicit
benefit tax rate, means that less income is sacrificed by not working, and so
the price of consuming leisure time falls. Together, the income and substitution effects are expected to result in reduced labor force participation. (As
discussed in chapter 3, this expectation may be altered by social regulation.)

Selecting the appropriate implicit benefit tax rate is the central design challenge of all NIT programs. Higher rates help target assistance to needy
households, but they also weaken incentives to work. Lower rates encourage
work among targeted groups, but they also extend benefits to relatively affluent families or households, thus increasing program costs.[11] The implicit
benefit tax rates of traditional welfare benefits, such as TANF, are often high.
But the work support system lowers the overall implicit benefit tax rate associated with the transition from welfare to work, and thereby encourages work.

The work support system slows the decline of the overall benefit package
that is available to those leaving welfare by providing means-tested benefits
that are initially constant or increase as earned income grows. School meal
programs and medical assistance provide a constant benefit package over the

9. Browning (1996).
10. Browning (1973).
11. Browning (1973).

range of incomes we consider. The federal EITC program provides benefits that are positively related to earned income, over a certain range, which offsets the reductions in means-tested benefits that needy workers experience in other programs (such as TANF, food stamps, and rental assistance). In the absence of federal EITC benefits, the implicit benefit tax rate would almost double to 44.7 percent in the average state, creating a substantial work disincentive; in fifteen states the implicit benefit tax rate would exceed 50 percent. This suggests that the EITC is an important part of the continuing efforts to encourage welfare clients to go to work.

The implicit benefit tax calculations presented in figure 6-1 are based on an optimistic scenario for receipt of work support benefits, and so may understate the implicit benefit taxes that many needy workers face in the real world. As people make the transition from welfare to work, they are transformed from a clientele that state social service departments are oriented to serving (welfare recipients) to one that they have not traditionally served (the working poor). Consequently, it may be more difficult than this analysis implies to continue to receive such benefits as food stamps and medical assistance, regardless of eligibility. The assumption underlying figure 6-1, that needy workers continue to receive all benefits for which they are eligible, is inconsistent with much of the program evaluation research discussed in chapter 2.

However, two other important considerations are relevant here. First, the benefit estimates for welfare participants were also based upon an optimistic scenario for participation. If welfare clients actually receive fewer benefits, our calculations may overstate implicit benefit tax rates. Second, needy workers are more likely to receive tax credits, medical assistance, and school meals than other work supports (as we show in chapter 7). These programs do not increase the implicit benefit tax over the income range we examine. Consequently, given actual patterns of program participation, our calculations may overstate the implicit benefit tax rates that most needy workers really face.

Beyond Minimum Wage Work

This analysis is a fair representation of the typical low-end outcome achieved by people moving from welfare work, as noted in chapter 4. But higher-income workers are likely to face higher implicit benefit tax rates. Most programs in most states reduce benefits as incomes increase: food stamp and TANF benefits vary inversely with earned income; once Transitional Medical Assistance is exhausted, eligibility for medical assistance is inversely related to earned income; and eligibility for free school meals is eventually exhausted as income increases. The only work support programs that run counter to this tendency are the federal and state EITC programs. Over a large income range, these benefits grow with earned income. However, at higher income levels EITC program benefits enter the phase-out range and are systematically reduced as income increases. At that point, the implicit benefit tax rate increases significantly.

By examining the benefit structure of the federal EITC program, it is possible to identify "tipping points" (the income levels at which the implicit benefit tax rate starts to increase significantly). These tipping points depend upon tax filing status and the number of qualified children claimed, and change from year to year, as EITC eligibility thresholds and benefit standards are adjusted to reflect living costs. Table 6-2 shows the modified adjusted gross income (MAGI) ranges that define the EITC benefit structure to identify the tipping points for 2004.[12]

For example, for married couples filing jointly, with two or more qualifying children, table 6-2 shows that the EITC phase-in begins with the first dollar earned and continues until MAGI equals $10,800. At that point, the EITC benefit is at its maximum ($4,300 in 2004). Over this income range, the implicit benefit tax rate associated with the EITC is negative. The benefit remains stable for income from $10,801 to $15,050. Over this range, the EITC implicit benefit tax rate is zero. When MAGI exceeds $15,051, the benefit phaseout begins. This is the key tipping point, because at this income level EITC benefits are reduced systematically until they are exhausted, when income reaches $35,458. Over this income range, the EITC program exhibits a positive implicit benefit tax rate.

Income Gains from Work

The analysis thus far has shown that compared to the traditional welfare system, the work support system encourages work by reducing the rate at which means-tested benefits are lost when welfare recipients make the transition to work. But this discussion only captures part of the story. The work support system also strengthens work incentives by allowing participants to combine means-tested benefits with earned income and thus improve their material well-being.

To measure the income gains that welfare recipients can expect once they move into work, we estimated the maximum benefits that welfare clients can receive in the fifty states and the District of Columbia and compared them to

12. Readers interested in the finer points of calculating MAGI may consult IRS publication 596, "Earned Income Credit."

Table 6-2. Tipping Points in Federal EITC Benefits, 2004[a]
Dollars

	Single, head of household, or qualified widow(er)			Married, filing jointly		
EITC benefit structure	No children	One child	Two children	No children	One child	Two children
Phase-in range	0 to 5,100	0 to 7,700	0 to 10,800	0 to 5,100	0 to 7,700	0 to 10,800
Stable range	5,101 to 6,400	7,701 to 14,050	10,801 to 14,050	5,101 to 7,400	7,701 to 15,050	10,801 to 15,050
Phase-out range	6,401 to 11,500	14,051 to 30,350	14,051 to 34,550	7,401 to 12,500	15,051 to 31,350	15,051 to 35,458
Maximum benefit	390	2,604	4,300	390	2,604	4,300

Source: Internal Revenue Service, "Earned Income Credit," Publication 596 (Department of the Treasury, 2004).
a. Ranges are given in terms of modified adjusted gross income.

the work support income and benefit total for half- and full-time minimum wage workers. Figure 6-2 presents the results of this analysis, using housing-cost-adjusted data.[13]

The figure indicates that half-time minimum wage workers who participate fully in the work support system are financially better off than welfare recipients in forty-eight states and the District of Columbia. Only Maryland and New Hampshire provide a lower income and benefit total for this group, and the loss is only about 1 percent of the maximum value of welfare benefits. Full-time minimum wage workers are better off than welfare recipients in all fifty states and the District of Columbia. In sum, the work support system provides an income and benefit package that is at least roughly equal to the benefits of welfare participation for half-time minimum wage workers. The figure also suggests that the package exceeds the value of welfare benefits for people who work more hours, because full-time workers enjoy significant income gains.

The combination of earned income and work support benefits compares favorably to welfare benefits in most states. In the average state the cost-adjusted welfare benefit total is $21,187. For half-time workers, the combination of earned income and work support benefits is $23,501.[14] This includes $5,536 in earned income, which represents 23.6 percent of the income and benefit total. The ratio of work supports to welfare benefits is 1.11, indicating that half-time work and work support benefits exceed the maximum welfare package by 11 percent in the average state. Of course, the ratios vary across states. The lowest ratios are 0.99 in Maryland and New Hampshire. In states such as Connecticut and Tennessee, the gains from leaving welfare to work half-time at the minimum wage are more than 20 percent. Full-time minimum wage workers fare even better. In the average state, they earn $11,051, which amounts to 41.0 percent of an income and work support benefits package worth $26,598. This represents a gain of 27.2 percent over the value of welfare benefits and a gain of 14.7 percent over the total for half-time workers. New Hampshire registers the lowest ratio of welfare benefits to work supports: 1.10. The highest ratio is 1.50, in Tennessee.

Although states make a variety of policy choices that influence the relative generosity of work support benefits, three decisions are key. One is the level

13. Strictly speaking, it is not necessary to use cost-adjusted estimates, because we are making comparisons within a given state. However, readers may be interested in comparing across states, for which purpose cost-adjusted estimates are more appropriate.

14. These are unweighted averages of the earned income and benefits provided in a given state. Since they are not weighted to account for differences in state-level participation, they are not national averages.

Figure 6-2. Welfare Compared to Work Supports

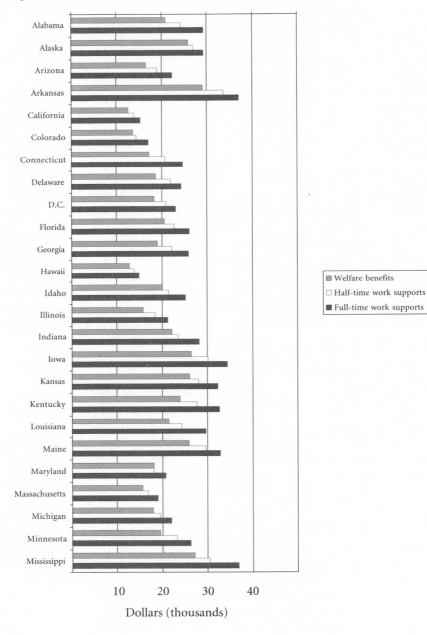

Dollars (thousands)

Figure 6-2. **Welfare Compared to Work Supports (continued)**

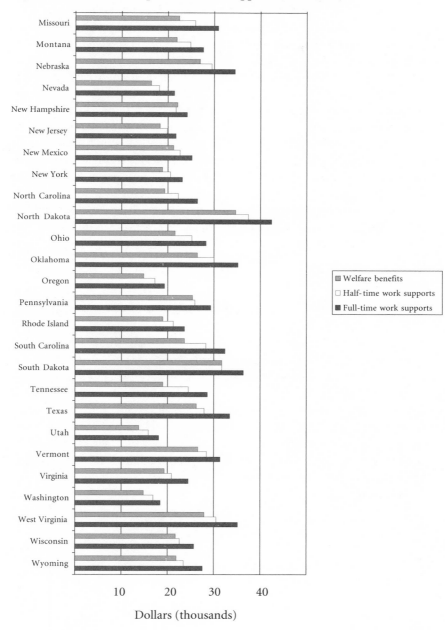

Dollars (thousands)

of TANF benefits provided to nonworkers compared to the level of TANF earned income disregards. If TANF benefits are high and there is a significant gap between TANF benefit payments for nonworkers and TANF earned income disregards, the welfare system tends to be more generous than the work support system. However, if TANF benefits for nonworkers are low or if there is only a slight gap between TANF benefits and TANF earned income disregards, the welfare system tends to be less generous than the work support system. States also influence work incentives by establishing their own minimum wage rates. States with a minimum wage above the federal minimum have more generous work support systems because half- and full-time minimum wage workers enjoy higher earned incomes. Although these higher earnings reduce the means-tested benefits that workers can receive, the earned income gains more than outweigh the benefit losses. Finally, states may decide to extend eligibility for medical assistance to minimum wage workers (they are compelled by federal requirements to extend such benefits to their children). States that do so have relatively generous work support systems.

Conclusion

The work support system creates positive incentives for people to leave the welfare system. This may not be immediately apparent, since welfare recipients must sacrifice means-tested benefits as they make the transition from welfare to work. The system, in other words, functions like a negative income tax, which normally reduces work incentives. However, when compared to the traditional welfare system, the work support system lowers the implicit benefit tax rate that welfare leavers face. Moreover, the system offers those leaving welfare the opportunity to make significant material gains by combining means-tested benefits with earned income. As a result, a well-designed work support system can encourage families to get out of and stay out of the welfare system—even when the rewards offered at the bottom of the labor market are declining.

Part 3

Evaluating Work Support Performance

7

Who Gets What?

The evidence presented in chapter 4 demonstrates that full-time, year-round minimum wage work combined with full participation in work support programs could result in significant material gains for needy working families. But this information does not necessarily indicate how the system actually performs. Do needy working families in fact participate in work support programs? How is program participation related to household characteristics? Do needy working families combine benefits from multiple work supports? Which programs do the most to help needy working families? In other words, who gets what from the work support system?

This chapter evaluates the work support system at the national level in terms of the material support it provides to poor and near-poor working families using a subsample we created from the March supplement of the 2002 Current Population Survey (CPS). The CPS March supplement is the principal data source for program participation, income, and work experience among Americans. Approximately 60,000 housing units are chosen for the main CPS sample, reflecting the labor force and demographic conditions of individual states. An additional 12,000 housing units are included in the March supplement.[1] In this chapter (and appendix C) CPS data are aggregated at the national level for individuals and households.

Our sample focuses on families with total incomes below 200 percent of the federal poverty standard. We linked these families to their individual members and the households in which they reside. We then determined whether any individual within the household was a "worker"; that is, had

1. Census Bureau (2002b).

earned income, including income from self-employment or farm self-employment. All households containing at least one worker were included in the subsample. Thus the sample is a set of households containing families with incomes below 200 percent of the federal poverty standard, in which at least one household member is a worker. By linking data on individuals and families to households and aggregating work support program participation data at the household level, we provide the most comprehensive picture of work support participation possible. The individuals, families, and households included in the subsample are described in appendix C.

There are two noteworthy limitations to the CPS data. First, the data are self-reported. If respondents have faulty recollections about the benefits they received, income sources, or work history, these faults are reflected in the data. Some respondents are reluctant to acknowledge participation in programs to which stigma is attached; this may reduce reported participation rates for some means-tested programs, especially Temporary Assistant for Needy Families (TANF), food stamps, and medical assistance. Second, CPS data are likely to systematically underestimate participation in the Children's Health Insurance Program (CHIP), because the Census asks about this only as a follow-up question for Medicaid participants.

Our sample is composed of households that contain poor and near-poor families that are supported by at least one worker. The composition of our sample reflects concerns about income and work effort that are common in studies of the relationships between work, poverty, and income support programs. The Department of Labor defines the working poor as "individuals who spent at least 27 weeks in the labor force (working or looking for work), but whose incomes fell below the official poverty level."[2] Our sample is more liberal in its income criterion but more strict in terms of work effort because merely looking for work is insufficient; to be included in our sample, someone in the household must be a worker. Gregory Acs, Katherin Phillips, and Daniel McKenzie have defined low-income working families as those with incomes below 200 percent of the federal poverty standard, with adult family members working an average of at least 1,000 hours per year.[3] Our sample uses the same income criterion but is more liberal regarding work effort because we do not require a minimum threshold of work hours.

Our evidence suggests that work support program participation is widespread but not extensive. Although many households that contain needy working families are touched by the work support system, few receive bene-

2. Bureau of Labor Statistics (2002).
3. Acs, Phillips, and McKenzie (2001).

Table 7-1. Household Participation Patterns, by Hours Worked

Percent

Number of work supports received	All households (N= 15, 879)	At least 2,080 hours of work (N= 9, 272)	Less than 2,080 hours of work (N= 6,607)
0	27.1	26.6	27.8
1	29.4	31.6	26.3
2	20.2	22.7	16.8
3	11.9	11.7	12.0
4	6.8	5.0	9.5
5	3.3	1.9	5.2
6	1.2	0.5	2.1
7	0.2	0.1	0.3

Source: Authors' calculations, as described in text.

fits from numerous programs. This finding is significant because the potential material gains described in chapter 4 were based on the assumption that families receive benefits from multiple work supports. For the work support system to be effective in helping the working poor and near poor to escape poverty and achieve self-sufficiency, needy working families must participate in the many programs for which they are eligible. If needy working families receive only a few work supports, the system is falling short of its potential.

Work Support Program Participation

Table 7-1 shows the percentage of households that received work support benefits among all households in the sample, among those households with 2,080 work hours or more annually (the equivalent of at least one full-time, year-round worker), and among those with fewer work hours. The CPS program participation data do not correspond exactly to the work support programs discussed in earlier chapters. Specifically, the CPS does not contain information about state earned income tax credit (EITC) benefits or free or reduced-price breakfast at school. In addition, in some cases its definitions of participation differ from ours. For example, only free school lunches are reported (whereas we also counted reduced-price lunches as a work support benefit). And rental assistance includes public housing as well as rental assistance vouchers, whereas our estimates focused on rental vouchers. However, the CPS does report receipt of the federal EITC, TANF, medical assistance, child care grants, and food stamps. In all, there is significant correspondence between the CPS program participation data and our list of work supports.

Table 7-1 indicates widespread participation in work support programs; 72.9 percent of all households receive some sort of work support benefit. However, the estimates of benefit generosity presented in chapter 4 assume that needy working families receive benefits from a variety of different programs. Our data show that although many households enjoy work support benefits, few participate in the "system" by combining benefits from numerous programs. A majority of households receive benefits from only one work support program or none at all, and approximately nine out of ten households receive benefits from three or fewer work supports. This finding confirms that the potential material gains presented in chapter 4 do not accurately represent how much needy working families actually receive from the work support system. Less than 5 percent of all households receive benefits from five or more work supports, and only 0.2 percent receive all seven work supports. In fact, only two out of 1,000 needy working families live in a household that could possibly experience the material gains we described in chapter 4.

A slightly different picture of participation emerges when we account for work effort. Although households in which people work more hours are equally likely to receive work support benefits, they tend to participate in fewer work support programs. The probability of receiving no work support benefits is about the same, regardless of total household work hours. However, households that participate more in the labor force have higher participation rates in one to three work support programs (66.0 percent) than households that participate less in the labor force (55.1 percent). Conversely, households with fewer work hours are likely to participate more extensively in work support programs. Households with lower labor force participation are more likely to receive benefits from four or more work supports (17.1 percent) than are households with higher levels of labor force participation (7.5 percent). The relationship between household work hours and the number of work supports that touch the household is statistically significant.[4]

Which work support programs are more likely to benefit needy working families? Table 7-2 presents program participation rates for all households and households with different levels of labor force participation for the seven

4. Chi square, $p < 0.05$. The p value reported for the chi square statistic indicates the probability that the null hypothesis is true. In this case, the null hypothesis is that work support program participation and labor force participation are not related or appear to be related only as a result of sampling error. The p value of less than 0.05 indicates that the chance the null hypothesis is true is less than five in 100. With this level of probability, the relationship is said to be statistically significant.

Table 7-2. Household Participation Rates in Selected Programs, by Hours Worked

Percent

Program	All households (N = 15,879)	At least 2,080 hours of work (N = 9,272)	Less than 2,080 hours of work (N= 6,607)
EITC	60.5	61.2	59.6
Medical assistance	34.3	30.7	39.3
Free school lunch	29.1	31.2	26.1
Food stamps	15.9	10.4	23.8
Rental assistance	10.0	6.5	15.0
TANF	4.1	2.2	6.7
Child care grants	3.2	2.4	10.4

Source: Authors' calculations, as described in text.

work support programs contained in the CPS databases.[5] Needy working families are most likely to use the federal EITC, medical assistance, and the school lunch program. Of these, the EITC program is by far the most popular: 60.5 percent of all households reported receipt of the EITC. This is not surprising, given the low hassle factor associated with the program, the absence of stigma, the lack of budget constraints on the program, and the fact that it is not necessary to have children in order to be eligible (though "qualifying children" do affect benefit generosity). Medical assistance (including both Medicaid and CHIP) is the second most frequently accessed work support benefit. A total of 34.3 percent of all households report medical assistance (that is, at least one person in the household received such assistance). This relatively high rate of use is somewhat surprising given that, as discussed in chapter 3, medical assistance benefits are subject to indirect budget constraints and accessing benefits may be a hassle and may carry a stigma. Participation in the school lunch program also is widespread; a total of 29.1 percent of households report that at least one member receives a free school lunch. The rate of school lunch participation is expected to be higher than the rates for most other work support programs because of the low hassle factor and limited stigma associated with participation. In addition, there are no budget constraints for the lunch program.

The relatively high participation rate for medical assistance requires further explanation. The discussion of program design in chapter 3 cited budget con-

5. Since the categories are not mutually exclusive, because a single household can (and many do) receive benefits from more than one program, the percentages do not sum to 100.

straints, hassle, bars to participation, and stigma to explain why those who are eligible may elect not to participate in work support programs. The present analysis is somewhat different, because it focuses on the programs that our sample households actually used. Eligibility varies from one program to another. Free school lunches are available only to families with children and with incomes below 130 percent of the federal poverty standard. Eligibility for medical assistance extends much further up the income scale, and adult-only households can receive benefits. In some states it is possible to receive CHIP benefits with an income that is 300 percent of the federal poverty standard. This suggests that more households in our sample were eligible to receive medical assistance benefits than free school lunches. The fact that our prediction that school meal participation should be greater than medical assistance participation was not borne out may be related to these differences in eligibility standards; more of the sample (which is composed of households containing families with incomes below 200 percent of the federal poverty standard) was eligible to receive medical assistance benefits.

Participation rates drop sharply for the remaining work support programs; food stamps and rental assistance provide benefits to only a small proportion of needy working families. The Food Stamp Program serves 15.9 percent of all households.[6] Although they are not budget constrained, food stamp benefits may carry a stigma, which could reduce both real and reported participation. It is also possible that food stamp participation rates are low because of the financial contributions that other household members make to total income (unlike other work support programs, food stamp eligibility is determined at the household level). However, in the vast majority of cases, the family and the household are one in the same, so this possibility is slight. Rental assistance also has relatively low participation rates. Only 10.0 percent of households in our sample receive some form of public housing assistance. As discussed in chapter 3, excessive demand in the face of budget constraints

6. There is evidence that among low-income working families, food stamp participation has recently increased. We analyzed data from the March supplement of the 2004 CPS, which reports program participation during 2003. Using the same selection criteria (families with incomes below 200 percent of the federal poverty standard in which at least one person was a worker), we find that food stamp participation increased to 17.5 percent of low-income working families. The participation gains were among households with incomes between 50 and 199 percent of the federal poverty standard. However, many factors, including macroeconomic conditions, can affect food stamp participation rates. The Bureau of Labor Statistics reports that between 2001 and 2003, the unemployment rate increased from 4.7 percent to 6.0 percent. It is possible that the participation gains we have noted reflect the effects of increased unemployment rather than those of program reforms enacted as part of the Farm Security and Rural Investment Act of 2002.

and bars to participation (such as closed wait lists) are the most likely explanations for these low participation rates; many more people would receive rental assistance if they could.[7]

Participation rates are dramatically lower for TANF and child care benefits; these programs assist only a tiny minority of households in our sample. Although TANF benefits were received by only 4.1 percent of all households, child care grants served the lowest proportion: only 3.2 percent of all households reported receiving such grants. The low participation rates for these programs are expected for several reasons, as discussed in chapter 3. Both of these programs are subject to budget constraints. This is especially true for child care grants, where demand clearly outstrips supply.[8] However, it is likely that reductions in TANF participation have decreased the relevance of budget constraints as a limiting factor for receipt of cash assistance. TANF participation has declined as a result of local social service departments' actively discouraging entry into and encouraging exit from the program. Consequently, factors such as hassle, administrative bars, and stigma are likely to depress the number of needy working families receiving cash assistance.

In sum, the federal EITC program is the work support that is most widely used by needy working families. This is no surprise. With one exception, the program participation rates we observe from the CPS data are consistent with the predictions we made based on program design. Needy working families are less likely to receive work support benefits when program resources are constrained, when applicants can be hassled for seeking benefits, when stigma is associated with receipt of benefits, or when there are administrative bars to participation. The EITC program is the most effective work support because it was designed to provide benefits to needy working families without budgetary or administrative constraints.

Participation among Privileged Groups

Not all needy working families are equal in the eyes of the work support system. Some groups are targeted for privileged access to work supports, specifically, children and people making the transition from welfare to work. Child care grants, school meal programs, CHIP, and TANF specifically target needy working families with children. People making the transition from welfare to work are eligible for TANF earned income disregards and transitional medical assistance (TMA); in addition, they are a priority target group for

7. Olsen (2003).
8. Department of Health and Human Services (1999a).

Table 7-3. Household Participation Patterns, by Presence of Children and TANF

Number of work supports received	Without children (N = 5,682)	With children (N = 10,195)	Received TANF (N = 652)	Did not receive TANF (N = 15,227)
0	57.6	10.1	n.a.	28.3
1	30.1	29.0	0	30.6
2	8.5	26.7	2.8	21.0
3	2.8	16.9	11.7	11.9
4	0.9	10.2	25.5	6.0
5	0.1	5.1	34.7	1.9
6	0.0	1.8	21.6	0.3
7	0.0	0.2	3.8	0.0

Source: Authors' calculations, as described in text.
n.a. = Not applicable.

child care grants and rental vouchers. How does the presence of children in the household affect the likelihood of work support participation? How does TANF participation affect participation in other work supports? What do these privileged groups get from the work support system?

Table 7-3 indicates that almost 90 percent of households with children are touched by the work support system, compared to only about 42 percent of households without children. The table also indicates that households with children are more likely to receive multiple work support benefits (more than 60 percent of households with children receive benefits from between two and seven programs). By contrast, almost 90 percent of households without children receive only one work support benefit or none at all.

Table 7-4 presents participation rates in various work support programs for households with and without children.[9] The participation rates for households with children surpass those of households without children for every relevant work support program. Households with children are far more likely to receive the EITC than are households without children (77.0 percent versus 31.0 percent). This difference is probably a consequence of eligibility criteria rather than benefit generosity. Although EITC benefits for childless workers are only about one-tenth as much as for workers with two or more children, the low hassle factor and absence of stigma are likely to result in many eligible people claiming the credit, regardless of whether they have children or not. However, the income caps that limit EITC eligibility are also quite a bit lower for childless workers. As we reported in chapter 2, the income

9. Because these programs are not mutually exclusive, percentages do not sum to 100.

Table 7-4. Household Participation Rates in Selected Programs, by Presence of Children and TANF

Percent

Program	Without children (N = 5,682)	With children (N = 10,195)	Received TANF (N = 652)	Did not receive TANF (N = 15,227)
EITC	31.0	77.0	80.4	59.7
Medical assistance	12.9	46.2	100.0	31.5
Free school lunch	n.a.	44.9	60.1	27.8
Food stamps	6.9	21.0	82.1	13.1
Rental assistance	7.2	11.6	33.4	9.0
TANF	n.a.	6.0	100.0	n.a.
Child care grants	n.a.	6.1	19.0	5.1

Source: Authors' calculations, as described in text.
n.a. = Not applicable.

limit for married couples filing jointly with two or more qualifying children in 2002 was $34,178; with one qualifying child, $30,201; and with no qualifying children, $12,060. It is likely that many of the childless families in our sample are not EITC eligible.

Medical assistance (including Medicaid and CHIP) is the second most frequently accessed benefit, regardless of whether children are present in the household or not. However, there is a clear difference in the participation rates for households with and without children; 12.9 percent of childless households and 46.2 percent of households with children received medical assistance. This large difference is not surprising, as children have been the targets of several recent policy changes that enhance access to medical assistance benefits. Recent changes include the federally mandated Medicaid expansion that required the states to offer coverage to children in families with incomes below the poverty standard, and the implementation of CHIP.

Only small minorities of households use food stamps and rental assistance, whether children are present or not. However, both programs show higher participation rates among households with children. The Food Stamp Program serves only 6.9 percent of childless households but 21.0 percent of households with children. One reason for the relatively low participation rates among childless households may be the work requirements of the 1996 Personal Responsibility and Work Opportunity Reconciliation Act (PRWORA) and the Balanced Budget Act of 1997; able-bodied adults without dependents must work at least thirty hours per week (and provide documentation to prove that they are doing so) to continue receiving food stamp benefits.

Households with children also are more likely to receive rental assistance. However, the difference between households with and without children is relatively small for rental assistance.

Overall, the differences in participation rates between households with and without children were statistically significant for all relevant programs: the EITC, medical assistance, rental assistance, and food stamps.

In chapter 1 we noted that people moving from welfare to work are granted privileged status as work support beneficiaries under the PRWORA. They enjoy exclusive eligibility for some work support benefits (TANF earned income disregards and TMA) and priority eligibility for some others (child care grants and housing assistance). For the current discussion, we define people in transition from welfare to work in our sample as those who received TANF benefits at any time during the past year.

Returning to table 7-3, although only 652 members of our sample received TANF benefits, it is clear that the households in which someone was in transition from welfare to work made far more extensive use of the work support system than did the others. It is striking that none of the households in transition from welfare to work received fewer than two work supports. This reflects the coordination of program access. TANF recipients qualify for Medicaid categorically; every household that reported TANF benefits also reported medical assistance. Beyond this, households in which people were making the transition from welfare to work were much more likely to receive benefits from four or more work supports (85.6 percent) than were the others (8.2 percent).

When participation is viewed by program (table 7-4), rates for most programs were markedly higher for those in transition from welfare to work than for those who were not. As noted above, all of the households that received TANF also received medical assistance. TANF recipients were also much more likely to receive food stamps. This result is consistent with studies sponsored by the Department of Agriculture (USDA) to assess restrictions to access to food stamps among the working poor.[10] Surprisingly, though, TANF recipients were more likely to claim the EITC, by a margin of 80.4 percent to 59.7 percent. This is probably a result of the facts that the incomes of people making the transition from welfare to work make them eligible and that all of these households have children.[11] In all cases, the differences in participation rates between households in transition from welfare to work and others were statistically significant.

10. Lerman and Wiseman (2002); Department of Agriculture (1999b).
11. Lens (2002); Zedlewski (2002).

It seems that if the work support system is working for anyone, it is for those making the transition from welfare to work. Why are those in transition out of the welfare system so much more likely to receive work supports? It is significant that many of the programs that we examine are also components of the welfare system.

Joe Soss has examined the participation decisions of recipients of cash assistance welfare and offers several pertinent observations: (1) programs can be designed to encourage or impede participation; (2) participation is more likely when people are exposed to an environment that is rich in information about the welfare process; (3) the process of claiming benefits is demeaning and difficult; and (4) case workers have significant discretion, which can be used to influence participation decisions.[12] His analysis has bearing on why people moving from welfare to work are more likely to receive work support benefits. First, they are eligible to receive more benefits because of their privileged status as TANF participants (this reflects program design decisions). Second, the USDA (the federal sponsor of the Food Stamp Program) and the Department of Health and Human Services responded to declines in program participation in the late 1990s by assiduously reminding the states that even though TANF was no longer an entitlement, food stamps and medical assistance remained so (this speaks to the influence of case workers in local social service departments). Advocacy groups have complemented these efforts by working to ensure that those leaving cash assistance welfare continue to enjoy access to other benefits. Third, it is possible that people who already have experience in navigating the welfare system are more capable of securing further benefits because they know the rules and do not perceive the system's hassles as insurmountable barriers.[13] For all these reasons, the work support system works best for people in transition from welfare to work.

The Benefits of Participation

In this section we estimate the benefits that different types of households are likely to receive from the work support system, given their participation patterns. The analysis above suggests that program participation depends critically upon the presence of children or someone who is making the transition from welfare to work in the household. We now present benefit estimates for households in three sub-categories: those with children, those

12. Soss (2000).
13. Zedlewski (2004); Woolridge and others (2003).

without children, and those in which someone is making the transition from welfare to work.[14]

Work support program participation among childless households is rare, and the benefits that such households receive if they do participate are quite modest. Among childless households, the modal dollar value of work support benefits is zero, because a majority of 57.6 percent receive no work supports whatsoever. For the minority that do receive work supports, the modal support package is receipt of the EITC only; 21.7 percent of all childless households and 51.1 percent of childless households that receive work supports get only EITC benefits. Even if one assumes that total earnings are within the range to qualify for maximum EITC benefits (and this will not be true for all households), the most generous work support package that most participating households could have received in 2000 was valued at less than $400 annually (in cash). Our estimates indicate that fully 83.4 percent of all households without children received less than $400 in work support benefits annually; most received nothing.

The situation among households with children is more complex, because the amount of work support benefits that a given household can receive depends upon the age and number of children present. Table 7-4 reveals that a strong majority of households with children receive benefits from three programs: the EITC, school lunch, and medical assistance. Table 7-5 presents estimates of the value of benefits that households with children are likely to receive under different combinations of these programs.

Work support participation among households with children varies significantly. Table 7-5 indicates that one in ten households with children received no work support benefits whatsoever; 3.9 percent received only a free school lunch (valued at $562 annually or less); and an additional 2.8 percent received medical assistance only (valued at $4,236 annually in the average state). The largest single group, 22.0 percent, constituted those who received the EITC only, a benefit that could have been worth as much as $3,888 annually in 2000. The exact EITC benefit received by a household depends upon earned income and the number of children present. Only families with two or more children with an income that places them in the maximum benefit range for the EITC receive the maximum payment. An additional 12.3 percent of households with children received the EITC in conjunction with a free school lunch, giving a nominal benefit value of no more than $4,450 annu-

---

14. We do not adjust benefits to reflect cost-of-living differences at the state level, because in this analysis benefit estimates are aggregated at the national level, making state-level differences in living costs irrelevant.

Table 7-5. Benefit Estimates for Households with Children

Benefit package	Percent of all households (N = 10,195)	Cumulative percentage	Benefit value (dollars)
No work support participation	10.1	10.1	0
School lunch only	3.9	14.0	562 (nominal cash value)
Medical assistance only	2.8	16.8	4,236 (nominal cash value)
EITC only	22.0	38.8	3,888 or less in cash
EITC and school lunch	12.3	51.1	3,888 or less in cash plus 562 (nominal cash value)
EITC and medical assistance	9.3	60.3	3,888 or less in cash plus 4,236 (nominal cash value)
EITC, medical assistance, and school lunch	8.7	69.0	3,888 or less in cash plus 4,798 (nominal cash value) access to medical care and free lunch for school-aged child
Other	31.0	100.0	n.a.

Source: Authors' calculations, as described in text.
n.a. =Not applicable.

ally for a family of three with two children, including one school-aged child. Thus, the majority of households with children (51.1 percent) received a benefit package worth $4,450 annually or less. Although this is more than ten times the value of the work supports that most childless households are likely to receive, it is a far cry from the material gains we estimated in chapter 4.

Households may receive more or less than $4,450, depending on the number and age of their children. A family with only one child who is of school age in 2000 could have received a maximum of $2,353 in cash from the EITC as well as the free school lunch, for a total nominal benefit of $2,915 annually. However, the potential gains in work support benefits for families with three or more children are limited to the additional benefits provided by the school lunch program, as the EITC does not provide increased benefits for families with more than two children.[15] Thus, households in which there are more than two school-aged children who are eligible to receive a free school lunch will see the annual nominal benefit total grow by only $562 per child.

If needy working families gain access to medical assistance benefits in addition to EITC payments, the value of their work support benefits increases

15. As mentioned earlier, the child tax credit provides additional refundable tax benefits to some families with more than two children. We did not include this credit in the benefit estimates.

markedly. The estimated nominal value of this package of benefits was $8,124 in 2000 ($3,888 for the EITC and $4,236 for medical assistance in the average state) for a family of three, though only one in ten households with children received this benefit package. To receive a benefit of this magnitude, the needy working family must contain at least two children and earned income must be in the maximum range for EITC benefits. Of course, the medical assistance benefit is a national estimate that represents the average value of benefits in the fifty states and the District of Columbia. Although the value of the federal EITC varies little, medical assistance benefits vary significantly from state to state.

When access to medical assistance is combined with the EITC and school lunch, the nominal benefit package can be worth as much as $8,686 ($3,888 for the EITC, $4,236 for medical assistance, and $562 for the free school lunch) for a family with two children, one of whom is school aged. However, only about one in ten households with children receives this benefit package. In all, approximately seven out of ten households with children received this level of benefits or less from the work support system.

Table 7-4 identifies the four programs that households in which someone is making the transition from welfare to work are most likely to use as work supports: TANF, medical assistance, food stamps, and the EITC. This pattern of participation is to be expected; TANF, medical assistance, and food stamps constitute the classic basket of benefits provided to welfare recipients, and the administrative system that supports these programs is designed to treat cash assistance as a gateway to the entire package. A substantial majority (68.4 percent) of households receive this package of four benefits or more from the work support system. Consequently, we estimate the minimum package of work support benefits typically received by households in which someone is making the transition from welfare to work as the sum of the benefits provided by these four programs.

People moving from welfare to work are the only group likely to realize significant material gains from the work support system. However, the benefits received by this privileged group are at the low end of the estimates presented in chapter 4. Of course, the national averages we use to generate this estimate do not reflect important differences in state generosity; in states that provide large TANF payments in comparison to others such as Connecticut and Alaska, benefits will be underestimated. Even with that caveat in mind, it is clear that the generosity of the work support system is remarkable when people are making the transition from welfare to work. The total value of the benefit package is at least $10,613 for a majority of full-time, year-round min-imum wage workers with a family of three, including two children, one of whom is school aged. Combined with after-tax earnings that average $10,187, a nominal income and benefit total of $20,800 is provided. This total exceeds the federal poverty standard for a family of three by a wide margin and exceeds the average of basic family budgets for low-cost areas.

Is the privilege enjoyed by those making the transition from welfare to work only temporary? The only benefit in this package that is explicitly time limited is TANF. Once TANF eligibility is exhausted, the value of the package will be reduced by $735. In some states, access to medical assistance is also time limited for this group. But if they reside in one of the states that feature adult eligibility for Medicaid, people making the transition from welfare to work can continue to receive medical assistance, for a total nominal work support benefit of $9,878 (93.1 percent of the total), in perpetuity. Moreover, these benefits are unlikely to lose their value over time, as both the EITC and food stamps are automatically adjusted for changes in living costs, and med-ical assistance (as an in-kind benefit) can lose value only if the menu of services is altered.

Conclusion

Our participation analysis indicates that although many low-income working families live in households touched by work support programs, the extent of participation and the generosity of benefits are slight, because few house-holds participate in several programs. The majority of households are likely to receive only EITC benefits, or nothing. The estimated total work support benefit received by a majority of needy working families in 2000 was less than $3,888.

The analysis also reveals important differences in participation for house-holds with and without children and households in which someone is making the transition from welfare to work. Households with children are more likely to receive work supports than childless households, and the benefits they receive are different. Households with children are likely to receive medical assistance benefits and free school lunches (often in conjunction with the EITC). Childless needy workers are not eligible for school lunch benefits, and their eligibility for medical assistance varies from state to state. However, the work support system reserves its greatest material benefits for people making the transition from welfare to work. Such households can perpetually enjoy sufficient work support benefits to escape poverty. But these are only a tiny minority of the households in which needy working families reside. For the overwhelming majority of needy working families, the work support system falls short.

8

Racing Up to the Bottom

This chapter evaluates the performance of the work support system at the state level. This is a significant concern because states have discretion over eligibility and benefit standards for many work support programs. In addition, their administrative practices influence program participation, even in programs that are governed by national standards. The data demonstrate significant variation in state-level performance, in terms both of how widespread and extensive work support program participation is and of how generous state-level benefits are.

Data

The General Accounting Office (GAO) has noted that the data sets available to study poverty and program participation at the state level suffer from two potential limitations: they either do not have a sufficient number of cases to draw reliable conclusions or do not cover of all fifty states.[1] The GAO notes that although most Census Bureau data sets have a sufficient number of cases to make reliable generalizations at the national level, individual state samples are insufficient for state-level analyses. But surveys that provide richer samples for individual states, such as the National Survey of American Families, limit the number of states studied.

To answer these concerns in estimating participation in the Children's Health Insurance Program (CHIP), the size of the Current Population Survey (CPS) sample was expanded during 2000 and 2001, so as to "produce statis-

1. General Accounting Office (2001b).

tically reliable annual state data."[2] The general CPS sample was increased from 55,000 to 60,000 "to meet the national and state reliability criteria," and an additional 12,000 households from the District of Columbia and the thirty-one states with the smallest samples were added to the CPS March supplement. Analysis of labor force participation statistics included in the CPS indicates that these changes improved those estimates as well, especially in states to which the additional 12,000 cases were allocated. Consequently, we used the March supplement of the 2002 CPS to evaluate state-level work support program participation and supplement the CPS data with the estimates of work support benefit generosity presented in chapters 4 and 5. Consistent with the rationale presented in chapter 5, we adjust the state-level benefit estimates for differences in the cost of living (using median housing value as the basis for adjustment) to better indicate the real value of the benefits that states provide.

State-Level Work Support Participation

In this section we measure how widespread is participation (the proportion of households that receive work supports) and how extensive is participation (the proportion of households that receive three or more work supports) among the households in our sample.[3] Significant differences exist in state-level participation rates. Table 8-1 illustrates these differences by reporting state-level summary statistics for the earned income tax credit (EITC), medical assistance (Medicaid and CHIP), school lunch, food stamps, child care grants, Temporary Assistance for Needy Families (TANF), and rental assistance.

Consistent with the analysis at the national level, participation rates at the state level are greatest for the EITC, medical assistance, and school lunch programs. The highest EITC participation rate was in West Virginia, where 69.2 percent of sample households reported they received EITC benefits. This contrasts with a low of 51.4 percent in Nebraska. However, in spite of these differences, the coefficient of variation indicates that the federal EITC program exhibits the least interstate variation of any work support program. Medical assistance had the greatest range in state-level participation rates. The highest rate (56.0 percent, in Vermont) is nearly 40 percentage points higher than the lowest rate (16.3 percent, in Nevada). However, the coefficient of variation suggests that there is little interstate variation; Nevada is an outlier in the

2. Census Bureau (2002a).
3. Sample selection is described in chapter 4.

Table 8-1. State-Level Program Participation Rates: Summary Statistics

Percent, except as indicated

Statistic	EITC	Medical assistance	School meals	Food stamps	Child care	TANF	Rental assistance
High	69.2	56.0	39.0	25.7	8.3	11.4	22.2
Low	51.4	16.3	17.5	5.0	0.7	1.0	3.7
Median	59.2	33.3	27.5	17.5	3.4	3.9	10.4
Mean	59.9	34.1	28.0	16.7	3.5	4.3	10.7
Range	17.8	39.7	21.5	20.7	7.6	10.4	18.5
Standard deviation	4.1	7.8	4.7	4.3	1.7	2.3	4.2
Coefficient of variation	.07	.23	.17	.26	.49	.53	.39

Source: Authors' analysis, as described in text.

distribution. School lunch participation rates were highest in Mississippi (39.0 percent) and lowest in Vermont (17.5 percent), and the coefficient of variation indicates a small amount of interstate variation. Thus, the results of the state-level analysis are consistent with the national analysis in two important ways: the same three programs emerge as the most popular work supports and (with the exception of the occasional outlier) the states exhibit little variation in participation rates. This implies that the federal EITC, medical assistance, and school meals are the most consistently accessed sources of material support for needy working families, regardless of state of residence.

Participation rates for the remaining work support programs also mirror the patterns found at the national level. Compared to the most popular work supports, participation rates in all fifty states and the District of Columbia are somewhat lower for the Food Stamp Program and rental assistance, and much lower for child care and TANF. The highest food stamp participation rate was 25.7 percent (Oregon) and the lowest was 5.0 percent (once again, Nevada). For rental assistance, the highest participation rate was 22.2 percent (Hawaii) and the lowest was 3.7 percent (once again, Nevada). The coefficient of variation for these rates indicates that food stamps and housing assistance exhibit a moderate amount of interstate variation compared to other work support programs. Child care participation rates ranged from 8.3 percent in Delaware to 0.7 percent in New Jersey. TANF participation was highest in Alaska (11.4 percent) and lowest in Florida (only 1.0 percent). The variation in receipt of child care and TANF benefits, as indicated by their coefficients of variation, was greater than for any other work supports. Participation rates are generally lower and vary more than other work supports. Thus, these are the least reliable sources of material support for needy working families.

We are interested also in how the extent to which needy workers enjoy access to any work support benefits varies from one state to the next. Table 8-2 presents the top ten and bottom ten states in terms of how widespread is work support participation, for all households and for households with children (eleven states are listed in the latter analysis, due to a tie for tenth place). We would have liked also to present state-level participation rates for those making the transition from welfare to work, as in the national evaluation in chapter 7. However, in many of the smaller states, low TANF participation rates resulted in too few cases in our sample to draw reliable generalizations at the state level.

Table 8-2 indicates that although considerable variation exists among the states, work support participation among all households is widespread, regardless of state of residence. The highest participation rate is in West Virginia, where 82.5 percent of sample households report benefits from at least one work support program. The lowest participation rate is in Maryland (63.0 percent). The range of state participation rates is 19.5 points, but three-fifths of all states have rates between 68.6 percent and 76.5 percent.

State-level work support participation is even more widespread among households with children. In Indiana, the state with the lowest participation rate, 83.0 percent of sample households with children report benefits from one or more work supports. The highest participation rate, 96.8 percent, is for New Mexico. The range of participation rates is 13.9 points, and three-fifths of all states have participation rates between 93.0 percent and 85.4 percent. State work support participation rates vary less among households with children than among all households. The participation rate for households with children in Indiana (the lowest) is 86 percent of the rate in New Mexico (the highest). However, among all households, the participation rate in Maryland (the lowest) is only 76.4 percent of the rate in West Virginia (the highest). Generally, this suggests that there is more variation in the extent to which states provide work supports to households without children.

We are also interested in the extent to which states offer needy working families the oppportunity to benefit from numerous work supports. Table 8-3 reports the extent of work support participation, as indicated by the proportion of all households and of all households with children that report benefits from three or more work support programs. A comparison of the rates of the top and bottom ten states suggests that there is significant interstate variation in the extent of work support participation. The data for all households indicate that in Mississippi, the state with the highest rate, almost one in three households reports receiving benefits from three or more work

Table 8-2. Rates of Partipation in Any Work Support Program, All Households and Households with Children

Percent

All households

Top states		Bottom states	
State	*Rate*	*State*	*Rate*
West Virginia	82.5	Ohio	68.6
Mississippi	79.3	New Hampshire	68.4
New York	79.1	Arizona	67.3
Vermont	78.2	Kansas	66.5
Alabama	78.1	Indiana	66.4
New Mexico	78.0	Colorado	65.7
Arkansas	77.9	Nebraska	65.7
California	76.9	Delaware	64.8
Texas	76.7	Wyoming	64.6
Massachusetts	76.5	Maryland	63.0

Households with children

Top states		Bottom states	
State	*Rate*	*State*	*Rate*
New Mexico	96.8	Nevada	85.4
West Virginia	96.4	Delaware	85.4
Mississippi	95.8	Utah	85.2
District of Columbia	95.2	Pennsylvania	84.9
Montana	95.2	South Dakota	84.6
Massachusetts	94.3	New Hampshire	84.3
Louisiana	94.2	Hawaii	84.0
Alabama	94.1	Virginia	83.9
Connecticut	93.4	Colorado	83.7
Oklahoma	93.0	Wyoming	83.4
Tennessee	93.0	Indiana	83.0

Source: Authors' analysis, as described in text.

supports. In Nevada, the state with the lowest rate, only about one in ten households reports receiving benefits from three or more work supports—less than three times as many as in Mississippi. The range of participation rates is 22.6 points; three-fifths of the states have rates between 18.3 percent and 28.2 percent.

As expected, participation is more extensive among households with children. The top rate is reported in the District of Columbia, where more than half of sample households with children receive three or more work supports.

Table 8.3. Rates of Participation in Three or More Work Support Programs, All Households and Households with Children

Percent

All households

Top states		Bottom states	
State	Rate	State	Rate
Mississippi	33.2	Wisconsin	18.3
Arkansas	32.5	Utah	18.2
Massachusetts	32.3	Maryland	17.9
Alabama	30.9	New Hampshire	17.8
West Virginia	30.0	Virginia	17.1
North Dakota	29.3	Arizona	16.7
Tennessee	29.2	Indiana	16.0
Vermont	29.1	Wyoming	15.6
Idaho	29.0	Colorado	13.5
Kentucky	28.2	Nevada	10.6

Households with children

Top states		Bottom states	
State	Rate	State	Rate
District of Columbia	52.4	Wisconsin	26.9
Massachusetts	46.8	New Jersey	26.7
Mississippi	46.7	Utah	25.4
Arkansas	45.8	New Hampshire	25.2
Tennessee	43.7	Arizona	25.1
Alabama	43.5	Virginia	25.0
Maine	43.3	Wyoming	22.8
Louisiana	42.8	Indiana	22.7
North Dakota	42.6	Colorado	21.7
New Mexico	41.8	Nevada	14.6

Source: Authors' analysis, as described in text.

The lowest rate, in Nevada, is 14.6 percent. The District of Columbia's rate is more than three and one half times that of Nevada. Although there is significant variation in the state-level rates (the range is 37.8 points), three-fifths of all states have rates between 41.8 percent and 26.9 percent.

A comparison of tables 8-2 and 8-3 shows that a number of states perform consistently on both dimensions of participation. West Virginia, Mississippi, Vermont, Alabama, Arkansas, and Massachusetts are ranked in the top ten states for both how widespread and how extensive is work support participation among all households. New Mexico, Mississippi, the District of Columbia, Massachusetts, Louisiana, Alabama, and Tennessee consistently score high on both participation dimensions among households with children. Alabama, Massachusetts, and Mississippi achieve high participation rates for all households and households with children, indicating that these states have the most comprehensive work support participation.

On the other hand, New Hampshire, Arizona, Indiana, Colorado, Wyoming, and Maryland all score low on both participation dimensions for all households. Nevada, Utah, New Hampshire, Virginia, Colorado, Wyoming, and Indiana score low on both dimensions among households with children. Colorado, New Hampshire, and Virginia have the dubious distinction of scoring low for both types of households; these states have the least comprehensive work support systems.

State Generosity Index

Our concept of work support generosity has two components: participation in work support programs and the maximum cost-adjusted value of income and benefits that needy working families could receive from the work support system. States are generous if they combine widespread and extensive participation with munificent benefits. Our state generosity index is a single indicator that combines work support program participation data and cost-adjusted income and benefit estimates at the state level.

The first step in creating the state work support system generosity index was to aggregate the program participation measures. We aggregated the data presented in tables 8-2 and 8-3 into a state participation index by calculating the product of the scores (expressed as proportions) on how widespread and how extensive is work support participation for all households in the fifty states and the District of Columbia. The range of scores is 0.189, and three-fifths of the states have scores between 0.194 and 0.113. The highest score is 0.263 (Mississippi) and the lowest is 0.074 (Nevada). Other states that exhibited high scores on the participation index are Alabama (0.241), Arkansas (0.254), and West Virginia (0.248). Other states with low scores were Colorado (0.089), Indiana (0.106), and Wyoming (0.101). The unweighted mean of state participation scores is 0.172, the median is 0.173.[4]

The second step in constructing the state generosity index was to multiply the state participation index by the cost-adjusted state work support income and benefit estimates (developed in chapter 5 and presented in figure 6-2).

---

4. The mean is unweighted because it does not account for state size.

The resulting index, presented in figure 8-1, measures the relative generosity of the fifty states and the District of Columbia in terms of the material support provided to needy working families. The state with the most generous work support system is Mississippi (11,550), and the state with the least generous work support system is Nevada (1,885). The average score is 5,967, the median score is 5,660 (Michigan). The range is 9,965, and the standard deviation is 2,288.

Explaining State Benefit Generosity

To explain variation in state work support system generosity, we performed a regression analysis. The dependent variable is the state work support generosity index (see figure 8-1). There are two independent variables. "Do-nothing state" is a dummy variable equal to one if a state does nothing to enhance work support benefit generosity, and equal to zero otherwise. The "do-nothing" states have no TANF earned income disregards for full-time minimum wage workers (in month thirteen of employment), no parental Medicaid eligibility for full-time minimum wage workers, maximum child care benefit payments below $6,000 annually, rental assistance payments below $4,800 annually, and no refundable state EITC program. (We draw this information from the analysis of state benefit generosity in chapter 4). There are ten do-nothing states: Alabama, Arkansas, Florida, Louisiana, Mississippi, New Mexico, Oklahoma, Texas, West Virginia, and Wyoming.

The second independent variable is a "threshold index" measuring state-level policies that influence access to work support programs. The index is based on state income eligibility thresholds for four work support programs: TANF, Medicaid, CHIP, and child care assistance. The TANF threshold is the maximum annual income an individual can earn and still be eligible for benefits.[5] The Medicaid threshold is the maximum annual income a working parent with two children can earn and still be eligible for benefits.[6] The child care threshold is the maximum annual income that a single earner in a family of three with two children can earn and still be eligible for child care assistance.[7] The CHIP threshold is the maximum annual income a family can earn and still be eligible to receive benefits.[8] We then summed the four income eligibility thresholds and divided the sum by state median income to produce

5. From the Urban Institute welfare rules database, as reported by Rowe (2000).
6. From Broaddus and others (2002).
7. From Children's Defense Fund (2001).
8. From the website of the Children's Defense Fund, www.childrensdefense.org/child-health/chip/default.aspx.

Figure 8-1. State Work Support Generosity Index

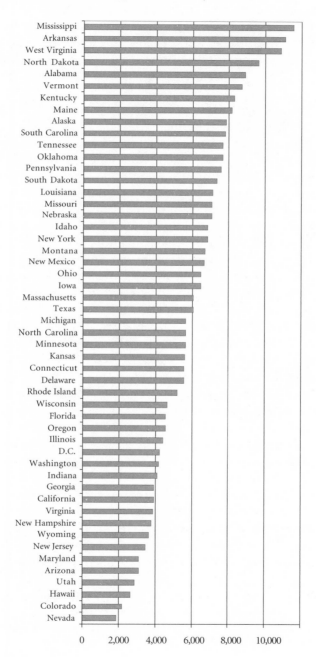

the index.[9] (We considered using these income eligibility thresholds as separate independent variables but found that because they are highly interrelated, this approach created multicollinearity problems in the regression analysis.)[10] The threshold index thus assesses work support program income eligibility thresholds in relation to income at the state level; a state is generous if income eligibility thresholds are large relative to the income of individuals in that state.

We initially planned to include two control variables. On the basis of our earlier finding that households with children are more likely than others to receive work supports, we decided to control for the proportion of households that contain children. We also expected that work support program participation varied with the severity of poverty, and consequently decided to control for the percentage of poor households.[11] However, we found that there were significant collinearity problems between these two variables; there was a close association between the proportion of sample households with children and the proportion of sample households that were poor. Consequently, we dropped the control variable for households with children.

The results of our regression analysis are reported in table 8-4. They indicate that all of the variables have a statistically significant relationship to the state work support generosity index, and all of these relationships are in the expected directions. The regression coefficient associated with the control variable indicates that more people get more work support benefits in states where more families are poor. This result is expected but uninteresting, because work support programs are means-tested. The relationship between the threshold index and work support system generosity also is straightforward. States that use their discretion to provide greater access to work support programs have more generous work support systems. Thus, controlling for the proportion of families in poverty in each state, states make significant decisions that affect access to work supports by establishing benefit eligibility thresholds.

The relationship between state work support system generosity and the do-nothing state dummy is also positive. At first this may seem counterintuitive. One would expect that states that do nothing to enhance work support benefit generosity are less generous. However, the positive relationship indicates that do-nothing-states are more generous. To interpret this finding, it is

9. Data on state median incomes are from the 2000 census.

10. States that have liberal eligibility thresholds for one program tend also to have liberal eligibility thresholds for the others, and likewise for ungenerous states.

11. We define poor households as those in which the total income of the primary family is below the federal poverty standard.

Table 8-4. Explaining State Benefit Generosity[a]

	Unstandardized coefficient	Standard error	Standardized coefficient	t value	Significance
Constant	−5,795.84	2,498.39		−2.32	0.025
Threshold index	2,055.62	684.94	0.333	3.00	0.004
Do-nothing state	1,622.66	666.18	0.284	2.44	0.019
Percent of households in poverty	22,353.78	6,817.49	0.384	3.28	0.002

a. Dependent variable is the state work support system generosity index. See text for details of all variables. Adjusted R^2 = 0.423. F = 11.493, significance = 0.000. (The F test indicates that the null hypothesis—that the combination of variables included in the regression model is not related to the dependent variable—can be rejected with confidence. The significance of the F test indicates that the probability that the null hypothesis is true is less than one in 1,000.)

important to recall that the work support system is a combination of programs that have federal eligibility and benefit standards (such as the EITC, food stamps, and school meals) and programs that feature state or local discretion over eligibility and benefits (TANF, child care, medical assistance, and rental assistance). We interpret the positive relationship to mean that when differences in living costs are considered, the real value of work support benefits in do-nothing states is greater because the *federal* benefits provided within those states have greater purchasing power.

States with low living costs tend to make few state-discretionary decisions that enhance work support benefit generosity. Other states, particularly those with high living costs, more often decide to enhance the generosity of work support benefits. However, as noted in chapter 5, the additional benefits provided by these states typically are insufficient to make up for the high cost of living.

This finding suggests three important implications about state discretionary policies for the work support system. First, state discretionary policies do not define the upper limits of work support system generosity. The states that do little or nothing are the most generous because of the benefits provided by programs that are governed by national eligibility and benefit standards. The EITC and food stamps, in particular, enhance the generosity of do-nothing states, because although the nominal value of these benefits varies little from one state to another, their real value is affected by differences in living costs. Nevertheless, state policy decisions are not irrelevant. A second implication of the analysis is that states' decisions to enhance work support generosity are compensatory; they compensate needy workers for higher living costs. In this sense, state policy decisions are an important feature of the work support system, because they make the system more rational by diminishing the real disparities that would exist if all programs were governed by consistent national standards. Finally, the analysis suggests that states' resource constraints are significant. Although policymakers in high-cost-of-living states apparently are inclined to enhance work support benefit generosity, they are unable to do what is necessary to fully compensate needy workers for the higher living costs. Ultimately, work support benefits in do-nothing states are more generous.

Rethinking the Race to the Bottom

The 1996 Personal Responsibility and Work Opportunity Reconciliation Act (PRWORA) aroused concern in some circles that the devolution of policy-making authority to the states would touch off a destructive "race to the bottom" in welfare policy.[12] The expectation that states will race to the bottom is rooted in long-standing concerns about the constraints and incentives that states confront when making and financing redistributive policy.[13] The findings of our analysis provide a useful basis from which to reconsider the debate.

Paul Peterson has expressed the view that the national government should dominate the design and finance of redistributive policies, because of labor and capital mobility. "If the locality attempts in any serious way to tax the rich and give to the poor, more poor people will enter the locality even as the rich will depart."[14] A local policy is not sustainable because the in-migration of the poor will increase demand for assistance even as the out-migration of the rich reduces the capacity for redistribution. Although the situation is less dire for states because the cost of mobility is somewhat higher, the same essential dynamic applies. Peterson's view of "fiscal federalism" is that states will use their discretion to reduce benefits and restrict eligibility for redistributive programs in order to save money and avoid becoming welfare magnets—the theory sees state discretion as a source of redistributive constraints.

Little of our evidence is consistent with the theory of fiscal federalism. Many states took positive steps to enhance work support generosity: some created new programs to assist needy workers, some enhanced work support benefit generosity in existing programs, some improved access to existing work support programs by liberalizing eligibility requirements. However, our analysis does indicate that state generosity was constrained. Our regression

12. Edelman (1997); Children's Defense Fund (1998).
13. Wilensky (2002); Primus and others (1999); Bane (1997); Peterson (1995).
14. Peterson (1995, p. 27).

results suggest that cost-adjusted work support benefits are more generous in do-nothing states. This implies that the decisions states made to enhance work support generosity did not enhance generosity enough to fully compensate for higher living costs; in other words, state generosity was constrained.

Clearly, most states did not race to the bottom by reducing benefits or restricting eligibility. However, if states that do nothing to enhance work support generosity are at "the bottom," and if more generous cost-adjusted benefits are provided in do-nothing states, the high cost-of-living states that enhanced work support generosity but failed to provide sufficiently generous benefits to match the do-nothing states did, in a sense, race "up to the bottom." This was a consequence of three factors: (1) the value of program benefits governed by national standards; (2) the low cost of living in do-nothing states; and (3) the apparent constraints on state policymaking that limited the generosity of compensatory policies in high-cost states.

Part 4

Conclusion

9

A Work in Progress

Although expansion of the work support system has increased the resources devoted to helping needy working families, observers have suggested that there is room for improvement.[1] We have identified a variety of factors that limit the benefits that needy workers are likely to receive; some of these constraints reflect willful decisions by policymakers, while others appear to be unintended. In this chapter we review and discuss what we have learned about work support system performance and propose a series of reforms.

To a great extent our research tells a story of unrealized potential. We have demonstrated that work support programs can be an important source of material benefits for needy working families. Benefits can be quite generous. However, although participation is widespread, only a small fraction of needy working families participate in numerous work supports, and they typically receive far smaller benefit packages than they could. We also have demonstrated that the states are key participants in the work support system. States contribute to benefit generosity and influence access to programs. States with high living costs play a constructive, compensatory role in the system. However, our evidence also demonstrates that these efforts come up short because the additional benefits that the high-cost states do provide fail to fully compensate for higher living costs, particularly in urban areas. This suggests that it is important to consider inequities across and within states when reforming the work support system. Beyond this, our research has shown that there are significant inequities in terms of the benefits that different groups of needy

1. Congressional Budget Office (1998); Sawhill and others (2002); Sawhill and Haskins (2002a, 2002b); Zedlewski (2002); Haskins (2001); Greenstein and Guyer (2001).

workers are likely to receive. In particular, people making the transition from welfare to work are most likely to receive work supports and are likely to receive the most generous package of benefits. Inequity between groups is also an important matter to consider for work support system reform. The work support system is a work in progress.

Benefit Generosity

Our analysis of work support benefits has demonstrated that full participation in work support programs could lead to remarkable material gains for needy working families. Chapters 4 and 5 also showed that there is significant variation in both the nominal and the cost-adjusted values of earned income from minimum wage work and work support benefits in the fifty states and the District of Columbia. Variation in state benefit generosity for nominal benefits reflects differences in state-level policies. Variation in cost-adjusted benefits reflects the greater purchasing power in low-cost-of-living states of benefits from work support programs governed by national benefit and eligibility standards.

Although benefits vary with location, earned income, family size, family composition, and program participation, the material rewards of extensive participation in the work support system exceed the federal poverty standard by a wide margin. However, extensive participation is not necessary to escape poverty; a full-time minimum wage worker can enjoy an income above the federal poverty standard for a family of three by receiving the federal earned income tax credit (EITC) and food stamps. This is true in all fifty states and the District of Columbia, regardless of state policy choices. Even when states do nothing to enhance work support benefits, the combination of federal EITC benefits, food stamps, and full-time, year-round minimum wage work exceeds the federal poverty standard for a family of three in the average state by approximately 12 percent.

Nevertheless, states' discretionary policy decisions are important to work support generosity. It is common for high-cost-of-living states to use their discretion to compensate for higher living costs by providing additional work support benefits. This enhances the rationality of the work support system by reducing real benefit differentials between states. However, place of residence does matter a great deal in regard to what needy workers can expect to get from the system. Our comparison between work support benefits and basic family budgets demonstrated that work supports are less adequate in high-cost states and in high-cost areas within each state.

Program Participation

Many needy working families receive work support benefits. The program participation analysis in chapter 7 showed that about three out of four households containing a needy working family were touched by the work support system. However, few of these households received multiple work supports. A little more than one in ten households received benefits from four or more work support programs. Households with children were more likely to receive work support benefits and more likely to receive multiple work supports. However, the work support system was most generous to people making the transition from welfare to work; these households were much more likely to receive work support benefits and much more likely to receive benefits from multiple work support programs.

The three most widely accessed benefits were the federal EITC, medical assistance, and school meals. A series of policy decisions expanded eligibility for medical assistance and indexed and expanded EITC eligibility and benefit standards. The changes in medical assistance can be traced to two key decisions: (1) the federally mandated extension of Medicaid eligibility that was phased in from 1990 and currently requires coverage for children under age 19 in families with incomes below 100 percent of the federal poverty standard; and (2) the creation of the Children's Health Insurance Program (CHIP), state programs initiated in 1997 to expand children's eligibility for medical assistance through more liberal income eligibility standards than under Medicaid. Many poor and near-poor children now enjoy access to medical assistance as a result of these changes.

Two policy decisions contributed to making the EITC a viable and significant work support program: (1) the decision, as part of the 1986 Tax Reform Act, to index EITC benefits and eligibility thresholds to inflation, thus maintaining the value of benefits over time; and (2) program expansions in 1990 and 1993 that increased benefits, provided additional benefits for families with more than one child, and extended benefits to childless families. These changes have made the EITC the most important income supplement in the United States and thus have benefited millions of needy working families.

The other work support programs have much lower participation rates. In some cases this reflects program design decisions. Child care grants and rental assistance are budget constrained, which restricts participation. Budget constraints also exist for TANF, but other factors, in particular the emphasis placed by the 1996 Personal Responsibility and Work Opportunity Reconciliation Act on moving recipients out of the welfare system and into the workforce, has reduced their significance.

More surprising, food stamp participation levels are low compared to several other work supports. Because this program is an individual entitlement, largely financed by the federal government, budget constraints are not an issue. And because food stamp benefits are automatically adjusted for inflation, they retain their value over time. However, evaluation research suggests that the low participation rates are related to the organizational context in which the program is implemented.[2] Local social services departments are oriented toward driving down cash welfare participation rates and may inadvertently reduce food stamp participation in their zealous pursuit of that objective. Enhancing participation in the Food Stamp Program should be an important reform goal. The program is an important source of support for families with children, because benefits are adjusted for family size. In addition, it is one of the few work supports that will provide benefits to needy workers whether or not children are present.

Antipoverty Effectiveness

The good news is that the work support programs currently in place are sufficient to end poverty, as defined by the federal government, among full-time minimum wage workers. Our analysis indicates that in each and every state and the District of Columbia, participation in only two work support programs (the federal EITC and food stamps) is sufficient to lift a family of three out of poverty. These programs, as individual entitlements and tax expenditures, are not budget constrained. Consequently, resource constraints do not prevent the elimination of poverty among full-time minimum wage workers.

This optimistic conclusion deserves careful scrutiny. First, although resource constraints are not a concern, other factors do limit program participation. An end to poverty remains only a theoretical possibility unless needy working families can gain access to benefits. In addition, one must acknowledge the importance of regional and local differences in the cost of living, as well as the limitations of the federal poverty standard. The official measure of poverty is a national benchmark that fails to account for state or local cost-of-living differences. While the work support system has the potential to eliminate poverty thus defined, it is likely that needy workers in high-cost areas will continue to face privation. Beyond this, the poverty standard is an outmoded and unrealistic basis for judging economic self-sufficiency.[3] Research into basic family budgets suggests that the federal

2. General Accounting Office (1999); Lerman and Wiseman (2002).
3. Acs, Phillips, and McKenzie (2001).

poverty standard must be (at least) doubled to provide a realistic reflection of the needs of working families.[4] Even extensive participation in the work support system often comes up short of providing self-sufficiency as defined by basic family budgets.[5] This means that ending poverty by enhancing program participation is only an intermediate goal. In the long run, the work support system must be enhanced through reforms that provide additional benefits where living costs are high.

Do Work Support Programs Constitute a System?

Is the work support "system" really a system, or is it a patchwork of programs serving overlapping target groups? To social policy analysts, the answer may seem obvious—like other realms of U.S. social policy, work supports are too fragmentary to be considered a system. Perhaps it is more appropriate to ask whether the work support system displays any systematic characteristics at all.

We propose three standards to identify systematic tendencies among work support programs: administrative coordination, internal consistency, and coherence. If program administration is coordinated, organized and implemented in a manner that provides systematic access to benefits, then work supports constitute a system. However, there is little evidence that this is the case. Although four of the work support programs we examine typically are administered by local social service departments, separate bureaus administer the others, and there is scant effort to coordinate these programs or organizations (the one exception is the use of school lunch eligibility information as a basis for medical assistance outreach efforts). However, within local social service departments, administrative patterns associated with the operation of the welfare system do lead to administrative coordination among some work support programs. Receipt of cash assistance, for example, has traditionally been a gateway to a package of welfare benefits that has included medical assistance and food stamps. This legacy has influenced the operation of the work support system when TANF cash recipients make the transition from welfare to work; TANF recipients enjoy categorical eligibility for food stamps and medical assistance. (This helps to account for the pattern, reported in chapter 7, that only people emerging from the welfare system participated extensively in the work support system.) However, for the vast majority of needy working families outside the cash assistance welfare system, there is no such consistency of administration across programs.

4. Bernstein, Brocht, and Spade-Aguilar (2000); Boushey and others (2001).

5. We define minimal self-sufficiency as an income and benefit total that meets need, based on basic family budgets (see chapter 5).

Second, work support programs may compose a system because of their internal consistency, despite the lack of coordination. Consistency of eligibility and benefit standards across work support programs and locations would indicate that this were true. With the exception of the traditional welfare benefit package noted above, there is little evidence that work supports are systematic by this standard. Each program has its own eligibility and benefit standards, creating a scattershot of hits and misses in serving needy working families. In addition, state discretion undermines the internal consistency of many work support programs—families in the same circumstances are eligible to receive different benefits depending upon where they live.

Third, it is possible to see work support programs as a system if they complement one another to create a coherent, seamless, and robust service plan to meet the needs of needy working families. However, the evidence suggests that there are significant gaps in the benefits available to such families. For example, although medical assistance is widely accessible among low-income children, low-income parents, childless couples, and singles frequently do not qualify. Beyond this, a seamless system would not produce a participation pattern that is widespread but not extensive, as described in chapter 7.

Despite the advantages that people emerging from the welfare system enjoy, they encounter a seam in the system when making the transition from welfare to work. That transition transforms welfare clients into low-income workers. Thus they are moved from a group that local social service departments are oriented to serve to a group that local personnel are not oriented to serve. This reduces receipt of work support benefits even for this privileged group. Pamela Loprest reports that only a fraction of those making the transition from welfare to work receive many work support benefits, including food stamps and Medicaid.[6]

Robustness is a related concern. Robustness would be evident if the system worked well in bad as well as good economic times and regardless of the life circumstances of needy workers. While some aspects of the work support system do seem to be robust, its overall effectiveness is likely to vary with macroeconomic trends. Employment is necessary to receive most work support benefits, and certainly to receive federal EITC payments, the most widely accessed work support. In bad economic times, job loss will be compounded by the loss of work support benefits. The work support system is made fragile by the strong link policymakers have created between receipt of means-tested benefits and work.

The EITC benefit structure also demonstrates the limits to the robustness of the work support system, and this is significant, because it is the most

6. Loprest (2002).

widely accessed work support. The benefit has three different schedules: one for childless taxpayers, one for taxpayers with one qualifying child, and one for taxpayers with two or more qualifying children. This structure is somewhat coherent inasmuch as benefits increase when there is more than one child to support. However, the benefit does not increase when there are more than two children to support.[7] Whether this is a cost-control measure or a reflection of concerns about providing "incentives" for needy workers to have more children, the benefit schedule fails to respond to the life circumstances of many needy working families.

One element of robustness is evidenced when work hours are constrained. The analysis of the implications of half-time versus full-time minimum wage work in chapter 4 suggests that, in the aggregate, work support programs do help to compensate needy workers when work hours are limited. Half-time minimum wage workers who participate fully in the work support system can receive 79 percent of the estimated income and benefit total that full-time workers receive. Lower earned income and loss of tax benefits are offset by gains in TANF and food stamps, in the average state. On balance, the system protects workers whose hours are limited because means-tested transfer programs more than compensate for income and tax benefit losses. (We would not dispute the retort that this is a happy accident, not a clever design.) Once again, this demonstrates the advantage that those within the cash assistance welfare system enjoy over other needy workers; access to TANF is critical to compensate for the loss of income and other benefits when work hours are constrained.

Finally, although it is clear that state discretion is a source of differential treatment for needy working families (both in terms of eligibility criteria and benefit generosity), it does also make the work support system more robust by reducing the variation in the real value of work support benefits. In this sense, state discretion and federalism contribute to the coherence of the work support system.[8]

Work Supports and Welfare

As noted in chapter 3, in many ways the work support system reflects the concerns and priorities of the welfare system: many of its benefits target children and it often provides more generous benefits to families with children

7. This lack of robustness may be reduced for families that are eligible to receive the child tax credit.

8. This may not be accidental, but it is beyond the scope of our analysis to determine that here.

and people moving from welfare to work. This influence may be inevitable, given the historical development of the work support system, but separating the work support system from the welfare system may be critical to making the former more effective. Harold Wilensky has described the U.S. "welfare mess" as a "cobweb of overlapping, competing, and uncoordinated programs" that are characterized by inadequate benefits, gross inequalities in the distribution of benefits, means-testing as a basis for eligibility, excessive concern about fraud, and expensive, time-consuming, and intrusive administration.[9] In many ways this is also an apt description of the work support system; the same problems undermine its effectiveness. Our evaluation of the work support system has identified several factors that limit system effectiveness, many of which reflect Wilensky's depiction of the welfare mess.

—*The work support system is fragmented.* Needy working families are offered assistance from a variety of programs governed by different standards and implemented by different organizations. This patchwork undermines the system's effectiveness by making it more difficult for needy workers to get the benefits they need and often are entitled to receive.

—*The system is compartmentalized.* In particular, the programs that support needy workers are separated functionally and organizationally from the policy mechanisms that influence job opportunities. The lack of coordination between these policy domains can place needy workers in a serious bind; the loss of work may be compounded by the loss of work support benefits.

—*There is stigma associated with receipt of some work support benefits.* The association of work supports with the welfare system undermines the system's effectiveness because of the stigma that is associated with receipt of welfare benefits. Although many work supports are individual entitlements and therefore eligible persons have a legally enforceable right to receive them, many of these needy workers fail to receive benefits.[10] This is a consequence of welfare stigma and policies aimed at reducing cash welfare caseloads.[11]

—*The design of some work support programs leads to the inadequate provision of benefits.* Program financing arrangements are important in this regard. Although several work supports are individual entitlements (food stamps and Medicaid) or tax expenditures (the EITC), other programs (such as child care grants and rental assistance) must be rationed due to resource shortages.[12]

9. Wilensky (2002, p. 316).

10. Schott, Dean, and Guyer (2001); Weil and Holahan (2001); Lerman and Wiseman (2002); Lyter, Sills, and Oh (2002); Zedlewski (2002).

11. Kornfeld (2002); Moffitt (2002); Greenstein and Guyer (2001); General Accounting Office (1999).

12. King (2000).

—*Federalism can also constrain the adequacy of work support benefits.* Even for some entitlement programs, the role and financial incentives of the states can limit eligibility and benefit generosity.[13] Under Medicaid, for example, the states establish benefits and service standards and pay a portion of program costs for medical assistance. This creates an incentive for states to constrain costs by manipulating eligibility standards (who can receive benefits) and the menu of services (what benefits qualified participants receive). Our research suggests that federalism is a mixed bag: states' policy choices vary; many states make affirmative decisions to enhance work support generosity, whereas others do nothing.

As a consequence of these limiting factors, significant inequalities exist in the provision of work support benefits across states, within states, and across different target groups. Ironically, people exiting the welfare system to go to work are a privileged target group. Those who reside in low-cost-of-living areas or states are also at an advantage, because nationally determined benefits have more purchasing power in these locations. The most distressed needy working families are those outside the welfare system and residing in costly urban areas.

Toward a Better Work Support System

Our research suggests that the most compelling problem with the work support system is inequity, not a lack of generosity. There are geographic inequities and inequities across groups. Needy workers in high-cost states and in costly urban areas in all fifty states and the District of Columbia suffer. Enhancing the existing links between benefit generosity and living costs is a promising reform strategy to reduce geographic inequities. The primary inequity across groups is the program participation gap between people emerging from the cash assistance welfare system and other needy workers. Improving program access for needy working families outside the cash welfare system is a promising reform strategy to reduce inequities across groups.

Since the work support system provides income supports to needy working families, many of the reforms we might propose would cost money. Money is a problem. This is a difficult time to consider additional federal spending.[14] Both houses of Congress have Republican majorities that are currently focused on tax cuts and deficit reduction. The war in Iraq has been more costly than the Bush administration imagined it would be. The Medicare

13. Peterson (1995).
14. These observations were made in January 2005.

prescription drug benefit that will be implemented in 2006 is now forecast to cost nearly three times the administration's original estimate. The federal deficit is breaking records despite the fact that hundreds of billions of dollars spent annually are "off-budget." The administration is currently lobbying Congress to borrow $2 trillion to finance the president's plan to privatize Social Security. What hope is there for reform in this context?

There is little hope of assembling a congressional majority to enact costly new benefits for needy workers anytime soon, even though needy workers are the "deserving" poor. Fortunately, that is not necessary. An important implication of our estimates of work support benefits and program participation (chapters 4 and 7) is that new federal programs with new benefits are not required in order to significantly enhance the generosity of the work support system. That can be accomplished by improving access to existing program benefits. Our federal agenda for reform focuses on program participation.

To enhance work support program participation, the welfare-to-work agenda that was institutionalized with the implementation of the 1996 Personal Responsibility and Work Opportunity Reconciliation Act (PRWORA) and the cultural transformation it has brought to local social service departments must be embraced and expanded. Local social service departments must become work support service centers for needy working families. They should welcome low-income workers and develop new routines to integrate needy workers into the work support system, including outreach efforts and public education campaigns. The mission of local social service departments should be to prevent welfare dependency by integrating low-income workers into the work support system.

Reform of the Food Stamp Program should be an important part of the effort to enhance the access of needy working families to work support benefits. As reported in chapter 2, the Farm Security and Rural Investment Act of 2002 took several significant steps to reform the program, and the Department of Agriculture has compiled program guidelines of state "best practices" to encourage participation among the working poor.[15] These are constructive developments. However, comprehensive reform also requires a change in our collective vision of what the program is and can be. Because of its long association with the welfare system, it carries a stigma. Only when food stamps are reconceived as a support service for needy working families will poverty for full-time minimum wage workers come to an end.

Yet ending poverty is not enough. Two key questions for reforming the work support system are: How can high-cost states provide more generous

15. U.S. House of Representatives, Committee on Ways and Means (2004).

work supports? And how can the inequities between different groups of needy working families be reduced? Our research has shown that the tax system is the most effective way to deliver work support benefits. Providing refundable, means-tested tax credits that reflect state-level differences in living costs will enhance the coherence of the work support system. Tax credits are a promising reform vehicle because of their clear link to work and their widespread popularity.[16] Saul Hoffman and Laurence Seidman suggest that liberals view means-tested tax benefits as a complement to welfare payments and the minimum wage.[17] However, conservatives view them as an alternative to welfare for the non-elderly and the able bodied. Tax benefits are likely to attract a broad, bipartisan support coalition.

We have not said much about state EITC programs and in general we have downplayed their significance. Few states offer refundable EITC programs, and the benefits they provide constitute only a small fraction of the total work support package; as such, their effects may have been overlooked. Our research suggests that the states have played a compensatory role in the work support system, and that tax benefits are the most popular type of work support. If this is so, it may be appropriate to consider state EITC programs as a vehicle to reduce inter-state benefit inequities.

State EITC programs are linked to the federal EITC program and typically pay a fraction of the federal benefit. There are several advantages to this linkage. Like federal benefits, they are adjusted automatically to maintain their value over time. Similarly, they are targeted specifically at needy working families and are available regardless of whether a family has children. And benefits are not time limited. Most important, however, is their potential to complement the federal program. State EITC benefits can vary from one state to another. If high-cost-of-living states offered EITC benefits, the inequity that currently exists between high- and low-cost states could be reduced.

As of April 2003, seventeen states had EITC programs and twelve states had refundable credits.[18] Some of those with refundable credits were high-cost-of-living states: Colorado, Massachusetts, New Jersey, and New York, and also the District of Columbia. These five states are among the ten with the highest median housing prices. If the other five costly states—Hawaii, California, Washington, Connecticut, and Oregon—established refundable EITC programs, the coherence of the work support system could be enhanced.[19]

16. Johnson, Llobrera, and Zahradnik (2003).

17. Hoffman and Seidman (1990).

18. Center on Budget and Policy Priorities (2003); Johnson, Llobrera, and Zahradnik (2003).

19. Oregon currently has a nonrefundable EITC program.

The Center on Budget and Policy Priorities has estimated the cost of state EITC programs.[20] If the five remaining high-cost states were to create EITC programs that paid a state benefit equal to 20 percent of the federal benefit (an annual maximum of approximately $800 per family in 2000), the total estimated cost would be approximately $1 billion; 78 percent of this cost is incurred in California.

Financing is an issue, particularly since the states are only now recovering from the fiscal difficulties they experienced during the economic recession of 2001; Colorado suspended its EITC program in 2002, due to its fiscal challenges.[21] However, one option is for the states to finance these benefits using federal TANF block grant funds. Refundable state EITC programs can be financed in this way, though nonrefundable programs cannot. Analysis of 2003 data indicates that only about 3.5 percent of TANF funds are used for this purpose.[22] The federal government could encourage this approach by restricting the states' flexibility to reprogram TANF block grant funds.

Alternatively, if the federal government wanted to maintain state flexibility, a modest increase in the federal resources devoted to the block grant would be sufficient to finance the state EITC programs we have proposed. Between 1998 and 2000, the TANF block grant represented an average of 1.2 percent of federal outlays. The federal budget has grown substantially since the PRWORA was enacted. Although the TANF block grant has been constant in nominal terms, it has declined as a proportion of the federal budget. If the TANF block grant were currently funded at 1.2 percent of federal outlays, its value would increase by more than $4 billion. This level of federal support would provide ample funds to finance refundable EITC programs in high-cost states.

State funds also could be used to finance such programs without creating significant financial burdens as the recent state fiscal recovery continues. The PRWORA created state maintenance of effort (MOE) requirements: "in every fiscal year, each State must spend . . . at least 75 percent of what it spent in FY 1994 if it meets the minimum work participation rates."[23] The effect of the MOE requirement in most states was to freeze spending at between 75 and 80 percent of 1994 levels.[24] Because the requirements established 1994 as the base year, the proportion of state expenditures devoted to TANF has declined over time as overall state expenditures have risen. If the high-cost states had

20. Center on Budget and Policy Priorities (2003).
21. Johnson, Llobrera, and Zahradnik (2003).
22. Greenberg and Rahmanou (2005).
23. Department of Health and Human Services (2005).
24. Department of Health and Human Services (2004).

Table 9-1. Analysis of Maintenance of Effort Expenditures for the High-Cost States without a State Earned Income Tax Credit

Millions of dollars, except as indicated

State	Cost of refundable EITC	Percent of budget spent on MOE		2003 MOE spending		
		1998–2000 average	2003	Actual	Projected[a]	Difference
California	781	2.18	1.41	2,878.36	4,447.10	1,568.73
Connecticut	44	1.22	0.97	185.64	253.51	67.87
Hawaii	19	1.30	0.90	73.93	99.18	25.26
Oregon	61[b]	0.64	0.51	91.64	115.09	23.45
Washington	94	1.20	0.81	264.14	391.88	127.73

Sources: Data on the cost of refundable state EITC programs are from the Center on Budget and Public Priorities, "How Much Would A State Earned Income Tax Credit Cost?" April 28, 2003 (www.cbpp.org/11-11-99sfp.pdf). Data indicating state MOE expenditures and the percent of state budgets spent on MOE are from Census Bureau, "State Government Finances," 1998, 1999, 2000, and 2003 (www.census.gov/govs/www/state98.html; www.census.gov/govs/www/state99.html; www.census.gov/govs/www/state00.html; www.census.gov/govs/www/state03.html), and Department of Health and Human Services, "TANF Financial Data: Analysis of State MOE Spending Levels in FY 2003 through the Fourth Quarter" (www.acf.hhs.gov/programs/ofs/data/tableE_2003.html).

a. Based on 1988–2000 average.

b. This is an overestimate; see text for details.

maintained the same level of effort on TANF spending that they established during the initial years of the welfare reform legislation, a refundable state EITC program could now be financed with state funds.

To assess the affordability of state-financed benefits, we averaged the percentage of the total state budget that was composed of MOE expenditures from 1998 to 2000 in the five high-cost states that lack a refundable state EITC. We compared that average to the percentage of the state budget that was spent for MOE in 2003. The analysis presented in table 9-1 shows that if the percentage of the state budget spent on MOE during the period 1998–2000 were applied to the 2003 budget base, all of the high-cost states except Oregon would have ample funds to finance a refundable state EITC program.

Oregon is an exception for several reasons. First, it is the only one of the five high-cost states that already has a nonrefundable EITC program. The estimate we use in the table does not reflect the cost offset associated with the existing nonrefundable credit. Consequently, it overstates the net cost of creating a refundable program in Oregon. The Oregon Legislative Revenue Office, by comparison, estimates the cost of a refundable state EITC program paying a benefit equal to 20 percent of the federal EITC to be $47.6 million per year until 2011.[25] Second, according to the General Accounting Office, Oregon had unusually low levels of MOE spending in the years immediately following the enactment of the PRWORA.[26] Oregon had already reduced its cash assistance caseload substantially in the early 1990s, and the federal decision to base the TANF block grant on 1994 spending penalized the state by providing an unusually low basis for Oregon's share of TANF block grant funds. Consequently, Oregon always made the minimum effort that was required to claim TANF block grant funds. Using the cost estimate provided by the Oregon Legislative Revenue Office, the revenue shortfall in Oregon is approximately $24 million. To finance this shortfall, state MOE spending would have to increase to approximately 0.775 percent of the current state budget. That is higher than the base Oregon established in the years immediately following the enactments of the PRWORA, but it would be lower than the percentages required of any other state.

If TANF block grant or MOE funds were used to finance state EITC benefits in high-cost states, two equity problems of the current work support system would be mitigated: state-level differences in cost-adjusted benefit generosity and inequities between people making the transition from welfare to work and other needy workers in the level of work supports provided would both be reduced. In addition, as Stacy Dickert-Conlin and Douglas Holtz-Eakin have explained, work incentives and work opportunities would be enhanced.[27]

The creation of state EITC programs will not reduce the inequities that exist within states. The most promising policy vehicle to accomplish this sort of reform is housing policy. Rental assistance programs are distinctive as work supports because they provide benefits that reflect localized differences in living costs. We therefore propose that rental assistance be transformed into an entitlement program. This proposal may seem implausible for reasons of cost. However, Edgar Olsen has pointed out that the current eligibility and benefit structures would not need to remain in place. With this in mind, it is possible to design a rental assistance entitlement that could meet any budget constraint.[28] In other words, it is possible, as we propose, to design a cost-neutral entitlement to rental assistance. Although localized differences in eligibility and benefits must continue to be reflected in our reformed program, other aspects of the program could be changed. Olsen suggests several

25. Oregon Legislative Revenue Office (2004).
26. General Accounting Office (2001c).
27. Dickert-Conlin and Holtz-Eakin (2000).
28. Olsen (2003).

possibilities: "we do not have to make more than 40 percent of the population eligible for housing assistance; we can reduce the fraction of housing assistance delivered through programs that are cost-ineffective, and we can reduce subsidies at every income level."[29]

Olsen's plan for a cost-controlled rental assistance entitlement has three basic elements.[30] First, income eligibility for rental assistance must target the neediest households. Second, the resources of several existing programs must be consolidated and shifted from project- to tenant-based assistance. Third, the subsidy received by each household must be reduced as necessary to distribute available budgetary resources among the eligible households that want to receive assistance. These changes provide rental assistance to the neediest households and increase the number of households that can be served with any given resource base. Olsen has pointed out that rental assistance programs are already moving in this direction by emphasizing vouchers, increasing required tenant contributions, and giving priority to lower-income groups.[31]

Our proposal for a cost-neutral entitlement to rental assistance reflects Olsen's plan. We propose that rental assistance programs target households with incomes at or below 30 percent of local area median income (rental assistance programs refer to these as extremely low-income households). Limiting rental assistance to extremely low-income households will make some current recipients ineligible; their benefits would be eliminated. In addition, we propose that the official definition of income should be revised to include federal EITC benefits. Currently, EITC benefits are excluded from the income base that determines eligibility for rental assistance.[32] These proposed changes are consistent with Olsen's plan and appropriate to the work support system because they maintain the connection between eligibility and local median income. Consequently, eligibility to receive rental assistance will vary depending on local income differences. Because high-income localities also tend to have high costs of living, these changes will provide more liberal eligibility where living costs are higher.

Currently, more than 70 percent of households that receive rental assistance receive project-based assistance, but tenant-based assistance programs are less costly than project-based programs. Following Olsen, we propose that resources should be shifted from the latter to the former.[33] The resource trans-

29. Olsen (2003, pp. 428–29).
30. Olsen (2004).
31. Olsen (2003).
32. Department of Housing and Urban Development (2001).
33. The primary programs we would consolidate and transfer are the low-income hous-

fer from project-based assistance is expected to increase the number of households that can receive assistance.[34] Olsen predicts that cost efficiency will increase by a minimum of 20 percent; that is, even with a fixed budget, the resources available to provide rental assistance are expected to increase by 20 percent or more as a result of this transfer.

It is not possible to consolidate and transfer all of the project-based rental assistance resources immediately, because many forms of project-based assistance are multiyear commitments. Olsen suggests a list of specific actions to be taken over several years during the transition: contracts to subsidize private projects should be allowed to expire; operating subsidies provided to local housing agencies should be terminated; no additional money should be provided for Hope VI projects; no new construction programs should be initiated; and existing publicly owned housing projects should be sold by local housing authorities. In addition, he suggests that the low-income housing tax credit and all local tax credits should be terminated, and no new tax credits should be enacted. All of the federal resources that are consolidated should be reprogrammed to the housing choice voucher program, and Congress should mandate that no additional project-based assistance could be provided under this program (currently local housing agencies may divert as much as 20 percent of their voucher budgets to provide project-based assistance).[35]

The more efficient use of existing resources will allow more extremely low-income households to enjoy rental assistance. However, it is not possible to know exactly how many eligible households will choose to participate. Certainly, the existing waiting lists and the fact that the lists are closed from time to time due to excessive demand imply that demand for rental assistance currently exceeds supply. However, even if rental assistance were to become an entitlement, it is to be expected that participation would be less than 100 percent, due to stigma and transaction costs.[36] Uncertainty about the level of participation (and therefore costs) suggests that it will be necessary to adjust benefit levels as more information becomes available.

---

ing tax credit; federal operating, maintenance, and modernization subsidies for public housing (including HOPE VI and Section 8 new construction and substantial rehabilitation); subsidies for private developments that set aside a portion of the units for low-income renters (Section 236); and Section 515, a rural housing program managed by the Department of Agriculture. Olsen's (2004) proposal also includes low-income homeownership programs and housing programs that target the elderly and disabled. We do not consider these programs because our research focuses on programs that target needy workers.

34. Olsen (2003, 2004); General Accounting Office (2001d).

35. Olsen (2004).

36. Olsen (2004).

Table 9-2. Cost Control Mechanism for a Rental Assistance Entitlement

Dollars, except as indicated

Monthly adjusted income	Portion of income paid as rent	Monthly rent payment	Monthly fair market rent	Monthly rent subsidy	Annual rent subsidy
1,200	0.30	360	400	40	480
	0.35	420	400	0	0
1,000	0.30	300	400	100	1,200
	0.35	350	400	50	600
800	0.30	240	400	160	1,920
	0.35	280	400	120	1,440

Source: Authors' calculations, as described in text.

An appropriate way to accomplish this while controlling costs is to use a national regulatory standard to manipulate the proportion of the adjusted income base that participants are required to pay for rent. At present, rental assistance programs typically pay the difference between 30 percent of the recipient's adjusted income and the estimated local fair market rent. It is important to retain a payment structure that reflects local differences in rental costs if this reform is to rationalize the work support system. When local subsidies reflect local living costs, these benefits help to reduce locational differences in total cost-adjusted work support benefits. However, to keep costs within budget constraints, so as to ensure that the program can be implemented in a cost-neutral fashion, the federal government may regulate the proportion of their income that participants are required to pay as rent. Increasing the proportion will eliminate the subsidy for the most affluent participants and reduce the subsidy for others (except for participants with zero income).[37]

Table 9-2 demonstrates the operation of this regulatory mechanism for three levels of adjusted monthly income ($800, $1,000, and $1,200) and two alternative proportions of income (0.30 and 0.35) to be paid as rent. If local median income is $50,000, households at any of these three income levels will qualify as extremely low-income households. All three income levels qualify for a subsidy when program participants are required to contribute 30 percent of their adjusted income toward rent. However, when that proportion is increased to 35 percent, participants at the highest income level see their subsidy eliminated, and the subsidy for the other participants is reduced.

37. In this context, TANF recipients who have no earned income do not have zero income, because eligibility standards for rental assistance count TANF benefits as income.

Using this mechanism, the percentage of income that recipients must pay for rent can be gradually increased until rental assistance wait lists disappear.[38] The standard can be raised or lowered periodically to reflect changing demand and keep program costs within budget constraints.

Finally, the federal government must continuously redistribute housing vouchers to reflect local participation. As the regulatory standard governing the proportion of adjusted income that participants are required to contribute is changed to manage costs, different local participation outcomes are created. Some housing agencies will fulfill local demand before others do. When this occurs, vouchers must be reallocated from those local housing agencies where supply exceeds demand to those local housing agencies where demand still exceeds supply.

The creation of a cost-neutral rental assistance entitlement would enhance the work support system by adjusting work support benefits to reflect local differences in costs of living. By limiting eligibility to the neediest households, making more efficient use of existing resources, adjusting benefit payments to reflect participation decisions, and redistributing vouchers to reflect local demand, the horizontal equity of rental assistance programs can be enhanced within existing budget constraints.[39]

Conclusion

The work support system is a work in progress with tremendous potential to assist needy working families now and in the future. Our proposals to enhance program participation, create new state EITC programs, and transform rental assistance are designed to build on recent progress. It is possible to end poverty for full-time minimum wage workers and provide additional material assistance to support needy working families in high-cost areas while encouraging work and expanding work opportunities.

The continuing development of the work support system could herald a watershed in U.S. social policy. New possibilities for redistributive generosity are created when means-tested benefits are linked to earned income. The rewards provided by the labor market have always acted as a brake on redis-

38. Advocates of rental assistance may object to the idea of increasing the share of income that needy households must contribute to their monthly rent. However, in the current political and budgetary environment it is unlikely that additional resources will be devoted to enhancing the generosity of rental assistance programs. The choice is whether to provide a more generous subsidy to lucky households and no subsidy to the rest, or to provide a more modest subsidy to the most needy households. .

39. Olsen (2004).

tributive generosity. That brake has been set since the mid-1970s, when the rewards provided at the bottom of the labor market started to decline. As labor market rewards declined, the idea that redistributive programs undermined work incentives became more plausible and popular; concern about welfare dependency increased among policymakers even as the real value of welfare benefits decreased.[40] Soon the material well-being of a large segment of the population was being held hostage to declining wages and benefits. An effective work support system has the potential to transform the politics of redistribution in the United States by joining redistribution and work.

The reforms we have proposed will enhance work support programs, but they will not complete the system. The most glaring deficiency is our failure to fully integrate concerns about employment opportunities. By linking work and means-tested benefits, policymakers have encouraged people to move from welfare to work and have enhanced the material supports that needy workers enjoy. But this fragile system presumes that only individual incentives and personal responsibility determine whether or not people will work. Thoughtful people understand that macroeconomic conditions sometimes undermine work opportunities. The work support system will not truly support needy workers until a link is forged between work requirements and work opportunities.

The road to self-sufficiency cannot end in a job that provides too little to support a family. However, welfare reform and declines in the rewards provided at the bottom of the labor market have made this possibility all too real for too many working Americans. By combining earned income with means-tested tax and transfer benefits, the work support system truly can make work the way up and out of poverty. That is one step along the road that can and should be taken.

40. Handler (1995); Jencks (1992).

Appendix A:
Estimating State Benefit Generosity

This appendix explains the sources and methods that we used to estimate the income and benefits provided by work support programs. As we stated in chapter 4, the income and benefit estimates are based upon a family of three with two children and one adult. The adult emerged from the cash assistance welfare system a little more than one year ago and became a minimum wage worker. In addition, to establish the family's eligibility for the school breakfast and lunch programs and the need for child care, we assumed that one child was of school age and the other was pre–school age. Finally, to estimate the amount of rental assistance, we assumed that a two-bedroom apartment was appropriate housing for the family. Except where noted, the eligibility guidelines and benefit estimates we present reflect the value of program benefits and the status of policies that were in effect in 2000.

The nominal estimates we present in chapter 4 are based upon tables 7-11 and 7-12 in the 2000 *Green Book,* which provide state-level estimates for a single parent with two children for several work support programs, including federal EITC payments, TANF earned income disregards in month thirteen of employment, and food stamps.[1] We complemented that analysis with estimates of the value of earned income from minimum wage work (less federal and state income taxes and federal payroll taxes), refundable state EITC benefits, medical assistance, child care grants, school lunch and breakfast programs, and rental assistance.

---

1. U.S. House of Representatives, Committee on Ways and Means (2000) (hereafter, *Green Book*).

Earned Income Less Taxes

Earned income was calculated by multiplying the minimum wage rate for each state by 2,080, representing forty hours per week of year-round employment; or 1,040, for year-round, half-time employment. Based on the specific assumptions we made about family structure, we estimate that none of the minimum wage workers has a federal personal income tax liability. The highest gross income provided by minimum wage employment was $13,520 in the states of Oregon and Washington. It was assumed that the workers were heads of household and qualified for the $6,450 standard deduction, as well as $2,800 for each of three exemptions, for a total of $14,850 in income adjustments, leaving no income to tax. We estimated FICA taxes by multiplying gross earned income by 0.0765, representing the employee's share of these taxes.

To estimate state income tax burdens, we relied on the work of Zahradnik, Johnson, and Mazerov, who report state income tax burdens for full-time minimum wage workers with two dependent children.[2] For states that do not have a state income tax, a value of zero was entered. To estimate the state income tax burden of half-time workers, the tax thresholds of the states that taxed full-time workers were examined; we determined that no state taxes the income of a half-time minimum wage worker with two children.

School Lunch and Breakfast Programs

The estimate of the value of school meal programs was applied to state income and benefit totals only for the one child who was assumed to be of school age. (This assumption is important also for establishing the need for child care benefits.) The value of these benefits depended upon whether full-time workers on state-level minimum wages were eligible to receive free or reduced-price lunches for their children. Recipients of TANF and food stamp benefits are categorically eligible for free school lunches. For others, eligibility is based upon income guidelines.[3]

The school lunch and breakfast programs have one set of income eligibility guidelines for the forty-eight contiguous states and the District of Columbia and special guidelines for Alaska and Hawaii. Table A-1 shows the income thresholds for benefit eligibility that were in effect from July 2000 to

2. Zahradnik, Johnson, and Mazerov (2001).

3. The initial scenario presented in the analysis assumes TANF participation; consequently, the child is categorically eligible for a free lunch. However, later scenarios make different assumptions about program participation, and so income eligibility guidelines are relevant.

Table A-1. Income Thresholds for School Nutrition Programs for a Family of Three[a]

Dollars

	Reduced-price meals		Free meals	
Location	Annual income	Monthly income	Annual income	Monthly income
48 States and D.C.	26,178	2,182	18,395	1,533
Alaska	32,727	2,728	22,997	1,917
Hawaii	30,100	2,509	21,151	1,763

Source: U.S. Department of Agriculture, www.fns.usda.gov/governance/notices/iegs/IEGS00-01.pdf.
a. Eligibility extends to children with family incomes up to and including the amounts shown.

June 2001. Eligibility is determined monthly.[4] For the purposes of determining eligibility among those who are not TANF or food stamp participants, income is defined to include earnings from work; welfare payments, child support, and alimony; pensions or retirement income, including Social Security payments, Supplemental Security Income, and veterans' pensions; any other income from rents, royalties, annuities, interest, or dividends.

For workers outside the welfare system, only income earned from work was considered. We assumed that there were no other sources of income and that income was earned regularly over the year, so that monthly income variation was irrelevant. Children of minimum wage workers in all fifty states and the District of Columbia were deemed eligible for free lunch and breakfast.

Once eligibility was determined, we estimated the per meal value of benefits by applying reimbursement rates paid to the states by the federal government for free lunches and breakfasts. We excluded the value of the basic lunch subsidy and commodity donations, because these benefits are not means tested (they are provided for all school meal participants, regardless of income), and so we do not consider them work support benefits. The reimbursement rates, published in the *Federal Register,* are uniform for the forty-eight states and the District of Columbia, but higher in Alaska and Hawaii. Between July 1, 1999, and June 30, 2000, the reimbursement rates for free lunches were $1.98 in the forty-eight contiguous states and the District of Columbia, $3.21 in Alaska, and $2.32 in Hawaii. For free breakfasts, the rates were $1.09, $1.74, and $1.27, respectively.[5] We multiplied these daily estimates for free and reduced-price school meals by 180 to establish a total annual value of school nutrition benefits per child.

4. Department of Agriculture (2001).
5. *Federal Register,* vol. 64, no. 131 (July 9, 1999), p. 37091

Child Care Grants

We based our estimates of child care grants for needy workers on a report by the Children's Defense Fund that reviewed state policies regarding eligibility and benefits.[6] A minimum wage worker with two children was eligible for child care assistance in every state and the District of Columbia, according to the income eligibility guidelines contained in the report. However, in addition to income eligibility, some states required more than twenty hours of work per week in order to qualify for benefits: Georgia and Pennsylvania required twenty-five hours, Iowa required twenty-eight hours, New Jersey required thirty hours, Arkansas required thirty-five hours, and Tennessee required forty hours. All of these states, except Tennessee, were scored zero for child care benefits for half-time workers.

In Tennessee, the transition from welfare to work is a complicating factor in determining eligibility. Families making the transition from welfare to work are only required to work twenty hours per week for the eighteen-month transition period in order to qualify for child care benefits. Since our estimates are for benefits provided by the work support system for month thirteen, transition families in Tennessee are qualified for child care benefits that other low-income working families are not able to receive. The benefit total for half-time workers in Tennessee includes child care benefits.

Having established eligibility, we considered state-level reimbursement rates and required copayments to estimate the benefits low-income workers may receive. In addition, benefit payments were adjusted according to family structure and the amount of time the parent worked. School-aged children do not require day care for so long a period as preschool children. To estimate the amount of child care that would be eligible for reimbursement, we assumed that wrap-around care for school-aged children would require 33 percent of the time (three out of nine hours), and hence the cost, of full-time child care. Thus, disregarding required copayments, our family of three was expected to receive benefits equivalent to 133 percent of the maximum state per child benefit if the parent was a full-time worker, and 67 percent if the parent was a half-time worker.

The Children's Defense Fund's report presents required copayments for parents who earn $7,075 and $14,150 per year, by state. We created a linear model with these two data points and used it to calculate the estimated copayment for the income levels in our scenarios. For example, in Alabama, parental copayments are $22 at $7,075 earned and $65 at $14,150. The model estimates that the copayment increases by about $6.08 per $1,000 income gained.

6. Children's Defense Fund (2001).

A full-time minimum wage worker in Alabama earns $9,893, and therefore has an estimated monthly copayment of $39.13; that is, (0.00608 * [$9,893 − $7,075]) + $22. The copayment was subtracted from the benefit to arrive at the estimated dollar value of state child care grants.

State Earned Income Tax Credits

Although, as noted in chapter 2, Johnson identified seventeen states with state tax credits for low-income workers, only those states that were identified in tables 7-11 and 7-12 of the 2000 *Green Book* were considered in this analysis, to maintain consistency in the periodization of our estimations.[7] According to the *Green Book*, eleven states had EITC programs in 2000: Colorado, Iowa, Kansas, Maryland, Massachusetts, Minnesota, New York, Oregon, Rhode Island, Vermont, and Wisconsin. Of these, only Colorado, Kansas, Maryland, Massachusetts, Minnesota, New York, Vermont, and Wisconsin offered a refundable credit. All but these eight states were scored zero on this component of work support.

With three exceptions, states express their EITC benefits as a fraction of federal EITC payments and follow federal eligibility rules. Colorado's EITC payments are contingent on a trigger based on state revenue levels. It is possible that payments in Colorado are not as generous as our estimate implies when the state is under fiscal stress. Minnesota devised a more complicated benefit payment scheme after state officials discovered that some of the intended beneficiaries experienced "no net gain" in income because state EITC benefit payments were offset by the loss of other social program benefits (such as food stamps). Although Minnesota has made its EITC more generous as a result, the change affects earned income levels higher than those of minimum wage workers. Consequently, we calculate benefits in Minnesota as a straight percentage of the federal benefit. In Wisconsin, more adjustments are made to benefits according to family size than under the federal EITC program. For our estimates for Wisconsin, we applied the benefit rate for a two-child family.[8]

For the states in our analysis, state EITC benefits as a percentage of the federal EITC are as follows: Colorado, 10 percent; Kansas, 10 percent; Maryland, 10 percent; Massachusetts, 15 percent; Minnesota, 25 percent; New York, 25 percent; Vermont, 32 percent; and Wisconsin, 14 percent.[9] These proportions were multiplied by the estimated federal EITC payments given in the 2000

7. Johnson (2001).
8. Johnson (2001).
9. Johnson (2001).

Green Book to arrive at estimated payments for state-level earned income tax credits.

Medical Assistance

The value of medical assistance benefits varies according to eligibility to receive medical assistance in the thirteenth month of employment and the dollar value of the assistance provided. A mandatory Medicaid expansion requires states to cover children under age 19 and born after September 30, 1983, with family income below the federal poverty standard.[10] All children in families with a minimum wage worker as the sole earner qualify by this standard, regardless of their state of residence. (Some states serve these children through a separate children's health insurance program that technically is not a Medicaid extension, but our estimates do not observe this distinction.)

All states provide transitional medical assistance (TMA) to those emerging from the cash welfare system and starting work. However, most states extend this benefit for only twelve months. In month thirteen of employment, the parent in our family of three may no longer be eligible for TMA, depending upon her state of residence. According to the Center on Budget and Policy Priorities, as of July 2000, fourteen states extended coverage beyond twelve months: Rhode Island and Tennessee for eighteen months; Arizona, California, Connecticut, Delaware, Georgia, Nebraska, New Jersey, North Carolina, South Carolina, and Utah for twenty-four months; and Missouri and Vermont for thirty-six months.[11] In these states, the estimated value of medical assistance includes coverage for the parent and both children.

In addition, some states have more liberal income eligibility standards for medical assistance than others. As of July 2000, twenty-two states and the District of Columbia had income eligibility standards that allowed the parent in our family of three to qualify for medical assistance (including some of those with extended TMA eligibility): Alaska, California, Delaware, the District of Columbia, Hawaii, Illinois, Iowa, Kentucky, Maine, Massachusetts, Minnesota, Missouri, Montana, Nevada, New York, North Dakota, Ohio, Oregon, Rhode Island, Tennessee, Vermont, Washington, and Wisconsin.[12] The

10. *Green Book* (2000).

11. Broaddus and others (2002).

12. This list was compiled by comparing the earned income for our hypothetical family to "income eligibility thresholds" presented in Broaddus and others (2002). The thresholds are the sum of state income eligibility guidelines and earnings disregards. This standard does not account for other disregards. Also, families with child care or child support expenses may qualify for medical assistance at higher income levels. Since July 2000, several additional states

estimated value of medical assistance in these states includes coverage for the parent and the children.

A total of thirty states and the District of Columbia thus provide a means for parents to receive medical assistance in month thirteen of employment. However, it is important to remember that TMA is only available to those emerging from the cash welfare system. For workers outside the cash welfare system, only twenty-two states provide parental medical assistance benefits.

The value of medical assistance benefits is estimated on the basis of data from the March supplement of the Census Bureau's 2002 Current Population Survey (CPS). The CPS estimates the market value of Medicaid services provided at the individual level. Medicaid beneficiaries were selected from the CPS sample pool, and the average value of individual state-level benefits was calculated.[13] For states in which both parents and children were eligible for Medicaid benefits, we multiplied this estimate by three to determine the value of benefits provided to the family. We multiplied the benefit estimate by two in states where only the children were eligible for medical assistance.

Rental Assistance

Estimation of the generosity of rental assistance requires additional assumptions about the lifestyle of our family of three. Housing subsidies typically restrict participants to "reasonable" accommodations and rental payments (on the basis of total income), but within these guidelines, some latitude exists, and this can create local differences in benefits provided. For the purposes of these estimates, we assume that the family of three lives in a two-bedroom apartment. The Department of Housing and Urban Development (HUD) has estimated the fair market rent of apartments in the metropolitan statistical areas (MSAs) and rural areas of the fifty states and the District of Columbia. We omitted the rural data and based our estimate of the benefits provided on HUD's median fair market rents for two-bedroom apartments in the MSAs of each state and the District of Columbia in 2000.[14]

---

have liberalized income eligibility standards. See Broaddus and others (2002) for additional details.

13. A drawback of this technique is the limited sample size for some of the smaller states. Indeed, our concern about this matter led us to use the 2002 survey, despite our goal of estimating the value of work support benefits in 2000. The Census Bureau has been improving the reliability of estimates in the CPS March supplement for several years and fully implemented adjustments to improve reliability in its sampling technique in the 2002 sample.

14. These data are available on HUD's website, www.huduser.org/datasets/fmr.html.

The benefit provided depends upon the income of the recipient. Local public housing authorities have some flexibility to define income and disregard some income sources. However, the federal government provides extensive guidance about what income can and cannot be taken in to account. According to HUD guidelines, annual income includes (but is not limited to) wages and salary; net business income; public benefits in place of earnings (such as unemployment compensation or disability payments); income from assets; periodic payments from Social Security, annuities, insurance policies, retirement accounts, and pensions; and alimony or child support. The following forms of income are excluded: EITC benefits; the value of food stamp benefits; child care grants provided under the Child Care and Development Block Grant (CCDBG); wages earned by family members under age 18; full-time students' earnings over $480; lump-sum additions to wealth; and sporadic income.[15]

Using these standards, we estimated the annual income by combining earnings from full-time minimum wage work and TANF earned income disregards benefits (if any). To identify the income base, this income total was reduced by $960, because the federal government mandates a deduction of $480 for each dependent child. Because most public housing authorities require participants to pay 30 percent of their income for housing, this income base was multiplied by .3 to calculate the participant's contribution. The amount of the subsidy is the rent estimate minus the participant's share.

15. Department of Housing and Urban Development (2001).

Appendix B:
Adjusting Basic Family Budgets

This appendix explains the steps we took to make basic family budgets compatible with our estimates of nominal work support system income and benefits in order to generate the self-sufficiency ratios that are presented in chapter 5. The problem is that the basic family budgets include some estimates of the income required to purchase services that work support programs provide (such as medical coverage and child care), and the extent to which the system provides these services varies from place to place. Depending on the participation scenario under consideration, we needed to subtract the estimated income required to purchase those services because we wanted budget differences to reflect differences in state policy, not differences in the estimated cost or value of the services.

Child care and health care are not always out-of-pocket expenses for the hypothetical family of three considered in this analysis. Under some work support participation scenarios in some states, selected family members qualify for Medicaid; and under some work support participation scenarios in all states, the family receives a child care grant. For the full participation scenario, we subtracted the estimated annual costs for health care and child care from the total basic family budget and from the work support income and benefit total. For the tax and entitlement scenario, we subtracted the estimated value of medical assistance from the total basic family budget and the work support income and benefit total. For the tax and school meals scenario, the basic family budget was used without modification.

Further adjustments were required to estimate health care expenses, depending upon state Medicaid eligibility policies. For states in which the parent in our hypothetical family of three was eligible for Medicaid, medical costs were excluded from basic family budgets for the full participation and tax and entitlements scenarios. However, in states that did not extend Medicaid eligibility to the parent, the estimated cost of health insurance for the parent was added back in to the basic family budget for the full participation and tax and entitlement scenarios. This cost was estimated by using quotes for health insurance coverage for a 35-year-old female nonsmoker obtained from www.ehealthinsurance.com (the source used in the construction of the original basic family budget estimates).[1] The cost of health insurance was estimated in the highest cost-of-living area in each state (selected on the basis of basic family budget information); when that was not possible, state capitals were used as the basis for the estimate. Such estimates were available for all required states except New Hampshire and West Virginia. To estimate the cost of health insurance in those two states, for each of the other states the insurance quote was divided by the estimated market value of medical assistance provided in that state (taken from the March supplement of the 2002 Current Population Survey). These proportions were averaged, and the average was multiplied by the estimated market values of medical assistance in New Hampshire and in West Virginia to estimate the costs of health insurance in those states.

Basic family budgets were also adjusted for child care expenses, depending upon state-level policies and participation scenario. In a few states, the cost estimate in the basic family budget was less than the maximum state child care grant. In such cases, the state copay requirement was added back into the basic family budget as the estimated child care cost for the full participation scenario. However, in most states and the District of Columbia, the maximum child care grant was less than the estimated cost of child care. In such cases, the net cost (the difference between the estimated market price and the maximum child care grant) was compared to the state copay requirement. If the copay requirement was less than net cost, net cost was added back into the basic family budget as the estimated cost of child care for the full participation scenario. If the required copay was greater than net cost, the copayment amount was added back into the basic family budget as the estimated cost of

1. For a discussion of the sources and methods used to construct basic family budgets, see Boushey and others (2001, app. A). We selected the lowest cost plan that offered a deductible of $500 (the lowest available). Except for the deductible, the features of the plan were not considered. Quotes are provided as monthly costs, and these cost estimates were multiplied by twelve to form annual cost estimates (no allowance was made for inflation). The prices were current in January 2003. Although the time difference suggests a concern about the validity of the data, the estimates we generated using this method were typical of the health insurance estimates generated for other states.

child care for the full participation scenario. No adjustments for child care were made for the other participation scenarios.

Finally, basic family budgets include funds to pay a variety of taxes, some of which we had already subtracted from earned income. Consequently, in all cases we added back into the income and benefit estimates the tax payments we had subtracted for federal and state income taxes and federal payroll taxes.

Appendix C:
Who Are Needy Workers?

This appendix describes the individuals, families, and households in our sample. The March supplement of the 2002 Current Population Survey (CPS) had 15,879 households that met the criteria specified in our definition. As explained in chapter 7, households were included in the sample if they contained a family with an income below 200 percent of the federal poverty standard and at least one household member was a worker. Of these households, approximately one-quarter contained multiple families. The most common family type was the female-headed family, which was the primary family in 48.8 percent of all households. Husband-and-wife families, the next most common type, constituted 35.9 percent of primary families in all households.

Strong majorities of households containing needy working families also contained children and only one worker. Children were present in 64.2 percent of households. Although most households had children, large families were uncommon; most households with children contained two or fewer children. A lone worker provided earned income to support 69.0 percent of all households. Although the remaining households contained a second worker, more than two workers were present in only a very small proportion of households.

A strong majority of families in our sample were not poor. Only 5,106 households (32.2 percent of all households) contained families with incomes below the federal poverty standard for their size. The remaining 10,773 households (67.8 percent of all households) contained families with incomes between 100 percent and 199 percent of the federal poverty standard. Female-headed families were more heavily concentrated in poverty, and the proportion of female-headed families increased consistently as poverty became more severe. Although female-headed families were the primary family type in 48.8 percent of all households, they comprised 62.4 percent of those in severe poverty (below 50 percent of the poverty level) and only 42.6 percent of the relatively affluent (150–99 percent of the poverty level). Conversely, the proportion of husband-and-wife families declined as poverty became more severe. Husband-and-wife families constituted 42.0 percent of the relatively affluent, but only 20.5 percent of the severely poor.

Several characteristics of husband-and-wife families explain their relative affluence: compared to others, they had more earners, worked more hours, and earned higher wages. The median number of hours worked in husband-and-wife families was 2,240; that was 12 percent more than the median for female-headed families and 16.7 percent more than the median for male-headed families. Moreover, 50.5 percent of husband-and-wife wife families were supported by a single worker, compared to 77.7 percent of female-headed families and 84.9 percent of male-headed families. And dividing the median hours worked by the median income earned, households with husband-and-wife families averaged $9.62 per hour, while households with female-headed families averaged $6.50 per hour and those with male-headed families averaged $6.25 per hour.

Among all households, labor force participation was significant. Most households (13,185, or 83.0 percent) had at least one worker who worked 1,000 hours per year, while 17.4 percent of the households had two or more workers who worked 1,000 hours per year. The typical number of hours worked in a household was 2,080, the equivalent of full-time, year-round work.

All of the households in our sample had at least one worker. We analyzed the characteristics of the income earners ("breadwinners") in each household. The "primary breadwinner" is the individual in the household who has the greatest earned income; this does not necessarily mean that the primary breadwinner earns the majority of the household's income. A "secondary breadwinner" is an individual with lesser earned income; a few households have several secondary breadwinners. There are 16,172 primary breadwinners and 13,289 secondary breadwinners in the sample. (There are slightly more primary breadwinners than households, because in 293 households two individuals tied as the top contributors of earned income.)

Although the primary breadwinner is equally likely to be male or female, secondary breadwinners are more likely to be female. Most primary breadwinners (70.5 percent) are of prime working age, between 25 and 54 years old.

Secondary breadwinners are typically younger than primary breadwinners; more than 38 percent of secondary breadwinners are age 24 or younger.

The average educational achievement of breadwinners is modest, though primary breadwinners typically have higher educational achievement than secondary breadwinners. Only 37 percent of primary breadwinners continued their education beyond high school. Educational achievement among secondary breadwinners was even more modest; only 32 percent of secondary breadwinners continued their education beyond high school. Nevertheless, more than one-third of primary breadwinners had attended or graduated college, and a small proportion held advanced degrees. Those with higher educational achievement are more likely to be primary breadwinners.

As one might expect, the tendency for households to have multiple bread-winners is inversely related to the severity of poverty; multiple workers are more common in households that contain relatively affluent families. Of families in severe poverty, 80.6 percent are supported by a lone breadwinner.

References

Acs, Gregory, Katherin Ross Phillips, and Daniel McKenzie. 2001. "Playing by the Rules, but Losing the Game: Americans in Low-Income Working Families." In *Low-Wage Workers in the New Economy*, edited by Richard Kazis and Marc S. Miller. Washington: Urban Institute Press.

Acs, Gregory, and others. 1998. *Does Work Pay? An Analysis of the Work Incentives under TANF*. Assessing the New Federalism project, Occasional Paper 9. Washington: Urban Institute.

Adams, Gina, and Monica Rohacek. 2002. "Child Care and Welfare Reform." Policy Brief 14. Brookings.

Baily, Martin Neil, Gary Burtless, and Robert E. Litan. 1993. *Growth with Equity: Economic Policymaking for the Next Century*. Brookings.

Bane, Mary Jo. 1997. "Welfare as We Might Know It." *American Prospect* (January–February): 47–53.

Beam, David R., and Timothy J. Conlan. 2002. "Grants." In *The Tools of Government: A Guide to the New Governance*, edited by Lester M. Salamon. Oxford University Press.

Bell, Stephen H. 2000. "The Prevalence of Education and Training Activities among Welfare and Food Stamp Recipients." New Federalism Project, B-24. Washington: Urban Institute.

Bernstein, Jared, Chauna Brocht, and Maggie Spade-Aguilar. 2000. *How Much Is Enough? Basic Family Budgets for Working Families*. Washington: Economic Policy Institute.

Bernstein, Jared, and Heidi Hartmann. 2000. "Defining and Characterizing the Low-Wage Labor Market." In *The Low-Wage Labor Market: Challenges and Opportunities for Economic Self-Sufficiency*, edited by Kelleen Kaye and Demetra Smith Nightingale. Washington: Urban Institute Press.

Bernstein, Jared, and John Schmitt. 2000. "The Impact of the Minimum Wage: Policy Lifts Wages, Maintains Floor for Low-Wage Labor Market." Briefing Paper 96. Washington: Economic Policy Institute.

Besharov, Douglas J. 2003. "The Past and Future of Welfare Reform," *Public Interest* 150 (Winter 2003): 4–21.

Blackorby, Charles, and David Donaldson. 1988. "Cash versus Kind, Self-Selection, and Efficient Transfers." *American Economic Review* 78 (4): 691–700.

Blank, Rebecca M. 1997. "Why Has Economic Growth Been Such an Ineffective Tool against Poverty in Recent Years?" In *Poverty and Inequality: The Political Economy of Redistribution*, edited by Jon Neill. Kalamazoo, Mich.: Upjohn Institute.

Blank, Rebecca M., David E. Card, and Philip K. Robbins. 2000. "Financial Incentives for Increasing Work and Income among Low-Income Families." In *Finding Jobs: Work and Welfare Reform*, edited by David E. Card and Rebecca M. Blank. New York: Russell Sage Foundation.

Blau, David M. 2003. "Child Care Subsidy Programs." In *Means-Tested Transfer Programs in the United States*, edited by Robert Moffitt. University of Chicago Press.

Boushey, Heather, and others. 2001. *Hardships in America: The Real Story of Working Families*. Washington: Economic Policy Institute.

Brauner, Sarah, and Pamela Loprest. 1999. "Where Are They Now? What States' Studies of People Who Left Welfare Tell Us." Washington: Urban Institute.

Broaddus, Matthew, and others. 2002. "Expanding Family Coverage: States' Medicaid Eligibility Policies for Working Families in the Year 2000." Washington: Center on Budget and Policy Priorities.

Browning, Edgar K. 1973. "Alternative Programs for Income Redistribution: The NIT and the NWT." *American Economic Review* 63 (1): 38–49.

———. 1996. "The Economics of Welfare Reform." Twelfth annual lecture in the Virginia Political Economy Lecture Series. Virginia Polytechnic University (March 15).

Bureau of Labor Statistics. 2002. "A Profile of the Working Poor." Report 957. Department of Labor.

Burkhauser, Richard V., and T. Aldrich Finegan. 1989. "The Minimum Wage and the Poor: The End of a Relationship." *Journal of Policy Analysis and Management* (Winter): 53–71.

Burtless, Gary T. 1994. "Rising Wage Inequality and the Future of Work in America." In W*idening Earnings Inequality: Why and Why Now?* edited by Janet L. Norwood. Washington: Urban Institute Press.

Burton, Larry. 2004. "An Improved Living Environment? Neighborhood Outcomes for HOPE VI Relocatees." Metropolitan Housing and Community Center Brief 3. Washington: Urban Institute.

Card, David, and Alan Krueger. 1995. *Myth and Measurement: The New Economics of the Minimum Wage*. Princeton University Press.

Carnevale, Anthony P., and Stephen J. Rose. 2001. "Low-Earners: Who Are They? Do They Have a Way Out?" In *Low-Wage Workers in the New Economy*, edited by Richard Kazis and Marc S. Miller. Washington: Urban Institute Press.

Carrington, William J., and Bruce C. Fallick. 2001. "Do Some Workers Have Minimum Wage Careers?" *Monthly Labor Review* (May): 17–27.

Census Bureau. 2000a. "Poverty in the United States: 1999." Economics and Statistics Administration, Report P60-210. Department of Commerce (September).

———. 2000b. "Current Population Survey Technical Paper 63: Design and Methodology." Department of Commerce.

———. 2002a. "Health Insurance Coverage: 2001." Economics and Statistics Administration, Report P60-220. Department of Commerce (September).

———. 2002b. "Poverty in the United States: 2001." Current Population Report P60-219. Department of Commerce (September).

Center on Budget and Policy Priorities. 1998. "Strengths of the Safety Net: How the EITC, Social Security, and Other Government Programs Affect Poverty." Washington.

———. 2001. "State Income Tax Burdens on Low-Income Families in 2000: Assessing the Burden and Opportunities for Relief." Washington.

———. 2003. "Estimating the Cost of a State Earned Income Tax Credit." Washington.

Children's Defense Fund. 1998. "Race to the Bottom: Plummeting Welfare Caseloads in the South and the Nation." Washington.

———. 2001. "A Fragile Foundation: State Child Care Assistance Policies." Washington.

Congressional Budget Office. 1998. "Policy Changes Affecting Mandatory Spending for Low-Income Families not Receiving Cash Welfare."

———. 2001. "Effective Federal Tax Rates, 1979–1997."

Crowley, Jocelyn. 2003. "The Gentrification of Child Support Enforcement Services: 1950–1984." *Social Service Review* 77 (4): 585–604.

Cunningham, Mary K. 2004. "An Improved Living Environment? Relocation Outcomes for HOPE VI Relocatees." Metropolitan Housing and Community Center, Brief 1. Washington: Urban Institute.

Currie, Janet. 2003. "U.S. Food and Nutrition Programs." In *Means-Tested Transfer Programs in the United States*, edited by Robert Moffitt. University of Chicago Press.

Daly, Mary C., and Richard V. Burkhauser. 2003. "The Supplemental Security Income Program." In *Means-Tested Transfer Programs in the United States*, edited by Robert Moffitt. University of Chicago Press.

Department of Agriculture. 1994. "Food Stamp Participation Rates: January 1992." Food and Nutrition Service.

———. 1999a. "The Thrifty Food Plan: Executive Summary."

———. 1999b. "The Reaching the Working Poor and Poor Elderly Study: What We Learned and Recommendations for Future Research."

———. 2000a. "Food Stamp Legislation." May 18.

————. 2000b. "Characteristics of Food Stamp Households: Fiscal Year 1998."

————. 2000c. "Improving Food Stamp Program Access: State Best Practices." Food and Nutrition Service (August).

————. 2001. "Eligibility Guidance for School Meals Manual."

Department of Health and Human Services. 1997. "Indicators of Welfare Dependence: Annual Report to Congress October 1997."

————. 1999a. "Access to Child Care for Low-Income Working Families."

————. 1999b. "State Children's Health Insurance Program (SCHIP) Status Report."

————. 2000. "Temporary Assistance for Needy Families: Third Annual Report to Congress, August 2000."

————. 2001. "Fiscal Year 2000 State Spending under the Child Care and Development Fund (CCDF) as of 9/30/2000."

————. 2004. "TANF Financial Data: Analysis of State MOE Spending Levels through the Fourth Quarter."

————. 2005. "Summary: Final Rule, Temporary Assistance for Needy Families (TANF) Program."

Department of Housing and Urban Development. 2004. "Housing Choice Vouchers Fact Sheet."

————. 2001. "Improving Income Integrity Guidance Booklet: Appendix A."

————. 2000. "Section 8 Tenant-Based Housing Assistance: A Look Back after 30 Years."

Devaney, Barbara and Thomas Fraker. 1986. "Cashing Out Food Stamps: Impacts on Food Expenditures and Diet Quality." *Journal of Policy Analysis and Management* 5 (4): 725–741.

Dickert-Conlin, Stacy, and Douglas Holtz-Eakin. 2000. "Employee-Based versus Employer-Based Subsidies to Low-Wage Workers: A Public Finance Perspective." In *Finding Jobs: Work and Welfare Reform,* edited by David Card and Rebecca Blank. New York: Russell Sage Foundation.

Dubay, Lisa, Ian Hill, and Genevieve M. Kenney. 2002. "Five Things Everyone Should Know about SCHIP." Report A-55. Washington: Urban Institute (October 1).

Edelman, Peter. 1997. "The Worst Thing Bill Clinton Has Done." *Atlantic Monthly* 279 (March): 43–58.

Garfinkel, Irwin. 2001. "Child Support in the New World of Welfare." In *The New World of Welfare,* edited by Rebecca Blank and Ron Haskins. Brookings.

General Accounting Office. 1999. "Food Stamp Program: Various Factors Have Led to Declining Participation." GAO/RCED-99-185.

————. 2001a. "Federal Taxes: Information on Payroll Taxes and Earned Income Tax Credit." Statement of Michael Brostek, Director of Tax Issues, before the Committee on Finance, U.S. Senate (March 7). GAO-01-487T.

————. 2001b. "Welfare Reform: Data Available to Assess TANF's Progress." GAO-01-298.

————. 2001c. "Welfare Reform: Challenges in Maintaining a Federal-State Fiscal Partnership." GAO-01-828.

————. 2001d. "Costs and Characteristics of Federal Housing Assistance." GAO-01-901R.

————. 2002a. "Food Stamp Program: States' Use of Options and Waivers to Improve Program Administration and Promote Access."

————. 2002b. "Welfare Reform: States Provide TANF-Funded Work Support Services to Many Low-Income Families Who Do not Receive Cash Assistance." Statement of Cynthia M. Fagnoni, Director, Education, Workforce, and Income Security Issues, before the Committee on Finance, U.S. Senate (April 10). GAO-02-615T.

Gilens, Martin. 1999. *Why Americans Hate Welfare: Race, Media, and the Politics of Antipoverty Policy.* University of Chicago Press.

Greenberg, Mark, and Hedieh Rahmanou. 2005. "TANF Spending in 2003." Washington: Center for Law and Social Policy.

Greenstein, Robert, and Jocelyn Guyer. 2001. "Supporting Work through Medicaid and Food Stamps." In *The New World of Welfare,* edited by Rebecca Blank and Ron Haskins. Brookings.

Gruber, Jonathan. 2003. "Medicaid." In *Means-Tested Transfer Programs in the United States,* edited by Robert Moffitt. University of Chicago Press.

Gueron, Judith M., and Gayle Hamilton. 2002. "The Role of Education and Training in Welfare Reform." In *Welfare Reform and Beyond: The Future of the Safety Net,* edited by Isabel Sawhill and others. Brookings.

Handler, Joel F. 1995. *The Poverty of Welfare Reform.* Yale University Press.

Haskins, Ron. 2001. "The Effects of Welfare Reform on Family Income and Poverty." In *The New World of Welfare,* edited by Rebecca Blank and Ron Haskins. Brookings.

Haveman, Robert. 1997. "Welfare Reform—1996 Style." In *Poverty and Inequality: The Political Economy of Redistribution,* edited by Jon Neill. Kalamazoo, Mich.: Upjohn Institute.

Health Care Financing Administration. 2000. "Chart Book 2000: A Profile of Medicaid." Department of Heath and Human Services.

Hoffman, Saul, and Laurence Seidman. 1990. *The Earned Income Tax Credit: Antipoverty Effectiveness and Labor Market Effects.* Kalamazoo, Mich.: Upjohn Institute.

Hotz, V. Joseph, and John Karl Scholz. 2003. "The Earned Income Tax Credit." In *Means-Tested Transfer Programs in the United States,* edited by Robert Moffitt. University of Chicago Press.

Howard, Christopher. 2002. "Tax Expenditures." In *The Tools of Government: A Guide to the New Governance,* edited by Lester M. Salamon. Oxford University Press.

Internal Revenue Service. 1999. *Earned Income Credit (EIC).* Publication 596. Department of the Treasury.

Jencks, Christopher. 1992. *Rethinking Social Policy: Race, Poverty, and the Underclass.* Harvard University Press.

Johnson, Nicholas. 2001. "A Hand Up: How State Earned Income Tax Credits Help Working Families Escape Poverty in 2001." Washington: Center on Budget and Policy Priorities.

Johnson, Nicholas, Joseph Llobrera, and Bob Zahradnik. 2003. "A Hand Up: How State Earned Income Tax Credits Help Working Families Escape Poverty in 2003." Washington: Center on Budget and Policy Priorities.

King, Desmond. 1995. *Actively Seeking Work? The Politics of Unemployment and Welfare Policy in the United States and Great Britain*. University of Chicago Press.

King, Ronald F. 2000. *Budgeting Entitlements: The Politics of Food Stamps*. Georgetown University Press.

Koppell, Jonathan. 2003. *The Politics of Quasi-Government: Hybrid Organizations and the Dynamics of Bureaucratic Control*. Cambridge University Press.

Kornfeld, Robert. 2002. "Explaining Recent Trends in Food Stamp Program Caseloads: Final Report." Department of Agriculture, Economic Research Service.

Ladd, Everett Carll, and Karlyn H. Bowman. 1998. *Attitudes toward Economic Inequality*. Washington: American Enterprise Institute.

LaLonde, Robert J. 2003. "Employment and Training Programs." In *Means-Tested Transfer Programs in the United States*, edited by Robert Moffitt. University of Chicago Press.

Leman, Christopher K. 2002. "Direct Government." In *The Tools of Government: A Guide to the New Governance*, edited by Lester M. Salamon. Oxford University Press.

Lens, Vicki. 2002. "TANF: What Went Wrong and What to Do Next." *Social Work* 47 (3): 279–90.

Lerman, Robert I., and Elaine Sorensen. 2003. "Child Support: Interactions between Private and Public Transfers." In *Means-Tested Transfer Programs in the United States*, edited by Robert Moffitt. University of Chicago Press.

Lerman, Robert I., and Michael Wiseman. 2002. "Restructuring Food Stamps for Working Families." Department of Agriculture, Economic Research Service.

Loprest, Pamela J. 2002. "Making the Transition from Welfare to Work: Success but Continuing Concerns." In *Welfare Reform: The Next Act*, edited by Alan Weil and Kenneth Finegold. Washington: Urban Institute Press.

Lyter, Deanna M., Melissa Sills, and Gi-Taik Oh. 2002. "Children in Single-Parent Families Living in Poverty Have Fewer Supports after Welfare Reform." Publication D451. Washington: Institute for Women's Policy Research (September).

May, Peter. 2002. "Social Regulation." In *The Tools of Government: A Guide to the New Governance*, edited by Lester M. Salamon. Oxford University Press.

McMurrer, Daniel P., and Isabel V. Sawhill. 1998. *Getting Ahead: Economic and Social Mobility in America*. Washington: Urban Institute Press.

Mead, Lawrence M. 1986. *Beyond Entitlement: The Social Obligations of Citizenship*. New York: Free Press.

———, ed. 1997. *The New Paternalism: Supervisory Approaches to Poverty*. Brookings.

Melnick, R. Shep. 1994. *Between the Lines: Interpreting Welfare Rights*. Brookings.

Meyers, Marcia K., Janet C. Gornick, and Laura R. Peck. 2001. "Packaging Support for Low-Income Families: Policy Variation across the United States." *Journal of Policy Analysis and Management* 20 (3): 457–83.

Michalopoulos, Charles. 2001. "Sustained Employment and Earnings Growth: Experimental Evidence on Earnings Supplements and Preemployment Services." In *Low-Wage Workers in the New Economy*, edited by Richard Kazis and Marc S. Miller. Washington: Urban Institute Press.

Moffitt, Robert A. 1989. "Estimating the Value of an In-Kind Transfer: The Case of Food Stamps." *Econometrica* 57 (2): 385–409.

———. 2000. "Lessons from the Food Stamp Program." In *Vouchers and the Provision of Public Services*, edited by C. Eugene Steuerle and others. Brookings.

———. 2002. "From Welfare to Work: What the Evidence Shows." Policy Brief 13. Brookings.

———. 2003. "The Temporary Assistance for Needy Families Program." In *Means-Tested Transfer Programs in the United States*, edited by Robert Moffitt. University of Chicago Press.

Murray, Charles. 1984. *Losing Ground: American Social Policy 1950–1980*. New York: Basic Books.

Neumark, David, Mark Schweitzer, and William Wascher. 2000. "The Effects of Minimum Wages throughout the Wage Distribution." Working Paper 7519. Cambridge, Mass.: National Bureau of Economic Research.

Neumark, David, and William Wascher. 1997. "Do Minimum Wages Fight Poverty?" Working Paper 6127. Cambridge, Mass.: National Bureau of Economic Research.

Okun, Arthur. 1975. *Equality and Efficiency: The Big Tradeoff*. Brookings.

Olsen, Edgar O. 2003. "Housing Programs for Low-Income Households." In *Means-Tested Transfer Programs in the United States*, edited by Robert Moffitt. University of Chicago Press.

———. 2004. "Fundamental Housing Policy Reform." Unpublished paper. University of Virginia, Economics Department (March).

Oregon Legislative Revenue Office. 2004. "Impact of the 1997 Legislation: Earned Income and Working Family Child Care Tax Credits in Oregon." Research Report 6-04. Salem, Ore.

Peterson, Paul. 1995. *The Price of Federalism*. Brookings.

Phelps, Edmund S. 1994. "Low-Wage Employment Subsidies versus the Welfare State." *American Economic Review* 84 (2): 54–58.

———. 1997. *Rewarding Work: How to Restore Participation and Self-Support to Free Enterprise*. Harvard University Press.

Piven, Frances Fox, and Richard A. Cloward. 1993. *Regulating the Poor: The Functions of Public Welfare*, 2nd ed. New York: Vintage Books.

Primus, Wendell, and others. 1999. "The Initial Impacts of Welfare Reform on the Incomes of Single-Mother Families." Washington: Center on Budget and Policy Priorities.

Rangarajan, Anu. 2001. "Staying On, Moving Up: Strategies to Help Entry-Level Workers Retain Employment and Advance in Their Jobs." In *Low-Wage Workers in the New Economy*, edited by Richard Kazis and Marc S. Miller. Washington: Urban Institute Press.

Reagan, Michael. 1987. *Regulation: The Politics of Policy*. Boston: Little, Brown.

Roberts, Paula. 1994. "Child Support Enforcement and Assurance: One Part of an Anti-Poverty Strategy for Women." *Social Justice* 21 (1): 76–79.

Rosso, Randy. 2003. "Characteristics of Food Stamp Households: Fiscal Year 2001." Food and Nutrition Service Report FSP-03-CHAR. Department of Agriculture.

Rowe, Gretchen. 2000. "The Welfare Rules Databook: State TANF Policies as of July 1999." Assessing the New Federalism project. Washington: Urban Institute.

Salamon, Lester M. 2002a. "The New Governance and the Tools of Policy Action: An Introduction." In *The Tools of Government: A Guide to the New Governance*, edited by Lester M. Salamon. Oxford University Press.

————. 2002b. "Economic Regulation." In *The Tools of Government: A Guide to the New Governance*, edited by Lester M. Salamon. Oxford University Press.

Sard, Barbara, and Jeff Lubell. 2000. "How the Statutory Changes Made by the Quality Housing and Work Responsibility Act of 1998 May Effect Welfare Reform Efforts." Washington: Center on Budget and Policy Priorities.

Sawhill, Isabel, and Ron Haskins. 2002a. "Welfare Reform and the Work Support System." In *Welfare Reform and Beyond: The Future of the Safety Net*, edited by Isabel Sawhill and others. Brookings.

————. 2002b. "Welfare Reform and the Work Support System." Policy Brief 17. Brookings (March).

Sawhill, Isabel, and Adam Thomas. 2001. "A Hand Up for the Bottom Third: Toward a New Agenda for Low-Income Working Families." Brookings.

Sawhill, Isabel, and others. 2002. "Problems and Issues for Reauthorization." In *Welfare Reform and Beyond: The Future of the Safety Net*, edited by Isabel Sawhill and others. Brookings.

Schiller, Bradley R. 1994. "Moving Up: The Training and Wage Gains of Minimum-Wage Entrants." *Social Science Quarterly* (September): 622–36.

Schneider, Anne Larson, and Helen Ingram. 1997. *Policy Design for Democracy*. University of Kansas Press.

Scholz, John K. 1994. "The Earned Income Tax Credit: Participation, Compliance, and Anti-Poverty Effectiveness." *National Tax Journal* 47 (1): 63–87.

Schott, Liz, Stacy Dean, and Jocelyn Guyer. 2001. "Coordinating Medicaid and Food Stamps: How New Food Stamp Policies Can Reduce Barriers to Health Care Coverage for Low-Income Working Families." Washington: Center on Budget and Policy Priorities.

Schwartz, Rebecca, and Brian Miller. 2002. "Welfare Reform and Housing." In *Welfare Reform and Beyond: The Future of the Safety Net*, edited by Isabel V. Sawhill and others. Brookings.

Smeeding, Timothy M. 1984. "Approaches to Measuring and Valuing In-Kind Subsidies and the Distribution of Their Benefits." In *Economic Transfers in the United States*, edited by Marilyn Moon. University of Chicago Press.

Smith, Ralph E., and Bruce Vavrichek. 1992. "The Wage Mobility of Minimum Wage Workers." *Industrial and Labor Relations Review* (October): 82–88.

Solow, Robert. 1994. "Introduction." In *Widening Earnings Inequality: Why and Why Now?* edited by Janet L. Norwood. Washington: Urban Institute Press.

———. 1998. "Guess Who Pays for Workfare?" *New York Review of Books* 45 (17): 27–37.

Soss, Joe. 2000. *Unwanted Claims: The Politics of Participation in the U.S. Welfare System.* University of Michigan Press.

Steuerle, C. Eugene, and Eric C. Twombly. 2002. "Vouchers." In *The Tools of Government: A Guide to the New Governance*, edited by Lester M. Salamon. Oxford University Press.

Stoker, Robert P. 1991. *Reluctant Partners: Implementing Federal Policy.* University of Pittsburgh Press.

Strawn, Julie, and Karin Martinson. 2001. "Promoting Access to Better Jobs: Lessons for Job Advancement from Welfare Reform." In *Low-Wage Workers in the New Economy*, edited by Richard Kazis and Marc S. Miller. Washington: Urban Institute Press.

Tanner, Michael, Stephen Moore, and David Hartman. 1995. "The Work versus Welfare Trade-off: An Analysis of the Total Level of Welfare Benefits by State." Policy Analysis 240. Washington: Cato Institute (September 19).

Tullock, Gordon. 1997. "The Reality of Redistribution." In *Poverty and Inequality: The Political Economy of Redistribution,* edited by Jon Neill. Kalamazoo, Mich.: Upjohn Institute.

Turner, Margery Austin. 2003. "Strengths and Weaknesses of the Housing Voucher Program." Testimony before the Subcommittee on Housing and Community Opportunity of the Committee on Financial Services, U.S. House of Representatives (June 17). Washington: Urban Institute.

U.S. House of Representatives, Committee on Ways and Means. Various years. *Green Book: Background Material and Data on Programs within the Jurisdiction of the Committee on Ways and Means.*

Ventry, Dennis J. 2000. "The Collision of Tax and Welfare Politics: The Political History of the Earned Income Tax Credit, 1969–99." "The Earned Income Tax Credit," special issue, *National Tax Journal* 53 (4): 983–1026.

Weil, Alan, and John Holahan. 2001. "Health Insurance, Welfare, and Work." Policy Brief 11. Brookings (December).

Weir, Margaret. 2004. "Challenging Inequality." *Perspectives on Politics* 2 (4): 677–81.

Wilensky, Harold L. 2002. *Rich Democracies: Political Economy, Public Policy, and Performance.* University of California Press.

Wilson, William J. 1987. *When Work Disappears: The World of the New Urban Poor.* New York: Alfred Knopf.

Winston, Pamela. 2002. *Welfare Policymaking in the States: The Devil in Devolution.* Georgetown University Press.

Woolridge, Judith, and others. 2003. "Interim Evaluation Report: Congressionally Mandated Evaluation of the State Children's Health Insurance Program." Princeton, N.J.: Mathematica Policy Research.

Zahradnik, Bob, Nicholas Johnson, and Michael Mazerov. 2001. "State Income Tax Burdens on Low-Income Families in 2000: Assessing the Burden and Opportunities for Relief." Washington: Center on Budget and Policy Priorities.

Zedlewski, Sheila. 2002. "Family Incomes: Rising, Falling, or Holding Steady?" In *Welfare Reform: The Next Act*, edited by Alan Weil and Kenneth Finegold. Washington: Urban Institute Press.

———. 2004. "Recent Trends in Food Stamp Participation among Poor Families with Children." Assessing the New Federalism project, Discussion Paper 04-03. Washington: Urban Institute.

Zedlewski, Sheila, and Sarah Brauner. 1999. "Declines in Food Stamp and Welfare Participation: Is There a Connection?" Discussion Paper 99-13. Washington: Urban Institute.

Index